Unions, Equity, and the Path to Renewal

Edited by Janice R. Foley and Patricia L. Baker

Unions, Equity, and the Path to Renewal

UBCPress · Vancouver · Toronto

20 19 18 17 16 15 14 13 12 11 10 09   5 4 3 2 1

Printed in Canada with vegetable-based inks on FSC-certified ancient-forest-free paper (100% post-consumer recycled) that is processed chlorine- and acid-free.

Library and Archives Canada Cataloguing in Publication

Unions, equity, and the path to renewal / Janice R. Foley and Patricia L. Baker, eds.

Includes bibliographical references and index.
ISBN 978-0-7748-1680-9 (bound)
ISBN 978-0-7748-1681-6 (pbk.)
ISBN 978-0-7748-1682-3 (e-book)

1. Labor unions – Canada. 2. Labor unions – Social aspects – Canada. 3. Women in the labor movement – Canada. 4. Equality – Canada. 5. Labor unions – Social aspects. 6. Women in the labor movement. 7. Equality. I. Foley, Janice R. (Janice Ruth), 1955- II. Baker, Patricia Louise, 1955-2007

HD6524.U55 2009	331.880971	C2009-900918-8

Canadä

UBC Press gratefully acknowledges the financial support for our publishing program of the Government of Canada through the Book Publishing Industry Development Program (BPIDP), and of the Canada Council for the Arts, and the British Columbia Arts Council.

This book has been published with the help of a grant from the Canadian Federation for the Humanities and Social Sciences, through the Aid to Scholarly Publications Programme, using funds provided by the Social Sciences and Humanities Research Council of Canada.

UBC Press
The University of British Columbia
2029 West Mall
Vancouver, BC V6T 1Z2
604-822-5959 / Fax: 604-822-6083
www.ubcpress.ca

This book is dedicated to the memory of
PATRICIA LOUISE BAKER,
whose life and academic work were guided by feminist ideals.

*Her kindness, gentle heart, and steadfast support
were a comfort to all who knew her.*

Patricia will be sorely missed.

Contents

Figures and Tables

Acknowledgments

I wish to thank all the contributors to this volume, and the Faculty of Business Administration at the University of Regina as well as the Canadian Federation for the Humanities and Social Sciences for making this publication possible. Special thanks go to Linda Briskin and Anne Forrest for their extra editorial support. I would also like to thank the editorial staff at UBC Press, particularly Emily Andrew, Randy Schmidt, and Ann Macklem, for their assistance.

Unions, Equity, and the Path to Renewal

Introduction

Janice Foley

Equity within unions is not just one of several prerequisites for union renewal but, rather, the *central* prerequisite. Current renewal strategies, most recently summarized in Kumar and Schenk (2006a, 36), overlap significantly with those that female union activists have practised for many years in an effort to advance equity for marginalized members (e.g., Briskin 2002; Briskin and McDermott 1993; Briskin and Yanz 1983). That they are being touted as "new" indicates that the many ways female and equity activists have contributed to union strength in the past have gone largely unnoticed within the larger union community. Deep-seated gender and race biases, which have been an unfortunate but well-documented part of the history of organized labour (e.g., Creese 1999; Forrest 2001, 2007; Kainer 1998; Sugiman 1994), may account for this, but it has now become imperative to eradicate these biases.

Labour force demographics have changed considerably in the past thirty years, resulting in a much more diverse union membership today, and diversity is expected to increase in the future as well (Luffman and Sussman 2007; Statistics Canada 2005, 2008). The labour force has "feminized" (Briskin and McDermott 1993), and unions must now cater to the needs of women and racialized and Aboriginal groups if they hope to attract new members, satisfy and retain existing ones, increase membership participation levels, and develop strong ties with their local and international communities. Organizing the service sector, where the majority of the unorganized and many previously unionized workers are now working as a result of economic restructuring, must be prioritized for social justice reasons and for union renewal. These jobs tend to be poorly paid, part-time, and insecure (Broad and Antony 2006; Zeytinoglu and Muteshi 2000a), yet unions have focused most of their organizing efforts elsewhere (Yates 2006).

To renew union strength, a new model of unionization is required that is inclusive, truly democratic, responsive to the needs of all members, and committed to improving the lot of workers everywhere. The difficulties of transitioning to the new model should not be underestimated, however, for changing the status quo will interfere with existing feelings of entitlement, creating conflict, and affecting union solidarity.

Insights that arise from an equity sensitive analysis of union renewal strategies, which are presented here, add considerably to the debate on union renewal. The contributors to this book document the equity deficit within the Canadian labour movement; suggest how union cultures, practices, and structures might be changed to enhance union solidarity and promote renewal; identify issues around which successful political action might be mobilized; and provide examples of how to reposition organized labour as a central institution in the lives of workers. A feminist vision of unions as instruments of social justice for all workers, and an appreciation of union and feminist activists' efforts over the past thirty years to build union democracy, solidarity, and strength by organizing women and other equity group members within Canadian unions, inform the discussion. "Equity" as defined here derives from the 1984 Royal Commission on Equality in Employment. Commissioner Rosalie Abella (1984, 3) concluded that "sometimes equality means treating people the same, despite their differences, and sometimes it means treating them as equals by accommodating their differences." As Briskin (2006a, 13) puts it, "Equity refers ... to what is fair under the circumstances."

The idea for this book arose from the 2005 workshop "Advancing the Equity Agenda Inside Unions and at the Bargaining Table," sponsored by the Centre for Research on Work and Society at York University. More than 120 unionists, academics, students, individuals with human rights or equity responsibilities, and members of the general public gathered to discuss the degree of equity progress achieved within Canadian unions to date, barriers to progress, and strategies for moving forward. The workshop made it clear that equity in unions remains a work in progress, although significant advances have been made since the early 1970s, when the second wave of the women's movement gained momentum in Canada.

Equity Progress to Date

Other recent publications in the mainstream literature (e.g., Hunt and Rayside 2007; Kumar and Schenk 2006a) have documented the many advances on the equity front that have occurred since the 1970s. Some of the important gains include the higher priority given to equity initiatives today; union constitutions that now employ inclusive language and afford members protection from discrimination and harassment by other members; equity structures of all types that exist in most unions; increasing numbers of women and other equity group members in formal leadership positions; a union bargaining agenda that embraces many issues not considered legitimate before, such as violence against women and work-life balance; and protection against harassment and discrimination in the workplace that recognizes the multiple forms of oppression that can occur when gender, race, and class intersect (Briskin 2006a; Zeytinoglu and Muteshi 2000b).

However, legislative interventions that legitimated, for instance, the bargaining of gay rights and harassment protection contributed to some of these outcomes (Kumar 1993). Also, progress has been uneven (Rayside 2007), with women and public sector workers in particular, and more recently men and women with diverse sexual preferences, being the primary beneficiaries. Unionized part-time workers have yet to fully benefit from the fair-pay principles espoused by unions (Forrest 2007; Kainer 1998), and significant inequity is still faced by people of colour, racialized minorities, youth, and Aboriginals (Zeytinoglu and Muteshi 2000a). Implementing equity policy at the local level still poses difficulties (Briskin 2007). The "overt sexism" (Briskin 2006a) that has long prevented equal participation by women and equity group members in union affairs (Briskin and McDermott 1993) still exists. Babysitting services, for instance, are not automatically provided at all union events, and meetings continue to be scheduled at times that fail to accommodate domestic responsibilities.

Although unions have substantially broadened their bargaining agenda, the other equity concerns identified in Briskin and McDermott (1993) remain, affecting women as well as other equity group members. While exceptions exist, unions still help to perpetuate a gender-segregated labour market, one in which males hold the full-time, high-paying jobs, while women work part-time, often with inferior wage scales and benefits (Creese 1999; Kainer 1998). Unions continue to adhere to outmoded views of male breadwinners, male-headed families, and generic workers (Briskin 2006a), which is apparent in their reluctance to advocate on behalf of the newer membership classes if more traditional members will be negatively affected (Forrest 2001, 2007). Union structures and practices continue to marginalize non-traditional members, and although there has been some effort in the past fifteen years to correct inequities, many equity advocates feel that more should have been done (Forrest 2007; Haiven 2007). Too often women and other equity group members feel that their concerns are taken too lightly by their leaders and that they are effectively shut out of union decision-making processes (Foley 2006; Kumar and Schenk 2006b; also Clarke Walker; Edelson; Wall; this volume). There is still much room for improvement on the equity front within the Canadian labour movement.

Equity and Union Renewal
Contemporary union renewal strategies include organizing the unorganized, increasing member participation to facilitate mobilization for change, coalition formation within the external community and other social movement organizations to increase the efficacy of political action, merging to

free up resources, more training to improve leadership effectiveness and membership commitment to union goals, and partnering with employers and government to advance and protect member interests (Kumar and Schenk 2006a, 36). The mainstream literature has started to recognize the connection between equity and union renewal (e.g., Buttigieg, Deery, and Iverson 2008; Lévesque, Murray, and Le Queux 2005), but female union equity advocates have been employing many of the "new" renewal strategies for a long time.

For example, Briskin (2002) indicates that union women have for several decades actively built coalitions with community groups, social movement organizations, and politicians to attain equity goals. These coalitions have proven highly instrumental in achieving such advances as equal pay for work of equal value, employment equity legislation, higher minimum wages, and reproductive choice. Pressure exerted by coalition partners and equity advocates has expanded the union bargaining agenda to include the general concerns of workers (Forrest 2001). Coalition building has kept unions abreast of emerging community concerns likely to resonate with their members, which has supported collective action. It has also strengthened community support and enhanced union legitimacy within the local community and in society in general, thus facilitating organizing drives and moving unions further along the path of social unionism, deemed essential to their survival.

Overcoming participatory and democratic deficits within unions, acknowledged as intrinsic to the renewal problem (Canadian Auto Workers 2003; Fairbrother 2006; Johnson and Jarley 2004; Lévesque and Murray 2006; Lévesque, Murray, and Le Queux 2005), has been another goal of these advocates. They have pressured union leaders to introduce affirmative action processes for staff hiring, filling educational seats, and accessing leadership positions (Briskin 2006a, 2006b). But they have also identified the limitations of doing so, cautioning that numerical strategies by themselves do not ensure strong equity group representation on union executive committees or in staff positions such as union organizer, believed critical to the success of organizing in new sectors (Curtin 1997; Yates 2006). Activists have therefore strongly pushed for the elimination of exclusionary structures and practices that limit the talent pool for leadership and staff positions. They have also taken up the issue of union merger as renewal strategy, pointing out its potential downsides in terms of member satisfaction (Waddington 2005).

In addition, advocates have pushed for other structural changes targeted at democratizing unions, such as equity conferences and women-only educational events and the like, as well as the establishment of women's and other equity committees (Briskin and McDermott 1993). These committees, modelling more democratic practices, have given marginalized workers voice and provided opportunities for confidence building and the development of group-based political identities. Because of the confidence-building, identity-formation possibilities associated with separate organizing, this type of organizing is a vehicle for recruiting equity group members to leadership and staff positions (Briskin 2006b). Equity advocates have advised that these committee structures must be sufficiently integrated into traditional union structures to prevent organizational marginalization, yet sufficiently autonomous to allow strong demands for change to be formulated.

In a further attempt to improve union democracy, equity advocates have encouraged coalition building within unions, across equity committees (Briskin 2007), to ensure that the marginalization of any group's concerns does not occur and that common interests can be more vigorously pursued. They have also pushed for structural linkages between the committees, the union executive, and negotiating committees, to increase the power of these committees to achieve changes that protect and advance the interests of their members. For instance, they have tried to ensure that committee demands go directly to the negotiating table, that each identity group is fairly represented there, and that the leadership backs these demands (Briskin 2006b).

Therefore, it can be seen that efforts to advance equity have provided insights regarding the utility of some of the contemporary union renewal recommendations, and have identified equity as the prerequisite for their success. By pursuing an equity agenda, advocates have positioned unions for renewal by targeting exclusionary practices and structures, improving organized labour's image in the community, supporting efforts to organize the unorganized, increasing membership involvement and support for equity initiatives, strengthening equity group members' attachment to the union, improving labour's potential to mount effective campaigns to secure a more labour-friendly political environment, and developing leaders who are more sensitive to and accountable for meeting the needs of equity group members.

Assessing Organized Labour's Capacity for Renewal

In keeping with the view that union renewal is an organizational change initiative (Kumar and Schenk 2006b; Orfald 2006), and because the organizational strategy literature indicates that such initiatives are usually implemented following an analysis of the organization's resource strengths and weaknesses and an assessment of the opportunities and threats that exist in the environment (Thompson, Strickland, and Gamble 2007), it seems appropriate to examine organized labour's capacity to renew along those lines, using the insights generated by the contributors to this book.

According to the contributors, who have examined the issues around equity and union renewal from a social justice perspective, a number of strengths, weaknesses, opportunities, and threats exist. In the strength category, potent resources include equity structures and the years of experience feminist union activists have had in democratizing union practices to encourage non-traditional workers to join and participate in unions, increase their participation therein, and encourage them to stay. The alliances female activists maintain with external constituency groups, locally, nationally, and internationally, and with community groups, constitute another strength that must be maintained. Separate organizing as a means of growing equity-sensitive leaders and cross-constituency organizing as a vehicle for building solidarity across equity groups are also viewed as strengths.

Some of the major weaknesses are union structures and cultures that, in addition to marginalizing many members' interests, create representational deficiencies within leadership ranks, fail to recognize the leadership afforded by female union activists, and produce leadership skill deficits when it comes to advancing the equity agenda. Systemic barriers such as inadequate equity training budgets for members and leaders exacerbate these problems. Another weakness is the outmoded view that the membership is one homogeneous mass. That view continues to flourish at least in part because of a failure to document the growing diversity within union ranks. The lack of documentation allows leaders to escape their obligations to represent diverse viewpoints, which is a serious problem in itself. But more significantly, this outmoded vision reinforces traditional union values and existing structures and ensures that diverse membership needs go unmet, and that existing gender, race, and class biases go unchallenged (Zeytinoglu and Muteshi 2000b). The result is the erosion of union solidarity, the growth of membership apathy, and problems with organizing and retaining members, all of which threaten union security and political effectiveness.

One opportunity that exists is the possibility of capitalizing on the changing labour force demographics and diversification of the membership by embracing the recommendations of the Canadian Labour Congress' anti-racism task force. Along the same lines, the increasingly difficult working conditions that prevail in the service sector where most new jobs are being created, and more general problems emerging within the workforce in regard to work-family balance and the plights of non-standard workers and new immigrants, provide a strong incentive for workers to unionize and/or mobilize, if the labour movement can address these concerns. The opportunity also exists to take action to expand union capacity to renew by enhancing leader capabilities. Developing the necessary training programs and removing systemic barriers to get more minority-group members into leadership are two options. Increasing funding to equity groups would also facilitate the development of potential leaders.

Finally, some real threats that could materialize if the pace of progress toward achieving equity within Canadian unions does not pick up were identified. The first is that the slow progress on equity is making some equity-seeking groups turn to worker centres and community groups, rather than unions, to achieve gains for workers. This is eroding union strength and legitimacy. A second is that the legal environment has changed with the passage of the Canadian Charter of Rights and human rights laws. The state-granted autonomy that has allowed unions to devise ways of addressing the needs of their members without interference could be taken away if unions do not prove themselves capable of conducting their day-to-day business in a manner that satisfactorily upholds the rights of non-traditional members. At that point, moving the equity agenda forward will no longer be an option – it will be mandated not by the membership but by the state.

Overview of the Book

The twelve chapters in this book are organized into four parts. Three chapters are written by black female trade unionists, while the remainder are written by some of the foremost feminist or equity scholars and union activists in the world. The voices of women of colour are privileged over those of other equity-seeking groups in this book because, despite the Canadian Labour Congress anti-racism task force recommendations tabled in 1997 (Canadian Labour Congress 1997), progress on the race dimension has been slow to materialize (Rayside 2007).

Part 1: The Equity Struggle – Past and Future

Chapter 1, by Jan Kainer, summarizes thirty years of effort by equity advocates to realize a feminist-inspired vision of a union movement that is inclusive and democratic, and that seeks to advance the interests of *all* working people, unionized or not. Here the many contributions women have made to union revitalization via means such as coalition building, rank-and-file activism, and adaptation to the new worker identities and forms of work that have emerged over the past two decades are summarized. Kainer argues that the union renewal literature has not acknowledged the gendering of the labour movement, or the role that women's organizing has played in transforming the labour movement and helping it reposition itself in the face of neo-liberal globalization, thus assuring its future survival.

Chapter 2, by Marie-Josée Legault, presents one highly undesirable possible future for the labour movement that *could* materialize if unions continue to underplay the importance of equity. Legault examines the implications for unions of the federal and provincial human rights legislation and the Canadian Charter of Rights. She points out that there are now two competing definitions of equity, one that is satisfied by equal treatment and another, based on the new human rights legislation, that demands equality of results and therefore preferential treatment for certain groups. She notes that as membership diversity increases, unions can no longer justify their actions on the basis of majority rule or seniority. She warns that unless unions find acceptable ways to deal with the increasingly diverse interests of their members, conflict could ensue that could remove unions' legal right to represent certain minority interests, as well as destroy union solidarity. She describes one such conflict currently moving through the courts, which arose from the negotiation of a two-tier wage clause that is allegedly discriminatory. This is a cautionary tale that highlights the link between union revitalization and equity.

Part 2: The Equity Struggle – Black Trade Unionists Speak Out

Chapter 3, which opens Part 2, consists of an interview conducted by Miriam Edelson with Beverley Johnson, a long-time union activist, and her daughter, Marie Clarke Walker, currently an executive vice-president with the Canadian Labour Congress. It documents the historic and ongoing struggle for equity waged by people of colour, and the continuing acute problem of racism in Canada and within unions. They issue a warning that if better progress on equity does not materialize soon, people of colour will turn to institutions other than unions to seek redress, with obvious consequences for union membership numbers and union renewal.

In Chapter 4, Carol Wall, another long-time union activist and person of colour, presents statistics documenting the changing face of Canada's labour force, which is projected to become more feminized, more racialized, and more Aboriginal. She points out that the labour movement has been slow to keep up with changing demographics to date and asserts that, in order to maintain its vitality, the movement will have to approach the issues confronting it from an equity perspective, rather than from the perspective of straight, white, Anglo-Saxon males. She warns that many of the most underprivileged workers are already turning to worker advocacy centres for help, rather than to unions, because of unions' continuing failure to respond to their needs. She believes that it is time to turn leadership over to "people who look and think differently" because the continuation of this trend could put the future of the labour movement at risk.

In Chapter 5, the final chapter in Part 2, Marie Clarke Walker draws on her experiences in the Canadian Labour Congress and the Ontario labour movement to elaborate on the causes and consequences of the limited progress made in advancing equity for racialized people within the labour movement. She asserts that many changes of a substantive nature are needed to accelerate progress but recognizes that if the leadership continues to deny that equity within unions is a problem, the necessary changes are unlikely to materialize. Like Wall, she warns that the consequences could be severe if these changes are not made. She sets out a ten-point action plan to rectify this situation and insists that the committees, working groups, and designated positions that have been created must be better resourced to advance the equity agenda.

Part 3: Equity, Solidarity, and Union Renewal

The three chapters in Part 3 all target internal union practices and structures that affect equity progress and union renewal by impacting membership participation rates and union solidarity, the underpinnings of collective action. Chapter 6, by Anne Forrest, examines what types of issues unions should pursue in an effort to mobilize what is, at present, a largely complacent or indifferent union membership (Canadian Auto Workers 2003, 6). Forrest points out that acting as a "sword of justice" has strengthened unions in two past periods, the 1930s to 1950s and the 1970s to 1980s. As she sees it, organized labour today is putting the interests of the most advantaged workers (generally white, highly skilled, and employed full time) ahead of those of other workers, many of whom are equity group members, contingent job holders, and not unionized. Noting that union leaders have historically been drawn primarily from the advantaged group, she argues convincingly that the future survival of the labour movement lies with improving the lot of the most disadvantaged.

Chapter 7, by Janice Foley, summarizes two research studies, both based on data collected from female union activists. These studies sought an explanation for why, despite a great deal of effort since the early 1970s to achieve equitable treatment for non-traditional union members, and substantial growth in their numbers since then, equity remains elusive. Even though a decade separated her two studies, she found that the perceived obstacles to equity progress remained relatively constant. Her analysis resulted in the development of a conceptual model of equity progress within unions, as well as the propositions that the formal leadership plays a significant role in determining to what extent equity is or is not achieved and that failure to vigorously pursue equity objectives will imperil union revitalization.

In Chapter 8, Linda Briskin examines how coalition building between and across equity-seeking groups *within* unions contributes to union revitalization by building solidarity. Her main focus is on what types of organizing structures contribute to unity in diversity, for example, by protecting the particular interests of each equity-seeking group while enabling a common equity agenda to be advanced. She believes these structures must reflect a deep understanding of intersectional oppressions and white skin privilege. Drawing her insights from case studies of the Canadian Union of Public Employees (CUPE), the Canadian Union of Postal Workers (CUPW), and the British Columbia Teachers Federation (BCTF), she describes three possible types of cross-constituency organizing structures and how they initially appear to be working out. She concludes that what she calls a dual structure, one that supports constituency organizing but also establishes an umbrella committee with representation from each of the equity-seeking groups, may be the most effective. She emphasizes that union renewal and equity initiatives are inextricably entwined.

Part 4: International Perspectives on Equity and Union Renewal
In Part 4, the focus shifts from a Canadian to an international perspective on equity and union renewal, and how it can be achieved. Chapter 9, by Barbara Pocock and Karen Brown, explores the unique characteristics of Australian unions, their relationship with the Labor Party, and the strategies they have employed to advance equity since the early 1980s under governments that, at times, have been less than labour friendly. They describe a recent community-based campaign organized around a gendered discourse of fairness that was hugely successful in re-establishing the Australian labour movement as a central institution in the lives of workers. They point out, however, that in focusing declining union resources on this campaign, other previously hard-won gains were sacrificed, highlighting the need for fair representation strategies to ensure agreement exists on what are acceptable trade-offs. Their chapter identifies work-family balance as a new priority area for the Australian labour movement.

Chapter 10, by Mary Margaret Fonow and Suzanne Franzway, links union revitalization to the presence of separate spaces where women can identify and articulate their needs, create feminist politics, and develop the will and ability to contest existing power structures within unions. They offer three examples of how union feminists in Canada, the United States, and Australia have created such spaces in unlikely places and by so doing have secured workplace rights and economic and social justice for women. Echoing Briskin's chapter, they suggest that these separate spaces constitute mobilizing structures that allow solidarity to be developed internally, as well as externally with the women's movement, and that a better understanding and appreciation of mobilizing structures and strategies like these, which encourage women's participation in unions, would help to revitalize the labour movement.

In Chapter 11, Anne McBride and Jeremy Waddington examine the European evidence on how union amalgamations affect women's representation within unions and whether they lead to union renewal. They examine three types of amalgamations: those involving unions with exclusively female members, those with unions where the majority of members are male, and those they call "big bang," or transformative. They find that although amalgamations can contribute to renewal by reforming union structures to make them more representative of and therefore more attractive to women and thereby safeguard member retention, those outcomes are contingent on whether or not they enhance member satisfaction. They point out that the needs of members, rather than structural considerations per se, should be the focus of union renewal efforts and that more research is needed to determine what structures, procedures, and practices are most appropriate for female trade unionists' representation.

Part 4 concludes with a chapter by Jane Parker that, drawing upon several empirical studies of UK unions, addresses the contributions women's committees can and do make to union revitalization, which she feels go largely unnoticed. She contends in Chapter 12 that these committees not only facilitate organizing efforts but also generate support for union campaigns and enhance the empowerment and representation of neglected constituents. She notes that these outcomes are hard to quantify but result in greater political influence for the labour movement and enhance internal efficiency. She further contends that women's committees can teach unions a great deal about inclusivity, coalition building, alternative ways of operating, and solidarity, and should therefore be held in greater esteem, echoing Fonow and Franzway's belief. The volume ends on a high note, with Parker pointing out that when both quantitative and qualitative indicators of union health are considered, the labour movement is in better shape than is commonly believed, and that women's committees provide a great many resources upon which the union movement can draw as it seeks to renew.

References

Abella, R. 1984. *Report of the Commission on Equality in Employment.* Ottawa: Ministry of Supply and Services Canada.

Briskin, L. 2002. The equity project in Canadian unions: Confronting the challenge of restructuring and globalisation. In *Gender, Diversity and Trade Unions: International Perspectives,* ed. F. Colgan and S. Ledwith, 28-47. London: Routledge.

–. 2006a. Equity bargaining/bargaining equity. Working Paper Series 2006-01, Centre for Research on Work and Society, York University.

–. 2006b. *Union Leadership and Equity Representation.* http://www.genderwork.ca.

–. 2007. Afterword. In *Equity, Diversity, and Canadian Labour,* ed. G. Hunt and D. Rayside, 244-55. Toronto: University of Toronto Press.

Briskin, L., and P. McDermott. 1993. *Women Challenging Unions: Feminism, Democracy and Militancy.* Toronto: University of Toronto Press.

Briskin, L., and L. Yanz. 1983. *Union Sisters: Women in the Labour Movement.* Toronto: Women's Educational Press.

Broad, D., and W. Antony, eds. 2006. *Capitalism Rebooted? Work, Welfare and the New Economy.* Halifax: Fernwood.

Buttigieg, D., S. Deery, and R. Iverson. 2008. Union mobilization: A consideration of the factors affecting the willingness of union members to take industrial action. *British Journal of Industrial Relations* 46, 2: 248-67.

Canadian Auto Workers. 2003. Union resistance and renewal. Paper presented at the triennial CAW constitutional convention, Toronto.

Canadian Labour Congress. 1997. *Challenging Racism: Going Beyond Recommendations.* Ottawa: Canadian Labour Congress.

Creese, G. 1999. *Contracting Masculinity: Gender, Class and Race in a White-Collar Union, 1944-1994.* Don Mills, ON: Oxford University Press.

Curtin, J. 1997. Engendering union democracy: Comparing Sweden and Australia. In *The Future of Trade Unionism,* ed. M. Sverke, 195-210. Aldershot, UK: Ashgate.

Fairbrother, P. 2006. Union democracy: Processes, difficulties and prospects. Paper presented at the "Union Democracy Reexamined" conference, Seattle.

Foley, J. 2006. Advancing equity in Canadian unions. In *Proceedings of the 34th Annual Conference of the Administrative Sciences Association of Canada*, ed. H. Kelley, 50-64. Banff, AB: Administrative Sciences Association of Canada.

Forrest, A. 2001. Connecting women with unions: What are the issues? *Relations industrielles/ Industrial Relations* 56, 4: 647-75.

–. 2007. Bargaining against the past: Fair pay, union practice, and the gender pay gap. In *Equity, Diversity, and Canadian Labour*, ed. G. Hunt and D. Rayside, 49-74. Toronto: University of Toronto Press.

Haiven, J. 2007. Union response to pay equity: A cautionary tale. In *Equity, Diversity, and Canadian Labour*, ed. G. Hunt and D. Rayside, 75-100. Toronto: University of Toronto Press.

Hunt, G., and D. Rayside, eds. 2007. *Equity, Diversity, and Canadian Labour.* Toronto: University of Toronto Press.

Johnson, N., and P. Jarley. 2004. Justice and union participation: An extension and test of mobilization theory. *British Journal of Industrial Relations* 42, 3: 543-62.

Kainer, J. 1998. Gender, corporate restructuring and concession bargaining in Ontario's food retail sector. *Relations industrielles/Industrial Relations* 53, 1: 183-206.

Kumar, P. 1993. Collective bargaining and women's workplace concerns. In *Women Challenging Unions: Feminism, Democracy and Militancy,* ed. L. Briskin and P. McDermott, 207-30. Toronto: University of Toronto Press.

Kumar, P., and C. Schenk, eds. 2006a. *Paths to Union Renewal: Canadian Experiences.* Peterborough, ON: Broadview Press.

–. 2006b. Union renewal and organizational change: A review of the literature. In *Paths to Union Renewal: Canadian Experiences*, ed. P. Kumar and C. Schenk, 29-60. Peterborough, ON: Broadview Press.

Lévesque, C., and G. Murray. 2006. How do unions renew? Paths to union renewal. *Labour Studies Journal* 31, 3: 1-13.

Lévesque, C., G. Murray, and S. Le Queux. 2005. Union disaffection and social identity: Democracy as a source of union revitalization. *Work and Occupations* 32, 4: 400-22.

Luffman, J., and D. Sussman. 2007. The Aboriginal labour force in Western Canada. *Perspectives on Labour and Income* (January). Statistics Canada catalogue no. 75-001-XIE.

Orfald, D. 2006. Learning to change? Union renewal and the challenge of intentional organizational change. Master's thesis, Carleton University.

Rayside, D. 2007. Equity, diversity and Canadian labour: A comparative perspective. In *Equity, Diversity, and Canadian Labour,* ed. G. Hunt and D. Rayside, 208-43. Toronto: University of Toronto Press.

Statistics Canada. 2005. Study: Canada's visible minority population in 2017. *The Daily.* 22 March. http://www.statcan.ca/Daily/English/050322/d050322b.htm.

–. 2008. Unionization. *Perspectives on Labour and Income* (August). Statistics Canada catalogue no. 75-001-XIE.

Sugiman, P. 1994. *Labour's Dilemma: The Gender Politics of Auto Workers in Canada, 1937-1979.* Toronto: University of Toronto Press.

Thompson, A., A. Strickland, and J. Gamble. 2007. *Crafting and Executing Strategy.* Boston: McGraw-Hill.

Waddington, J., ed. 2005. *Restructuring Representation: The Merger Process and Trade Union Structural Development in Ten Countries.* Brussels: P.I.E. – Peter Lang.

Yates, C. 2006. Women are key to union renewal. In *Paths to Union Renewal: Canadian Experiences,* ed. P. Kumar and C. Schenk, 103-12. Peterborough, ON: Broadview Press.

Zeytinoglu, I., and J. Muteshi. 2000a. A critical review of flexible labour: Gender, race and class dimensions of economic restructuring. *Resources for Feminist Research* 27, 3/4: 97-121.

–. 2000b. Gender, race and class dimensions of nonstandard work. *Relations industrielles/ Industrial Relations* 55, 1: 133-67.

Part 1
The Equity Struggle – Past and Future

1

Gendering Union Renewal: Women's Contributions to Labour Movement Revitalization

Jan Kainer

Since the onset of neo-liberal globalization, unions have lost members and labour movements have struggled to retain their legitimacy. The problem of union recovery has created a large literature on how labour movements can survive in the new global economy (e.g., Boeri, Brugiavini, and Calmfors 2001; Fairbrother and Griffin 2002; Fairbrother and Yates 2003; Frege and Kelly 2004; Kumar and Schenk 2006; Harrod and O'Brien 2002; Jose 2002; Rose and Chaison 2001; Verma and Kochan 2004). This chapter summarizes key themes in the union renewal literature and argues that the contributions of women's labour organizing are given scant consideration in the current debates on labour revitalization.[1] Most of the scholarship on union renewal starts with the premise that alternative forms of organizing are a recent response to labour movement decline. Coalition building, organizing the unorganized, diversifying rank-and-file activism, and other core elements of renewal are typically presented as an outgrowth of the "new" social unionism, emerging from struggles to advance the labour agenda in an era of economic globalization. It is suggested here that significant aspects of labour renewal predate contemporary revitalization efforts. Many feminist initiatives challenging labour on diversity, equity, and social justice organizing can be traced to women's labour activism starting in the 1970s. Given that union feminists developed alternative models of organizing that are similar to or even the same as those proposed by renewal scholars, there needs to be greater acknowledgement of the lessons to be learned from their experience. Yet, surprisingly, there is often little or no discussion of the implications of decades of women's labour organizing for union renewal.

As shown below, at least two reasons can be offered to explain this absence. First, the union renewal literature tends to begin analysis in the late 1980s or the 1990s, thereby missing earlier feminist engagement challenging unions. As a result, the contemporary literature on renewing labour movements borrows heavily, albeit unconsciously, on the traditions and successes of women's labour organizing as potential strategies for renewal, without according credit to these historic origins. A second reason for this gap is that the feminist literature on women and unions (e.g., Adamson, Briskin, and McPhail 1988; Beccalli 1996; Briskin 1994, 2002; Briskin and McDermott 1993; Briskin and Yanz 1983; Cobble 1993, 2004, 2007; Colgan and Ledwith 2002; Crain 1994; Creese 1999; Franzway 2000a, 2000b; Parker 2002; Spalter-Roth, Hartmann, and Collins 1994; Warskett 1996; White 1993) seems to exist independently of the work of contemporary scholars interested in union revitalization. In some instances, reference to women's labour activism is entirely absent (e.g., Fairbrother and Hammer 2005 on labour internationalism); in other cases, limited attention is paid to women's past experience in the realm of union organizing (e.g., organizing the unorganized); but most important, there is a tendency to neglect the implications of *gendering* as a coherent force for political mobilization and change – a process that has tremendous transformative potential for labour movements. This chapter serves as an intervention in the ongoing debates on union renewal and is intended to establish the significance of the labour feminist political project for labour movement revitalization.

Since the second-wave women's movement, women's labour organizing has exhibited a dynamic political struggle to redefine the gender politic of labour movements, what I refer to as "gendering" labour. Women unionists, in alliance with women's movements, issued a feminist challenge to make visible, and resist, the social structures and processes that systematically place men and women in different and often unequal social locations. The feminist challenge to traditional unionism was driven by feminist praxis and activism in coalition with social movements committed to a vision of social justice. Informed by gender-difference ideology, gendering is linked to a broader change project to oppose social inequities within and outside labour movements (see Acker 2006, 10). A feminist-inspired equity agenda promoting substantive equality gains for equity-seeking constituencies (e.g., women, racialized groups and the disabled),[2] and represented in policies such as pay equity and affirmative action, established a tangible political program for feminist mobilization. Equity-organizing strategies have injected greater internal union democracy and built membership support for a social movement model of unionism, furthering social and economic justice.

Although gendering operates as a progressive political force for accomplishing transformational change within labour movements, it has not been a smooth or unchallenged process. As Rayside (2007) observes, labour movements have been far more committed to discussion and debate on policy and process than they have to substantive changes regarding participation and implementation of labour feminist (e.g., equity) policy and procedure. Clarke Walker, Edelson, and Wall (chapters, this volume) make the same point about equity action plans and the representation of racialized minorities in the Canadian labour movement. Gendering labour movement policy and practices involves contestation; it entails struggle over inclusion of women and equity groups in labour movement organizational structures and in labour resistance strategies. Especially contentious are attempts to fully integrate the fights of minorities for social and economic equality in the political action of labour movements. Invoking a gender lens when examining labour movement organizational practices challenges traditional unionism and may produce alternative approaches to union structure and policy, but it simultaneously creates intense conflict, internal and external to labour movements, over the implementation of an equity program. This gender dimension of trade union activity has not been adequately documented by labour renewal scholarship even though it has been ongoing for several decades within many labour movements, and in coalitions between the new social movements, in many industrialized economies.

Themes in the Union Renewal Literature

The literature on union renewal is very large and continues to grow, but broadly, two major themes run throughout. Wide-ranging subjects relate to the problem of union decline (e.g., decreasing union density, diminishing bargaining power, the weakening influence of labour in the global political economy), while another set of topics focuses on ways to bolster unionism (e.g., cross-border solidarity, corporate campaigns, union mergers, improving labour law). The primary trajectory in the renewal literature is to determine optimal strategies for rebuilding labour movements. Reference is often made to assessing best practices (Kumar and Schenk 2006, 19) in relation to union structures, policies, and organizational features of labour organizations or developing a "bigger tool kit," "both old and new," that challenges conventional ways of doing things, to revive labour movements (Turner 2004, 4).

In general, arguments about developing strategic capacity based on vision, agenda, and discourse; promoting internal solidarity (enlarging membership participation); and promoting external solidarity through labour and community alliances or coalitions are repeated themes in much of the literature. Typically, if gender-specific or feminist issues are acknowledged, it is in reference to expanding union membership and promoting an inclusive organizational culture for women and other equity-seeking groups that have tended to be ignored and under-represented by labour organizations (e.g., Behrens, Hamann, and Hurd 2004; Yates 2003, 2006a). The issue of inclusive representation is frequently identified as a key factor in renewal strategies. Another common observation is that union growth depends upon devising a broader worker agenda that will appeal to a wide constituency "informed by a broader set of values incorporating the importance of membership involvement, equity and social justice" (Lévesque and Murray 2006, 121).

There is considerable agreement between renewal scholars and labour feminists on the overall strategic direction needed for labour movement revitalization. For instance, both literatures point to the importance of re-vamping union structures to promote greater internal union democracy and inclusive participation of members, as well as revisioning labour move-ment ideology in a more radical direction (e.g., Robertson and Murningham 2006). There is also recognition by some authors of the importance of or-ganizing women workers in unions and their potential for union renewal (e.g., Clawson 2003; Hurd 2004; Yates 2006a, 2006b). Where the two litera-tures diverge is in documenting and recognizing women's previous (historic) contributions, especially in relation to the development of a gender or equity lens. The process of gendering not only involves organizing "women as women" but also entails mobilizing and applying a "difference" feminist perspective in the organization of labour movement activity. "Gendering" has a broad meaning and refers to the progressive transformation of labour movement strategy, policy, and practices through the application of a femin-ist agenda (see, e.g., Briskin, 1994, 2002; Cobble, 2007; Colgan and Ledwith, 2000, 2002).

By not acknowledging second-wave labour feminist activism in relation to equity organizing, and by not recognizing it as a mobilizing force in union transformation, there remains confusion about what should be considered new and effective renewal strategies. Moreover, as seen below, many strategies identified as new or innovative have been tried, sometimes successfully but oftentimes unsuccessfully because of competing interests within the labour movement and also external forces. It is important to recognize the organ-izing strategies that have been ongoing for some time and to acknowledge their strengths and limitations if we are to really determine what will move union renewal efforts forward.

In this chapter I emphasize gender as a category of analysis to illustrate how and why women's organizing is particularly relevant to evaluating ongoing debates on union revitalization. I argue that feminist unionist activ-ists and feminist labour scholarship offer an important perspective on understanding the strengths and weaknesses of renewal strategies. Labour feminists' views of what works and does not work for union revitalization should be seriously considered by union leaders and labour scholars inter-ested in rebuilding labour movements. I also argue that the transformative potential of gendering labour movement policy and practices must be better understood and acknowledged as a vital approach to achieving necessary change to ensure trade union survival.

The following discussion is a thematic overview of key historical develop-ments in the second wave of labour women's organizing, which attempts to show how labour movements have been gendered by feminist unionist politics. The Canadian labour movement is primarily emphasized, with some comparisons from other national contexts. Given the huge literature on union renewal, it is not possible to offer an in-depth review of the many debates or provide detailed case examples of women's organizing; instead, the discussion is structured around key themes.[3] For organizational purposes, the narrative is structured under four broad headings; however, conceptually, the subjects overlap and interrelate.

The first theme addresses the importance of gender identity as a springboard for women's activism, explaining that feminist unionists revised traditional ideas of unionism based on analyses of "woman's" experience. Feminist unionists' political alliance with the women's movement also broadened and reconceptualized labour movement politics and labour reform ideology. Union women's involvement in organizing the unorganized is the second theme, and further demonstrates how gendering alters notions about who to organize and what organizational strategies to use, especially for workers in feminized occupations. Equity organizing is the third focus of discussion, demonstrating concretely how the equity agenda has operated to challenge internal union democracy by promoting new leadership and alternative democratic structures of representation. The final and fourth theme addresses labour internationalism, explaining the importance of global women's organizing on international union politics and global policy debates.

Women's Organizing: Gender Identity, Political Vision, and Coalition Building

Feminist analyses of women's labour organizing since the late 1960s show that feminist union activists actually initiated many revitalization strategies touted as new or innovative by renewal scholars. One strategy that can definitely be attributed to women's early organizing is coalition building. As the following narrative illustrates, building political power through alliances with groups outside labour circles that are committed to an ideology opposing patriarchal capitalism describes the historic trajectory of labour women's organizing. Yet, in the renewal literature, forming political and community coalitions with non-labour groups is regarded as a fairly recent innovation of labour movements. Reviews of union renewal refer to the importance of building coalitions with the non-labour community, including grassroots or community-based organizations and non-governmental organizations (NGOs) involved in the environmental, women's, and human rights movements (e.g., Milkman and Voss 2004; Voss and Sherman 2003). Kumar and Schenk (2006, 40) point out that "coalition-building is regarded as one of the most innovative strategies for union revitalization" and that links need to be drawn between "trade unions and other non-labour institutions in civil society." Others remark that, "in theory, unions might be able to increase their institutional power by accessing the power of social movements in civil society through building coalitions with these groups and therefore coalition building is our fifth union [revitalization] strategy" (Frege and Kelly 2004, 35). Further, renewal scholars point to the need to develop a "broad reform vision" or "strategic focus," in conjunction with political alliances, in order to build an effective social movement (e.g., Turner 2004, 2). The argument made here is that links with the women's movement by feminist trade unionists have influenced labour movements for many years; coalitions with women's movement groups, many of them grassroots organizations, built capacity for mobilization, expanded the constituency of labour organizing, reframed debates on union goals and unionism, and inspired visioning for social change. Out of this activism grew a broader trade union purpose, pushing labour in the direction of social movement unionism.

In Canada, women's union organizing, similar to what occurred in many other industrialized countries, first began during the second wave of the women's movement. In the late 1960s and early 1970s, union women responded to a dominant male leadership and masculine union culture by devising their own ways of organizing. In these early years of feminist unionism, mobilization revolved around promoting women as agents of political action within the labour movement. As more women entered the labour market and joined unions, particularly in the newly organized public sector of the 1970s, women struggled to define "women's issues," those that primarily advanced gender-specific equality. Union women initially focused their efforts on a woman-centred strategy that sought to eradicate union and labour market barriers preventing them from achieving equality with men. Through engagement with women's movement organizations, many women labour activists developed a feminist ideology and feminist praxis. Participation in consciousness raising groups radically altered the perception of women as an oppressed group in society, furthering their capacity to engage in collective struggle.[4] Consciousness raising legitimated women's subjective knowledge of their social experience and transformed their consciousness about the hegemony of male power in social relations. Identifying and defining sexual harassment in the workplace, for instance, was an outcome of consciousness raising (MacKinnon 1979).

By the 1980s, the involvement of labour women in women's movement organizations influenced how female labour activists thought about unions as organizations, and the role of labour in movement building. Feminist unionists participated in alliances with non-labour groups that adopted radical left political ideologies. For example, the International Women's Day Committee in the city of Toronto, a grassroots socialist feminist organization, argued that "capitalism must be fundamentally altered to achieve the liberation of women, that patriarchy and capitalism are interwoven, that mass action is necessary to win gains from the state, and that [we] need to make alliances with other progressive forces, particularly with the trade union movement, if [we are] to achieve [our] goals" (Egan 1987, 114-15).

Within feminist unionist circles it was increasingly understood that labour alliances with outside groups was a necessary strategy to challenging unequal power relations under capitalism (Connelly and Keddy 1989, 28-29). Over time, numerous coalitions in Canada of labour and women's organizations were developed on issues such as child care, abortion, free trade, welfare state entitlements, and employment standards legislation.[5]

Coalitions of organized labour and feminist groups were especially significant in the struggle for pay equity. In the 1970s, 1980s, and early 1990s, in large industrialized economies such as the United States, Canada, Australia, and those in Western Europe, women's groups engaged in widespread political action, demanding policy reforms to raise women's wages (e.g., Acker 1989; Burton 1991; Evans and Nelson 1989; Fudge and McDermott 1991; Gregory, Hegewisch, and Sales 1999; Lewis 1988). In the fight for pay equity in the United States, for example, trade unions joined with feminists in community-based coalitions in dozens of states across the country (e.g., Blum 1991; McCann 1994). The labour-feminist alliance (Cuneo 1990) demanding fair wages for women contributed enormously to the development of "new gender politics" within labour movements (Hallock 2001, 152). Because the pay equity process required systematic job comparison measuring the relative value of paid work performed by women in relation to men, unions were sensitized to the gender power imbalance experienced by women on a daily basis in the workplace. Pay equity analyses demonstrated how women are "differently" situated in the labour market. Job comparison showed the prevalence of a generic male standard (e.g., the "normal worker" modelled on a full-time, white, able-bodied, heterosexual breadwinner) as the benchmark against which the worth of women and other minority groups work contributions are judged (Acker 1990; Creese 1999; Steinberg 1992).

As labour began to seriously confront employers about their power to define the value of work performed by women, unions inevitably began to be challenged on their own gender labour practices (e.g., Acker 1989, 22). Pay equity provided the political space for union women to push forward on equity demands both in the area of labour market policy and in regard to internal union policy, especially concerning leadership and the gender-biased culture within labour movements.[6] In this sense, the pay equity struggle of the 1980s and 1990s marked an important turning point in transforming the gender power dynamic within labour movements, and it still remains a powerful strategic force for equity mobilization. That pay equity is regarded as a human right demonstrates the success of feminist equity organizing.[7]

On a strategic level, the labour movement learned that alliances with the women's movement could be an important tactical move for building mass support for labour issues. As Judy Darcy, a high-profile Canadian trade union leader points out, "It was the alliance with the women's movement that showed the first organizational commitment of the labour movement to social unionism. We were able to build recognition in the labour movement that women are a major ally. During the Eaton's [department store] strike, there was a rallying cry around women's issues. The Fleck [auto parts manufacturing] strike, too, was an important landmark, where people in the labour movement came to understand that there was another movement out there that could be an ally" (cited in Rebick 2005, 99). Strikes and organizing campaigns that were supported by women's movement organizations educated the labour movement and the wider public about the plight of women's work lives, especially the problem of systemic sexism observable in issues such as maternity leave, sexual harassment, and unequal pay for women (e.g., Briskin and Yanz 1983; Egan and Yanz 1983; Ritchie 1987, 76-78; White 1990).

From the beginning of women's organizing, then, conventional conceptions of a union issue, and *unionism,* were being questioned and redefined by feminist unionists. Women labour activists' direct involvement in the women's movement helped shape an alternative perspective of unionism. Links with the women's movement demonstrated that fighting for economic and social equality required more than engaging in struggle at the point of production (e.g., in the workplace), and that to broaden the base of labour activism it was necessary to move beyond the usual economic demands commonly associated with collective bargaining, to incorporate issues related to the social needs of all citizens. Feminist activists' demands steered unions away from a narrowly defined focus on bread-and-butter issues, the domain of conventional business unionism, to matters of family and sexuality and other issues within the sphere of women's movement politics. This was the beginning of gendering labour movements, as the concerns of women contrasted sharply with male interests, moving unions away from the long-established labour-management industrial relations bargaining framework (e.g., for improved wages and benefits) and toward innovative approaches to unionism and alternative models of organizing.

Organizing the Unorganized: Women Workers

As labour movements experienced union decline around the globe, renewal scholars queried whether there has been a change in unions' strategy and commitment to membership recruitment (e.g., Heery and Adler 2004). It is often observed that a shift occurred, usually thought to have started in the mid-1980s and continuing into the 1990s, toward a more aggressive stance on organizing new constituencies of workers (Behrens, Hamann, and Hurd 2004, 21; Kumar and Murray 2003, 207; Kumar and Schenk 2006, 37-39; Yates 2006a, 230). As Fairbrother and Yates (2003, 17) note, before the 1980s, "unions paid little strategic attention to, and invested few resources in, actively organizing the unorganized. Even in the United States, where membership decline was evident in the 1960s, much earlier than in the other [Anglo-American] countries, organizing was not a priority." Renewal strategists often suggest that women, who are predominantly employed in flexible, low-wage, and insecure jobs, increasingly typify the so-called model worker in the service-based economy and should be singled out for recruitment.

Although it is true that greater emphasis and additional resources have been dedicated to organizing in recent years, it is also important to recognize the historic continuities regarding *strategic* approaches to organizing the unorganized. Women have long been the target of unionization and new organizational methods. Many of the so-called innovative organizing models were created by feminist unionists as early as the 1960s and 1970s to appeal to a feminized workforce (e.g., Baker 1993; Ledwith and Colgan 2002; Tait 2005; Warskett 2004). Contrary to the views of many renewal scholars, labour women have significantly influenced recent trade union strategy. In Australia, Britain, Canada, and Sweden, as Howell and Mahon (1996, 500) explain, "strategies for renewal have often been influenced by modes of action, forms of organization, mechanisms of representation and communication and types of discourse that were originally developed with women wage earners in mind."

In the area of organizing the unorganized, women unionists made great strides in refashioning traditional organizing approaches to appeal to women workers. Unlike traditional union organizing, union campaigns were led by women and informed by feminist organizing principles. Women's groups focused on community identity, such as women's identity as service workers, to create solidarity and commitment to collective action. Women's organizing also recognized the social value of paid and unpaid reproductive labour, broadening the direction of labour campaigns. Connections were made between the devaluation of women's work in the home and the social construction of low-wage feminine or reproductive work, such as caring and personal service work, in the labour market. Women labour activists reached out to non-union women in these sex-typed occupations, forging alliances with grassroots local communities to organize and build movement support. Some examples from Canada and the United States show how early efforts to unionize working women fostered innovative organizing models, forerunners of sorts to alternative organizing strategies that were to emerge later in labour movements.

Many new and independent women's organizational structures emerged in the 1970s because of a lack of support for feminism within labour movements. In Canada, feminist women who supported labour struggle and wished to unionize women formed their own women-centred structures to overcome the obstacles they experienced from organized labour. In 1972 the Service, Office, and Retail Workers of Canada (SORWUC), a self-described "grassroots, feminist union" (Lowe 1980, 32), was formed by women labour activists to unionize workers in service sectors where women predominate. Despite a weak commitment by the Canadian labour movement to SORWUC, the union was able to certify a respectable number of bargaining units in the banking industry.[8] Other feminist groups with strong ties to the Canadian women's movement included the Association of University and College Employees (AUCE) and Organized Working Women (OWW). The AUCE successfully organized support staff at the University of British Columbia, bargaining a collective agreement in 1973 with "feminist stuff" such as a "personal clause about not having to run errands and make coffee" (Jean Rands, cited in Rebick 2005, 89). The OWW, established to promote women's issues in the labour movement, was instrumental in supporting a women's committee in the Ontario Federation of Labour, the first women-only committee to be formed in a labour central in Canada.[9]

In the United States, one of the better-known women-centred organizing models initiated in the 1970s was the 9to5 association. The organizing work of this association was groundbreaking in that it was one of the first to systematically direct its mobilizing efforts to the large, feminized, non-union, clerical workforce. The original aim of the association was not unionization per se, but creating group solidarity through community-based actions raising awareness of clericals' unfair pay and working conditions. By the end of the 1970s, 9to5 formed National District 925, in alliance with the Service Employees International Union (SEIU), to function nationwide as a union local "for women and by women." The association experimented with alternative organizing approaches, such as opening a workers' centre in Cincinnati to "test out the possibilities of city-wide sectoral organizing of clerical workers. From the union's perspective, it was to be a new way to get into the workplace, not to target particular employers, but to aim to unionize 1 percent of all clerical workers in Cincinnati, then 10 percent, then 30 percent" (Lipsig-Mumme 1999, 15). By seeing itself as an extension of the community and rethinking the role of the union (and union membership) as the sole mechanism for organizing, National District 925 successfully organized thousands of librarians; college and university support staff; and daycare, home health care, and other government workers across the United States.[10]

As these few case examples demonstrate, the traditional (post-Second World War) model of unionism started to be redefined and challenged by women's organizing as early as the 1970s. The very fact that women led campaigns organizing feminized service occupations, using their own unique organizing strategies involving feminist methods such as consciousness raising and non-hierarchical approaches to decision making, was a major, if not radical, shift from the traditional masculine approach of unionizing industrial male workers en masse in large factory settings. Feminist unionists were taking important steps toward gendering organizing strategy by altering the culture and objectives of labour struggle. Instead of a total emphasis on expanding the membership base, women's organizing concentrated on mobilizing women workers to undertake collective action, to reform their gender consciousness, and to bring them into a labour community focused not just on workplace issues but also on social movement change.

Women and Equity Organizing: Building Social Unionism

In the union renewal literature, the importance of rebuilding unions and labour movements by developing new strategies and organizational approaches to engage the participation of the general union membership is understood as a key reform for labour revitalization. Arguments are made about fostering greater internal democracy and vitality within labour movements through developing new approaches for involving union members in labour movement activism (e.g., Behrens, Hamann, and Hurd 2004, 22; Kumar and Murray 2003, 208; Schenk 2003, 248-50). Promoting rank-and-file involvement in union decision making, creating avenues for inclusive participation of minority or equity groups and advancing their leadership in the union hierarchy, as well as in union organizing campaigns, are recommended strategies for renewal offered in the literature (e.g., Milkman and Voss 2004; Sharpe 2004; Weir 2006; Yates 2006a).

However, it is not sufficiently recognized in this discussion that feminist union activists and feminist scholars have made these arguments before (e.g., Briskin 2002; Briskin and Yanz 1983; Colgan and Ledwith 2000; Darcy 1993; Ledwith and Colgan 2002; White 1990). In fact, considerable discussion and debate over the benefits and pitfalls for union democracy of creating alternative structures of representation, such as women's committees and caucuses, have permeated feminist discussions on women and unions. Although the debates are too involved to discuss here, it is often agreed (with the exception of Sweden – see Briskin and Eliasson 1999a) that women's committees and other equity structures of representation have gone a long way toward transforming the culture of labour organizations, especially on issues of gender discrimination and leadership, and have oriented labour movement goals toward social movement unionism. As I explain below, equity organizing, both historically and into the present, lies at the heart of women's labour activism and remains a key element of the equity agenda in unions.

Starting as early as the 1970s, labour women in Canada, the United Kingdom, the United States, and Australia, as well as in some European nations, formed women-only committees and reform caucuses where women could meet in a non-sexist culture to discuss concerns specific to women (e.g.,

Beccalli 1996; Beccalli and Meardi 2002; Briskin 1994, 1999, 2002; Colgan and Ledwith 2000, 2002; Franzway 2000b; Hunt 2002; Parker and Gruelle 1999; Tait 2005). Often referred to as separate organizing, these groups were structured in non-hierarchical and less bureaucratic ways to encourage women's participation and were a deliberate attempt to level power relations in unions so as to promote inclusive and collective decision making. In Canada, women's committees were instrumental in creating anti-discrimination policy prohibiting sexist and other discriminatory behaviour in union meetings.[11] Separate organizing raised awareness about union priorities that ignored and disempowered women, generating feminist response that promoted women into leadership roles. As one former member of Saskatchewan Working Women (SWW), a women's committee formed in the 1970s in that Canadian province, explains, "Women got confidence from each other. As a result, the future president of the SFL (Saskatchewan Federation of Labour) came up through SWW. The head of the Saskatchewan Government Employees' Union came from SWW, as did the chairperson of the Labour Relations Board. Nearly all the women staff reps in unions came from SWW" (S. Roberts, cited in Rebick 2005, 92). By the early 1980s, as a result of separate organizing, union women in Canada demanded and were successful in attaining affirmative action positions on the executives of central labour bodies (White 1993). Separate organizing proved to have far-ranging impact not only in challenging the masculine culture of unions but also in contesting the overall direction of labour movement goals. More than any other aspect of women's union activism, separate organizing provided the foundational bedrock for developing a gender and equity perspective of trade unionism (e.g., Briskin 2002; Hunt 2002; Ledwith and Colgan 2002; Sugiman 1994).

Women's union activism generated new approaches and perspectives about whom to organize. Community coalitions, especially with women's organizations, led to growing awareness of the need to take into account *differing* experiences among women and other minorities. Gender-specific labour demands that were first put forward based on a conception of a universal women's identity started to be re-evaluated in response to views of minority women whose experiences differed from the core constituency of white and typically middle-class women. The experience of racialized women in consciousness raising groups, for example, exposed different forms of oppression among women.[12] Although feminists had previously critiqued a universal male standard as unfair to women, now minority women began to criticize essentialist notions of universal womanhood. Within labour movements, recognition of diversity led to alternative equality strategies, not only for women but for all minorities. New constituencies such as racialized minorities, gays and lesbians, the disabled, and other marginalized union members sought political recognition and structures of representation similar to those that women had originally pursued inside labour movements (Briskin 1999, 551). Sexual minorities in Canada especially benefit from the organizing work of women who paved the way for gays and lesbians to form caucuses, thereby opening space to debate and propose policy initiatives challenging unions on issues of sexual orientation discrimination (Hunt 2002, 272).

Racialized constituencies, too, built upon the feminist challenge to rid labour movements and labour markets of systemic racism (Briskin 2002, 38; Clarke Walker, this volume; Das Gupta 2007, 192-93; Leah 1999, 114).[13] As equity-seeking groups continued to organize, affirmative action-designated seats were extended to racial minorities on central labour bodies in Canada by the early 1990s, and later in the same decade, for the disabled, gays and lesbians, and Aboriginals. Recently, Aboriginal organizing in Canada has begun to flourish. In some unions, collective agreement language to protect Aboriginal culture is being devised, alternative approaches to unionizing specific to Aboriginal communities are being developed, and employment equity plans are being formulated to better represent Aboriginals in the workforce (Moran 2005; Page 2005).

That women's organizing contributed to building and diversifying the constituency base of labour movements is not unique to Canada. As Hunt (2002, 273) observes about sexual diversity, "The Canadian experience has some parallels in countries such as Australia, Germany, Britain, the Netherlands, and to a lesser extent the United States ... [in that] early union activity has tended to follow progress on women's issues." In the United Kingdom, as Ledwith and Colgan (2002, 16) explain, "the Trades Union Congress has moved from running a women's conference, since 1925, to organizing a black members' conference and a lesbian and gay workers' conference in the 1990s. In 2000 it established a conference for disabled members."

Building equity constituencies also created a vehicle for reaching out to communities outside labour to engage in collective struggle for social and economic justice. In recent years, in the United States and Canada, unions have established coalitions with community-based groups such as those allied with immigrant and migrant labour communities, to press for better and more inclusive labour protections. These coalitions expanded the reach of organized labour to encompass groups difficult to organize (precarious workers) or the unorganizable (migrant workers), and encouraged labour organizations to engage in cross-border and international labour resistance strategies. In Canada, the Philippine Women Centre of BC follows feminist ideas to organize live-in migrant domestic caregivers on their employment rights by working with labour and establishing community-based programs and projects that empower Filipina-Canadian women (see Zaman, Diocson, and Scott 2007). The Toronto and York Region Labour Council, based in the city of Toronto, engages in municipal campaigns aimed at supporting immigrant workers, many of whom are low-paid women working in the private service sector, for example, in hospitality, garment, clerical, and health care sectors.

The council has launched campaigns to raise the economic and work standards for these low-paid workers by demanding an increase in the minimum wage to ten dollars per hour; by supporting mass mobilization and unionization with the goal of raising union density in the Greater Toronto Area by 1 percent; and by lobbying municipal, provincial, and federal politicians to improve social services (Toronto and York Region Labour Council 2005). STITCH, a US-based labour advocacy organization, builds links with the American labour and women's movements to forge international solidarity, and specifically engages in cross-border education and union actions with women activists in Central America.[14] Strategies such as these may reasonably be conceived of as a logical outgrowth of the feminist unionist equity agenda to achieve greater social equality for the marginalized, establishing the strategic capacity for social movement unionism.

Labour Internationalism

A fourth subject in the trade union renewal scholarship concerns the issue of international unionism and global labour solidarity (e.g., Harrod and O'Brien 2002; Munck 2002; Turner 2004). However, as Fairbrother and Hammer (2005, 406) point out, "Surprisingly, there has been relatively little discussion of international unionism in the debates about trade union renewal or revitalization." Given the relative lack of interest in labour internationalism, it is not surprising to see almost no discussion of global labour women's organizing, even though the work of international trade union women, and other women labour activists, has shaped policy discussions on matters of international trade, development policy, and international labour standards.

International women's groups began to systematically organize in the 1980s when structural adjustment policy, implemented by the World Bank and International Monetary Fund, severely altered the conditions of life for women (Antrobus 2004, 67). Women's groups caucused, networked, organized coalitions, and formed alliances with NGOs to debate strategy and formulate gendered analyses of women's socio-economic position within the global economy. Such analyses highlighted how women are super-exploited in the sphere of production, through export-led development in manufacturing that depends on low-wage, young, female, and flexible labour. In services, women are hired to perform exceedingly routinized (e.g., data and teleprocessing) work and experience extreme forms of oppression in personal service (e.g., domestic, sex trade) work. Transnational women's groups also pointed to the impact of neo-liberal development policy on the sphere of reproduction, showing that reductions in the delivery of state-funded social services such as education, health care, and general welfare programs harm the economic and social well-being of families and households (Petchesky 2003). A large part of the struggle for women's equality has been to insist that governments recognize women's unpaid labour in the household. United Nations conferences on women devoted discussion to this issue, resulting in member governments signing agreements in 1975 and 1985 to redress problems related to the devaluation of women's unpaid domestic work. However, by 1995, at the Beijing NGO conference, women from all 185 participating countries reported a decline in the position of women in their countries and noted that women's unpaid contributions had increased while policies and services designed to support them had, in almost all countries, been reduced or eliminated (Luxton 2005, 8).

These gendered analyses established the strategic groundwork for further global organizing. When the World Trade Organization (WTO) was launched in 1995, it became a focal point for women's organizing, particularly feminist labour organizing.[15] In 1996, when the WTO met to debate a proposal for a social clause, women's groups asked what "a social clause would mean for women and what its significance is in an overall campaign for workers rights" (Hale 1998, 28). This was the first time international attention focused on the specific gender impact of global free trade.

The organizing work of feminists also influenced the policy perspective of the international labour community, especially of global unions, such as the International Confederation of Free Trade Unions (ICFTU).[16] The ICFTU Women's Committee has repeatedly argued for the "inclusion of gender perspectives in all trade union policies and programmes" (ICFTU 2003, 13). It devised an ICFTU Charter of Rights of Working Women and has called for including women workers' rights in the policies of the WTO, World Bank, and regional trade agreements, as well as demanded that the policies of international agencies be assessed from a gender dimension. The ICFTU has asked affiliates to intensify efforts to target organizing women (who represent 80 percent of workers) in the export processing zones; to organize women, as well as youth, in precarious employment; and to protect the rights of migrant workers.

Inserting a gender lens in policy discussions on global development redefined the debates on important issues such as trade liberalization and global labour regulation. International women trade unionists, in alliance with the global women's movement, identified women as central actors in the global economy who, as highly exploited workers in the formal and informal economies, need protection from trade unions, as well as support from global institutions whose policies directly impact on the women's work and day-to-day lives. As in other areas of feminist union activism, alliances and coalitions with global women's movement organizations have proven to be a crucial strategy in the struggle to advocate for gender and social equality worldwide.

Gendering Labour: Toward an Equity Model of Unionism

As a result of women's organizing, the labour movement in Canada and elsewhere experienced decisive challenges to traditional unionism. These feminist challenges and reform efforts correspond to those that renewal scholars recommend. However, as the above review points out, the renewal scholarship tends to neglect the fact that, often, progressive change occurred whenever a gender lens and equity focus was brought to bear on the issues, structures, practices, and culture of labour organizations. As we have seen, the woman-centred strategy to eliminate sexism in unions evolved and expanded to a broader union equity base, generating a stronger commitment to social justice in labour movements. Various forms of feminist union activism, from advancing new constituencies into the union fold through encouraging greater rank-and-file participation, to mobilizing both union and non-union workers in coalitions with grassroots community groups, to developing an equity agenda to improve the situation of the marginalized inside, and outside, the labour movement, contributed to a coherent labour strategy to further economic and social justice. An equity agenda encompassing support for gender, racialized, and other minority group equality eventually extended equity issues to international labour and human rights, sustainable development, and global solidarity.

Women's organizing imparted to labour movement culture a gender politic – a discourse that incorporates recognition of difference and strives for substantive equality outcomes for women and other equity-seeking groups. For instance, as feminist unionists struggled to achieve greater union representation for women, it became evident that the industrial model of unionism in Canada and the United States is structured to secure unionization in male-predominant industries, thus neglecting the plight of precarious workers in many feminized sectors (e.g., Forrest 1995; Warskett 1996).

In the struggle for pay equity, gender biases in the workplace were uncovered, exposing a masculine ideal of the generic worker that serves as an implicit reference point for defining work standards. The struggle for recognition of women's unpaid work in the home caused a decisive shift in thinking about "women's work" that altered perceptions about the social value of women's paid and unpaid employment in the economy and led to mobilization around specific policy demands (e.g., pay equity, UN policy). Issues on child care, reproductive choice, and balancing the workday between home and work are now seen as key labour concerns (e.g., Beccalli 1996; Briskin 2002, 33; 2006).

Union women continuously work to genderize employment and welfare policy to be fairer to working women, thereby politicizing and gendering the meaning of welfare entitlements (e.g., Cobble 2004; Porter 2003). Although initially the basis of women's inequality was understood in relation to structural issues such as women's unequal earnings compared with those of men, or to an unequal gender division of labour that reinforced women's subordinate status in the workplace, in the union, and in the home, over time, the study and meaning of gender relations broadened to encompass the social processes and cultural value systems that lie behind inequities experienced by women and other equity-seeking groups in unions and within society.

Gendering facilitated a transformative labour strategy along two dimensions. First, by internally challenging trade union organizations, largely, though not exclusively, in relation to equity demands, traditional hierarchical and bureaucratic structures and conceptions of unionism were reformulated and re-envisioned. Feminist unionists' alliance with the women's movement broadened the labour agenda to incorporate gender equality and other social equity demands, enlarging and transforming the very basis of labour struggle. The meaning of a legitimate labour issue was transformed by challenging the masculine culture of unions and labour markets (e.g., the male breadwinner ideal), identifying the intersection between productive and reproductive labour (e.g., child care, work/life balance, parental and family leave), resisting low-wage feminized service work (e.g., precarious employment, gender wage equity, sex work), promoting human rights (e.g., international labour regulation, pay equity movements, same sex rights), and by international solidarity (e.g., women and global trade union issues).

Second, by opposing systemic inequities inherent in labour organizations, labour markets, and within society generally, women's activism moved labour in a direction of social justice unionism. Feminist unionism necessarily confronts fundamental gender power relations, driving labour in the direction of broader social change projects. Flowing from women's organizing is a type of equity model of unionism that promotes a transformative politic within labour movements.

Conclusion

How gender is incorporated into the union revitalization project was the central problematic of this chapter. The decades of struggle over the implementation of a feminist labour agenda is barely acknowledged in much of the union renewal literature, and therefore the successes and limitations of these past organizing efforts are not analyzed or integrated into this literature. It is worth emphasizing that women's labour organizing since the 1970s can be broadly described as encompassing the following internal and external movement strategies, all of which are frequently cited in renewal scholarship: coalition building (alliances with women's movement organizations and grassroots community groups), organizing the unorganized (e.g., non-union clerical and other service workers), political action campaigns (e.g., pay equity), inclusive democratic practices promoting greater membership participation (e.g., separate organizing of equity groups), diversifying labour leadership (e.g., increasing the presence of women and minorities), and labour internationalism and promoting an alternative vision of social change (e.g., feminist ideology and practice). All of these strategies contributed to a broader conception of unionism, altering how unions conceived of themselves and how they structured their organizations. An equality-driven framework, first introduced by union women during second-wave feminism, channelled labour struggle toward a transformative political program internally within the trade union movement, and externally as part of a larger social movement confronting globalization. Women's union organizing initiatives promote labour organizing as a social movement through its wide-ranging political program to further economic and social justice.

That the organizing work of women continues to have validity for the renewal project is emphasized by Christopher Schenk (2003, 253), who reminds us of "the need to support people's various identities as feminists, environmentalists, or members of a particular ethnic community and concomitantly to create the necessary unity to defend their needs and aspirations as workers." I obviously agree with Schenk that labour in Canada, and in other national contexts, must continue to represent and advocate for the needs and interests of feminists and equity groups, as well as of other social movement activists. But I would also point out that this has been an ongoing struggle that needs to be given full consideration in evaluating tactics and practices of union renewal. Equity organizing is seldom addressed as a coherent strategy for labour movement change, but rather it is understood as one factor among many for revitalizing unions. Simply inserting women and equity-seeking groups into the existing union structures without understanding that the equity project is part of a larger gender politic to transform labour as a social movement will not alter the policies and practices of trade unions.

Indeed, one of the implications of assessing feminist labour organizing as a renewal strategy is that change does not come easily in labour movements (Clarke Walker; Edelson; Foley, Chapter 7; Wall; this volume). The recent history of women's organizing in unions shows that gendered inequality and other inequality regimes are so fundamental and deeply rooted in labour organizations that change strategies must be continuously revised and adjusted to confront new barriers and shifting economic and social realities. Still, in the current era of labour struggle, where unions are losing ground as a force of political opposition to capital, women's organizing continues to hold out possibilities for labour movement change and needs to be considered in debates on the future of unions.

Notes

1 In this chapter the terms "women's organizing," "women's labour activism," "feminist unionism," "feminist unionist activism," "feminist trade unionism," and "women's organizing" refer to organizing initiatives and actions informed by feminist principles and feminist politics. For a discussion of feminism in unions see Colgan and Ledwith (2000).

2 The Canadian Labour Congress' report (1997) *Women's Work* uses the terms "equity" and "equality agenda." For a theoretical discussion of equity agenda and equity project see Linda Briskin (1994, 2002).

3 For a longer discussion of the literature see my working paper (2006) *Gendering Union Renewal: Women's Contributions to Labour Movement Revitalization*. For the Gender and Work Database, see http://www.genderwork.ca.

4 Consciousness raising was highly influential in feminist theorizing and feminist action, especially on questions of women's domestic labour and sexuality. See Beccalli (1996), MacKinnon (1989), and Rebick (2005, 12).

5 The Equal Pay Coalition advocated for legislated pay equity in the province of Ontario; the Childcare Advocacy Association of Canada continues its struggle for a federally funded national child care program for regulated child care centres; Women Against the Budget advocates for an alternative budget policy supporting a broad set of social programs beneficial to women and other vulnerable groups; Women Against Trade in the Pro-Canada Network mobilized an anti-free-trade campaign in the 1980s against greater trade liberalization with the United States.

6 Since the 1980s almost every dimension of labour market policy, from occupational health and safety to job training, apprenticeships, and employment standards, has been subject to a gender-sensitive analysis. On Canadian policy issues see, for example, Cohen (2003), Fudge (1991), and Porter (2003).

7 Historic continuities on the pay equity struggle are evident in Canada. In the province of Quebec, the right to equal pay for work of equal value first began with legislation in 1976, continuing into the 1980s and 1990s. In 1996, the women's and union movement won a proactive pay equity law – achieved, in part, by the 1995 Bread and Roses March; see Beeman (2004). On pay equity as a human right see the Canadian federal *Pay Equity Task Force 2004* (Canada, 2004), 7.

8 Eventually, limited resources and a legal decision restricting certification (unionized) units to small bank branches undermined the momentum of the campaign and the union was unable to continue its organizing efforts. See, for example, Baker (1993) and Warskett (1991).

9 The Ontario Federation of Labour formed the first women's committee in a labour central in Canada in 1961. On the formation of women's committees in Canada see White (1993, chapter 5).

10 In 2001, National District 925 restructured, merging with various other locals within SEIU. However, 9to5 continues to exist and organize, with a national office in Milwaukee, Wisconsin, focusing on campaigns such as family leave, sexual harassment and anti-discrimination, workfare and non-standard work; see http://www.9to5.org/.

11 In Canada, the women's committee in the Canadian Auto Workers (CAW) union devised anti-discrimination language in 1988 that is still used today. Interview, Peggy Nash, CAW, 31 October 2003, Toronto, Ontario.

12 Consciousness raising in the 1970s alienated many racialized women living in Canada whose experiences as immigrants and racialized minorities did not match those of white middle-class women, who tended to dominate these groups; see Agnew (1996, 76-82).

13 In the United States, the history of racial minority unionization began much earlier than in other national contexts, including that of Canada; see Tait (2005).

14 www.stitchonline.org/whowhat.asp.

15 Numerous feminist organizations and networks were developed to address the issue of gender and trade; see Antrobus (2004, 90) and Hale (1998, 17).

16 The ICFTU has a membership of 45 million workers, 40 percent of whom are women; see Fairbrother and Hammer (2005).

References
Acker, J. 1989. *Doing Comparable Worth: Gender, Class and Pay Equity*. Philadelphia: Temple University Press.

–. 1990. Hierarchies, jobs, bodies: A theory of gendered organizations. *Gender and Society* 4, 2: 139-58.

–. 2006. *Class Questions: Feminist Answers*. Toronto: Rowman and Littlefield.

Adamson, N., L. Briskin, and M. McPhail. 1988. *Feminist Organizing for Change: The Contemporary Women's Movement in Canada.* Toronto: Oxford University Press.

Agnew, V. 1996. *Resisting Discrimination: Women from Asia, Africa and the Caribbean.* Toronto: University of Toronto Press.

Antrobus, P. 2004. *The Global Women's Movement: Origins, Issues and Strategies.* Halifax: Fernwood.

Baker, P. 1993. Reflections on life stories: Women's bank union activism. In *Women Challenging Unions: Feminism, Democracy and Militancy,* ed. L. Briskin and P. McDermott, 62-86. Toronto: University of Toronto Press.

Beccalli, B. 1996. The modern women's movement in Italy. In *Mapping the Women's Movement,* ed. M. Threfall, 152-83. London: Verso.

Beccalli, B., and G. Meardi. 2002. From unintended to undecided feminism? Italian labour's changing and singular ambiguities. In *Gender, Diversity and Trade Unions: International Perspectives,* ed. F. Colgan and S. Ledwith, 113-31. New York: Routledge.

Beeman, J. 2004. Pay equity in Quebec: A right unknown to the women workers who need it most. *Canadian Woman Studies* 23, 3/4: 96-104.

Behrens, M., K. Hamann, and R. Hurd. 2004. Conceptualizing labour union revitalization. In *Varieties of Unionism: Strategies for Union Revitalization in a Globalizing Economy,* ed. C.M. Frege and J. Kelly, 11-30. Toronto: Oxford University Press.

Blum, L. 1991. *Between Feminism and Labor: The Significance of the Comparable Worth Movement.* Berkley: University of California Press.

Boeri, T., A. Brugiavini, and L. Calmfors, eds. 2001. *The Role of Unions in the Twenty-First Century: A Study for the Fandazione Rodolfo Debenedetti.* New York: Oxford University Press.

Briskin, L. 1994. Equity and restructuring in the Canadian labour movement. *Economic and Industrial Democracy* 15, 1: 89-112.

–. 1999. Feminisms, feminization, and democratization in Canadian unions. In *Feminist Success Stories,* ed. K. Blackford, M-L. Garceau, and S. Kirby, 73-92. Ottawa: University of Ottawa Press.

–. 2002. The equity project in Canadian unions: Confronting the challenge of restructuring and globalization. In *Gender, Diversity and Trade Unions: International Perspectives,* ed. F. Colgan and S. Ledwith, 28-41. New York: Routledge.

–. 2006. Equity bargaining/bargaining equity. Working Paper Series 2006-01, Centre for Research on Work and Society, York University.

Briskin, L., and M. Eliasson, eds. 1999a. *Women's Organizing and Public Policy in Canada and Sweden.* Montreal: McGill-Queen's University Press.

Briskin, L., and P. McDermott, eds. 1993. *Women Challenging Unions: Feminism, Democracy and Militancy.* Toronto: University of Toronto Press.

Briskin, L., and L. Yanz, eds. 1983. *Union Sisters: Women in the Labour Movement.* Toronto: Women's Press.

Burton, C. 1991. *The Promise and the Price: The Struggle for Equal Opportunity in Women's Employment.* Sydney: Allen and Unwin.

Canada. Department of Justice. 2004. *Pay Equity: A New Approach to a Fundamental Right: Pay Equity Task Force, 2004.* Ottawa: Department of Justice.

Canadian Labour Congress. 1997. *Women's Work: A Report by the Canadian Labour Congress.* Ottawa: Canadian Labour Congress.

Clawson, D. 2003. *The Next Upsurge: Labor and the New Social Movements.* Ithaca, NY: ILR Press.

Cobble, D., ed. 1993. *Women and Unions: Forging a Partnership.* Ithaca, NY: ILR Press.

–. 2004. *The Other Women's Movement: Workplace Justice and Social Rights in Modern America.* Princeton, NJ: Princeton University Press.

–. 2007. *The Sex of Class: Women Transforming American Labor.* Ithaca, NY: Cornell University Press.

Cohen, M., ed. 2003. *Training the Excluded for Work: Access and Equity for Women, Immigrants, First Nations, Youth and People with Low Income.* Vancouver: UBC Press.

Colgan, F., and S. Ledwith. 2000. Diversity, identities and strategies of women trade union activists. *Gender, Work and Organization* 7, 4: 243-44.

–, eds. 2002. *Gender, Diversity and Trade Unions: International Perspectives*. New York: Routledge.

Connelly, P., and M. Keddy. 1989. Fifty years a feminist trade unionist: Interview with Madeleine Parent. *Studies in Political Economy* 30, Fall: 13-36.

Crain, M. 1994. Gender and union organizing. *Industrial and Labor Relations Review* 47, 2: 227-48.

Creese, G. 1999. *Contracting Masculinity: Gender, Class and Race in a White-Collar Union, 1944-1994*. Don Mills, ON: Oxford University Press.

Cuneo, C. 1990. *Pay Equity: The Labour-Feminist Challenge*. Toronto: Oxford University Press.

Darcy, J. 1993. Foreword. In *Women Challenging Unions: Feminism, Democracy and Militancy*, ed. L. Briskin and P. McDermott, vii-xi. Toronto: University of Toronto Press.

Das Gupta, T. 2007. Racism and the labour movement. In *Equity, Diversity and Canadian Labour*, ed. G. Hunt and D. Rayside, 181-207. Toronto: University of Toronto Press.

Egan, C. 1987. Socialist feminist activism and alliances. In *Feminism and Political Economy: Women's Work, Women's Struggles*, ed. H.J. Maroney and M. Luxton, 109-18. Toronto: Methuen.

Egan, C., and L. Yanz. 1983. Building links: Labour and the women's movement. In *Union Sisters: Women in the Labour Movement*, ed. L. Briskin and L. Yanz, 361-75. Toronto: Women's Press.

Evans, S., and B. Nelson. 1989. *Wage Justice: Comparable Worth and the Paradox of Technocratic Reform*. Chicago: University of Chicago Press.

Fairbrother, P., and G. Griffin. 2002. *Changing Prospects for Trade Unionism: Comparisons between Six Countries*. London: Continuum.

Fairbrother, P., and N. Hammer. 2005. Global unions: Past efforts and future prospects. *Relations industrielles/Industrial Relations* 60, 3: 405-31.

Fairbrother, P., G. Griffin, N. Hammer, and C. Yates, eds. 2003. *Trade Unions in Renewal: A Comparative Study*. London: Continuum.

Fairbrother, P., and C. Yates, eds. 2003. *Trade Unions in Renewal: A Comparative Study*. London: Continuum.

Forrest, A. 1995. Securing the male breadwinner: A feminist interpretation of PC 1003. In *Labour Gains, Labour Pains: Fifty Years of PC 1003*, ed. C. Gonick, P. Phillips, and J. Vorst, 139-62. Winnipeg: Society for Socialist Studies.

Franzway, S. 2000a. Women working in a greedy institution: Commitment and emotional labour in the union movement. *Gender, Work and Organization* 7, 4: 258-68.

–. 2000b. Sisters and sisters? Labour movements and women's movements in (English) Canada and Australia. *Hecate* 26, 2: 31-46.

Frege, C.M., and J. Kelly, eds. 2004. *Varieties of Unionism: Strategies for Union Revitalization in a Globalizing Economy*. Oxford and New York: Oxford University Press.

Fudge, J. 1991. *Labour Law's Little Sister: The Employment Standards Act and the Feminization of Labour*. Ottawa: Centre for Policy Alternatives.

Fudge, J., and P. McDermott, eds. 1991. *Just Wages: A Feminist Assessment of Pay Equity*. Toronto: University of Toronto Press.

Gregory, J., A. Hegewisch, and R. Sales, eds. 1999. *Women, Work and Inequality: The Challenge of Equal Pay in a Deregulated Market*. New York: Macmillan.

Hale, A., ed. 1998. *Trade Myths and Gender Reality: Trade Liberalisation and Women's Lives*. Uppsala, Sweden: International Coalition for Development Action.

Hallock, M. 2001. Pay equity: Did it work? In *Squaring Up: Policy Strategies to Raise Women's Incomes in the United States*, ed. M. King, 136-61. Ann Arbor: University of Michigan Press.

Harrod, J., and R. O'Brien, eds. 2002. *Global Unions? Theory and Strategies of Organized Labour in the Global Political Economy*. London: Routledge.

Heery, E., and L. Adler. 2004. Organizing the unorganized. In *Varieties of Unionism: Strategies for Union Revitalization in a Globalizing Economy*, ed. C.M. Frege and J. Kelly, 45-70. Oxford and New York: Oxford University Press.

Howell, C., and R. Mahon. 1996. Editorial Introduction – Special Issue on Strategies for Renewal: Women wage earners and the new exemplar? *Economic and Industrial Democracy* 17: 499-509.

Hunt, G. 2002. Organised labour, sexual diversity and union activism in Canada. In *Gender, Diversity and Trade Unions: International Perspectives*, ed. F. Colgan and S. Ledwith, 257-74. New York: Routledge.

Hurd, R. 2004. The failure of organizing: The new unity partnership, and the future of the labor movement. *Working USA: The Journal of Labor and Society* 8 (September): 5-25.

ICFTU (International Confederation of Free Trade Unions). 2003. *The Charter of Rights of Working Women*. Belgium.

Jose, A.V. 2002. Organised labour in the 21st century: Some lessons for developing countries. In *Organized Labour in the 21st Century*, ed. A.V. Jose, 1-20. Geneva: International Institute for Labour Studies.

Kumar, P., and G. Murray. 2003. Strategic dilemma: The state of union renewal in Canada. In *Trade Unions in Renewal: A Comparative Study*, ed. P. Fairbrother and C. Yates, 200-20. London: Continuum.

Kumar, P., and C. Schenk, eds. 2006. *Paths to Union Renewal: Canadian Experiences*. Peterborough, ON: Broadview Press.

Leah, J. 1999. Do you call me sister? Women of colour and the Canadian labour movement. In *Scratching the Surface: Canadian Anti-Racist Feminist Thought*, ed. E. Du and A. Robertson, 97-126. Toronto: Women's Press.

Ledwith, S., and F. Colgan. 2002. Tackling gender, diversity and trade union democracy: A worldwide project? In *Gender, Diversity and Trade Unions: International Perspectives*, ed. F. Colgan and S. Ledwith, 1-27. New York: Routledge.

Lévesque, C., and G. Murray. 2006. Globalization and renewal: Lessons from the Quebec labour movement. In *Paths to Union Renewal: Canadian Experiences*, ed. P. Kumar and C. Schenk, 113-26. Peterborough, ON: Broadview Press.

Lewis, D. 1988. *Just Give Us the Money: A Discussion of Wage Discrimination and Pay Equity*. Vancouver: Women's Research Centre.

Lipsig-Mumme, C. 1999. The language of organising: Trade union strategy in international perspective. Working Paper No. 20, Centre for Research on Work and Society, York University.

Lowe, G. 1980. *Bank Unionization in Canada: A Preliminary Analysis*. Toronto: Centre for Industrial Relations.

Luxton, M. 2005. Working class women and struggles around unpaid work. Paper presented at the "Labouring Feminism and Feminist Working-Class History in North America and Beyond" conference, Toronto.

MacKinnon, C. 1979. *Sexual Harassment of Working Women: A Case of Discrimination*. New Haven, CT: Yale University Press.

–. 1989. *Toward a Feminist Theory of the State*. Cambridge, MA: Harvard University Press.

McCann, M. 1994. *Rights at Work: Pay Equity Reform and the Politics of Legal Mobilization*. Chicago: University of Chicago Press.

Milkman, R., and K. Voss, eds. 2004. *Rebuilding Labor: Organizing and Organizers in the New Union Movement*. Ithaca, NY: ILR Press.

Moran, D. 2005. Partnerships and patience: Organizing strategies for Aboriginal communities. *Our Times: Canada's Independent Labour Magazine* 24, 2: 12-17.

Munck, R. 2002. *Globalisation and Labour*. London: Zed Books.

Page, H. 2005. Tools for change: Organizing Aboriginal communities. *Our Times* 24, 1: 19-22.

Parker, J. 2002. Women's groups in British unions. *British Journal of Industrial Relations* 40: 23-48.

Parker, M., and M. Gruelle. 1999. *Democracy is Power: Rebuilding Unions from the Bottom Up*. Detroit: Labor Education and Research Project.

Petchesky, R. 2003. *Global Prescriptions: Gendering Health and Human Rights*. London: Zed Books.

Porter, A. 2003. *Gendered States: Women, Unemployment Insurance and the Political Economy of the Welfare State in Canada, 1945-1997*. Toronto: University of Toronto Press.

Rayside, D. 2007. Equity, diversity and Canadian labour: A comparative perspective. In *Equity, Diversity and Canadian Labour,* ed. G. Hunt and D. Rayside, 208-43. Toronto: University of Toronto Press.

Rebick, J. 2005. *Ten Thousand Roses: The Making of a Feminist Revolution.* Toronto: Penguin Canada.

Ritchie, L. 1987. *Women Workers and Labour Organizations.* Paper commissioned by the Institute on Women and Work, City of Toronto.

Robertson, D., and B. Murnigham. 2006. Union renewal and union resistance in the CAW. In *Paths to Union Renewal: Canadian Experiences,* ed. P. Kumar and C. Schenk, 161-83. Peterborough, ON: Broadview Press.

Rose, J., and G. Chaison. 2001. Unionism in Canada and the United States in the 21st century: Prospects for revival. *Relations industrielles/Industrial Relations* 56, 1: 34-62.

Schenk, C. 2003. Social movement unionism: Beyond the organizing model. In *Trade Unions in Renewal: A Comparative Study,* ed. P. Fairbrother and C. Yates, 244-62. London: Continuum.

Sharpe, T. 2004. Union democracy and successful campaigns. In *Rebuilding Labor: Organizing and Organizers in the New Union Movement,* ed. R. Milkman and K. Voss, 62-87. Ithaca, NY: ILR Press.

Spalter-Roth, R., H. Hartmann, and N. Collins. 1994. What do unions do for women? In *Restoring the Promise of American Labor Law,* ed. S. Friedman, R.W. Hurd, R.A. Oswald, and R.L. Seeber, 193-206. Ithaca, NY: ILR Press.

Steinberg, R. 1992. Gendered instructions, cultural lag and gender bias in the Hay System of Job Evaluation. *Work and Occupations* 19, 4: 387-423.

Sugiman, P. 1994. *Labour's Dilemma: The Gender Politics of Auto Workers in Canada, 1937-1979.* Toronto: University of Toronto Press.

Tait, V. 2005. *Poor Workers' Unions: Rebuilding Labor from Below.* Cambridge, MA: South End Press.

Toronto and York Region Labour Council. 2005. *Toronto and York Region Labour Council Yearbook: A Million Reasons to Take Action.* Toronto: Toronto and York Region Labour Council.

Turner, L. 2004. Why revitalize? Labour's urgent mission in a contested global economy. In *Varieties of Unionism: Strategies for Union Revitalization in a Globalizing Economy,* ed. C.M. Frege and J. Kelly, 1-10. Oxford and New York: Oxford University Press.

Verma, A., and T. Kochan, eds. 2004. *Unions in the 21st Century: An International Perspective.* New York: Palgrave Macmillan.

Voss, K., and R. Sherman. 2003. You just can't do it automatically: The transition to social movement unionism in the United States. In *Trade Unions in Renewal: A Comparative Study,* ed. P. Fairbrother and C. Yates, 51-77. London: Continuum.

Warskett, R. 1991. Bank worker unionization and the law. *Studies in Political Economy* 34 (Spring): 219-33.

–. 1996. The politics of difference and inclusiveness within the Canadian labour movement. *Economic and Industrial Democracy* 17: 587-625.

–. 2004. Thinking through labour's organizing strategies: What the data reveal and what the data conceal. Paper presented at the "Gender and Work: Knowledge Production in Practice" conference, North York, ON.

Weir, J. 2006. Increasing inter-union co-operation and co-ordination: The BC Federation of Labour Organizing Institute. In *Paths to Union Renewal: Canadian Experiences,* ed. P. Kumar and C. Schenk, 295-305. Peterborough, ON: Broadview Press.

White, J. 1990. *Mail and Female: Women and the Canadian Union of Postal Workers.* Toronto: Thompson Educational.

–. 1993. *Sisters and Solidarity: Women and Unions in Canada.* Toronto: Thompson Educational.

Yates, C. 2003. The revival of industrial unions in Canada: The extension and adaptation of industrial union practices to the new economy. In *Trade Unions in Renewal: A Comparative Study,* ed. P. Fairbrother and C. Yates, 221-43. London: Continuum.

–. 2006a. Women are key to union renewal: Lessons from the Canadian labour movement. In *Paths to Union Renewal: Canadian Experiences,* ed. P. Kumar and C. Schenk, 103-12. Peterborough, ON: Broadview Press.

–. 2006b. Challenging misconceptions about organizing women into unions. *Gender, Work and Organization* 13, 6: 565-84.

Zaman, H., C. Diocson, and R. Scott. 2007. *Workplace Rights for Immigrants in BC: The Case of Filipino Workers.* Vancouver: Canadian Centre for Policy Alternatives.

2
Too Bad, You Were Too Late Coming In!
Marie-Josée Legault

Since the 1980s, and even more so since the 1990s, European researchers (e.g., Hyman 1992; 1997, 29; Müller-Jentsch 1988) and North American researchers (e.g., Creese 1996, 454; Crever 1993, 1998; Edwards 1986; Fudge 1996; Gagnon 1998; Kumar, Murray, and Schetagne 1998; White 1990; Zeytinoglu and Muteshi 2000) have been examining what is frequently referred to as a "crisis" in the union movement, in contrast to what was a fairly firm consensus on the unity and representative power of organized labour up until the late 1970s. Trouble in aggregating and recognizing common interests within both trade union locals and confederations has become fairly evident since this time (see also Clarke Walker; Edelson; Foley, Chapter 7; Wall; this volume).

This situation is closely tied to the emergence of new factors contributing to the segmentation of labour, which in turn may have the effect of segmenting the unionized community. Some of the segmentation factors stem from human resource management decisions: promoting worker and workplace flexibility; increasing the number of casual workplace statuses and forms of compensation; the practice of multi-tasking; disparities among workers in status and compensation levels, and so on. Other segmentation factors, however, originate among the workers themselves or are shared, appropriated, and promoted by them.

Under human rights charters and acts,[1] the case law that stems from them, and the more general spreading and promotion of their philosophy, some categories of labour demonstrate specific interests that are distinct from those of the larger group of unionized workers to which they belong, sometimes to the point of contesting what are regarded by others as important gains in union practices, or decisions based upon majority votes. A relevant example is the conflict raised by employees paid under what are known as orphan clauses in Quebec, or as two-tiered wage systems in other Canadian contexts.

In this chapter I attempt to show that where two-tiered wage systems are implemented, newly hired workers' demands and interests are sometimes so distinct from those of the majority of the union local that they affect solidarity and create conflict. First I present a discussion of two-tiered clauses as a general phenomenon. I then focus more sharply on a lawsuit that has advanced to the Supreme Court of Canada. It was initiated by a group of union members against their union, the Centrale des syndicats du Québec (CSQ), because the members felt they had been adversely affected by a two-tier wage clause the union had negotiated. The file is now closed (though unsettled).

I do not analyze here the substance of the case, nor the content of the refused out-of-court settlement,[2] but rather a previous decision of the Supreme Court of Canada inherent to the case; this decision has acknowledged that a conflict of interest exists between this group of workers and their union, and has denied the union the right to represent these workers as the case advances, as it could be held responsible for the situation and be required to face those workers in court. This case raises serious questions about who can legitimately speak on behalf of such workers, and emphasizes the need for more equitable representation of diverse member groups within unions.

Following the detailed discussion of this particular request from a group of union members and of the decision of the Supreme Court of Canada, I develop the difference between the concepts of equality and equity, the former being deeply rooted in union traditions, the latter recently brought into labour relations by the Quebec Human Rights charter and its philosophy.[3] In unionized environments the notion of formal equality, or equality of rights, is widespread if not universal. Similar in its application to the same concept in our liberal law and political life, it provides the foundation for democratic citizenship, in which decisions are supposed to be based on the primacy of a majority vote taken in a general meeting; in these, each individual enjoys a vote of equal weight. According to this notion, aiming at equality dictates that all union members be treated equally. On the other hand, with the notion of equity or equality of results set forth by the human rights laws, legislators recognize that it is sometimes necessary to treat the members of certain groups differently in order to increase their representation in work environments, for instance, to temporarily allow for preferential treatment to women (or other groups suffering discrimination) until a situation of equality of results has been established, regardless of the opinion of the majority, because human rights prevail over any other law. These conflicting conceptions of equality create serious difficulties for unions.

The consequences of two-tiered wage systems and their relationship to the concepts of formal equality and equity for unions' inner solidarity conclude the argument developed in this chapter. As we will see, the application of the equity concept in unions' practices requires a considerable change in the political decision-making process, a change that many union members do not see as fair.

Employees Paid under Two-Tiered Wage Scales (Orphan Clauses)

Matter at Issue

In response to the pressures of a new economic situation, such as the opening of markets and international competition for the private sector, and the pressure for debt reduction and labour cost-cutting targets set by the Quebec provincial government for the public sector, employers are seeking increased flexibility with monetary compensation for their employees. As a consequence, innovations such as merit pay, skill-based pay, broadbanding, and even the establishment of two-tiered wage systems based on date-of-hire (orphan clauses) (Collectif 1999), have been introduced.

Orphan clauses originated in the United States and saw their greatest spread during the 1980s. They were generally introduced in an effort to reduce costs while pacifying experienced employees, as saving jobs was sometimes invoked as an outcome of two-tiered wage systems. Two-tiered systems were still prevalent at the end of the 1990s in the Quebec municipal employment sector (e.g., present in 12.6 percent of the collective agreements in 1998) and in the Quebec retail trade sector (e.g., present in 13.7 percent of collective agreements in that same year) (Coutu 1998). They took on various forms, limited only by the creativeness of the parties to the agreements. Sometimes new hires were subjected to longer probationary periods, or different fringe benefits. Some collective agreements included arrangements that maintained pension levels for older employees (defined benefit plans versus defined contribution plans) but provided no such guarantees for newer employees – just the opposite, in fact. Other agreements reduced the wages of temporary workers or students, or abolished job security for workers to be hired under the new agreement. Some agreements placed new hires in contingent positions while suspending their right to arbitration.

The effects of orphan clauses could be temporary or permanent. For instance, in the education sector they were temporary, since new hires could eventually achieve the same pay ceilings as senior employees; the wage differential ended once the newly hired teacher resumed normal progression in the wage scale. But sometimes the effects were permanent, for instance, where whole new structures were created for the new hires, whose pay ceilings were permanently lower than those of senior employees. The characteristic all these two-tiered clauses shared was that they provided new hires with working conditions that were inferior to those negotiated for more senior colleagues in the same jobs, and implemented two different sets of rules governing employees' access to various benefits, plans, programs, and so on, based on date-of-hire. In other words, employees hired after day X could get lesser benefits, or wait longer to have access to benefits, or wait longer to reach the same level of benefits, than would employees hired before that day.

The Quebec Act Respecting Labour Standards (title VII.1, section 87.1 and following) now outlaws wage disparities based on date-of-hire, whether temporary or permanent, as long as the matter is dealt with by a standard stipulated in the act, namely wages and hours of work; statutory general holidays and non-working days with pay; paid annual leaves; rest periods; absences owing to sickness, accident, a criminal offence, or family or parental reasons; notice of termination of employment or layoff; and work certificate.[4] The standards pertaining to retirement (Division VI.1) are excluded from the application of section 87.1.

The Quebec Human Rights Commission also concluded that two-tiered wage clauses could have a directly discriminatory effect based on age, but also, in an indirect way, on sex and ethnic origin, because women and immigrants were more often newcomers in the labour market, ironically sometimes benefiting from equity programs. Age, sex, and ethnicity are all forbidden factors of discrimination under section 10 of the Quebec charter, which states that "Every person has a right to full and equal recognition and exercise of his human rights and freedoms, without distinction, exclusion or preference based on race, colour, *sex,* pregnancy, sexual orientation, civil status, *age* except as provided by law, religion, political convictions, language, *ethnic or national origin,* social condition, a handicap or the use of any means to palliate a handicap. Discrimination exists where such a distinction, exclusion or preference has the effect of nullifying or impairing such right" (Quebec charter, R.S.Q., C-12, s. 10, emphasis added).

Furthermore, under the charter, the use of date-of-hire as the basis for determining how various classes of employees are treated cannot be reconciled with what is known as a "rational work requirement," the defence allowed under the charter to employers who introduce a discriminatory rule. As section 20 states, "A distinction, exclusion or preference based on the aptitudes or qualifications required for employment, or justified by the charitable, philanthropic, religious, political or educational nature of a non-profit institution or of an institution devoted exclusively to the well-being of an ethnic group, is deemed non-discriminatory" (Quebec charter, R.S.Q., C-12, s. 20).

It follows, then, that if two-tiered wage systems do have a prejudicial effect on certain legally protected categories of workers, they can be contested because of their systemic discrimination effects. Moreover, if applied to wage structure, such clauses directly contravene Article 19 of the charter, whether temporary or permanent, which states: "Every employer must, without discrimination, grant equal salary or wages to the members of his personnel who perform equivalent work at the same place. A difference in salary or wages based on experience, seniority, years of service, merit, productivity or overtime is not considered discriminatory *if such criteria are common to all members of the personnel.* Adjustments in compensation and a pay equity plan are deemed not to discriminate on the basis of gender if they are established in accordance with the *Pay Equity Act"* (R.S.Q., c. E-12.001) (Quebec charter, R.S.Q., C-12, s. 19, emphasis added).

Lastly, it is important to bear in mind that Article 16 of the charter can also be relevant to this debate. It states, "No one may practise discrimination in respect of the hiring, apprenticeship, duration of the *probationary period,* vocational training, promotion, transfer, displacement, laying-off, suspension, dismissal or *conditions of employment* of a person or in the establishment of *categories or classes of employment"* (Quebec charter, R.S.Q., C-12, s. 16, emphasis added).

This clause rules out two-tiered systems that try to extend probationary periods for the newly hired if, for instance, plaintiffs can establish that the majority of the workers affected by a two-tiered system is part of the same age group (Coutu 1998). Furthermore, a clause that automatically grants newcomers (hired after day X) a temporary status and workers hired before that day permanent status would also not be in keeping with Section 16 (Commission des droits de la personne et des droits de la jeunesse du Québec 1998).

Despite the legal amendment of the labour standards act that has made many two-tiered systems illegal in Quebec, they remain a significant issue for unions for at least two reasons. First, not all two-tiered systems have disappeared because some of them are not, per se, related to working conditions covered by the law (employment status, for instance). Second, some of them are not set out in a business policy, a collective agreement, or a decree – for example, new rules for pension contribution levels can be included in a pension plan but not in the collective agreement; the plan may well be excluded from the negotiable field. According to the provisions in Quebec's human rights legislation that make these clauses discriminatory, where there is a clause in the collective agreement pertaining to pension contributions, if the contribution level is the same for all union members (defined contribution plans versus defined benefit plans), the requirements are met despite the fact that benefits will vary, depending on the generation of worker affected.

The second reason two-tiered systems remain relevant is that some of them generated lawsuits that have created strange situations in which groups of unionized workers have been at odds with the rest of the unionized workforce and with their union representatives, refusing to be represented by them when contesting the agreement, for obvious reasons. Thus, in the case at study here, the two parties to the contested collective agreements – that is, union and management – become the respondents before the court, whereas a group of workers and union members, gathered in a new association, are the plaintiffs. Thus, in these cases, union and management have temporarily joined forces before the courts to deal with these complaints. Court proceedings have resulted in union executive committees as well as management being challenged for failing to comply with the Canadian or the Quebec charter of human rights and freedoms (Coutu 2000). They could also have been challenged for not fulfilling their duty to provide fair representation under Section 47.2 of the Labour Code of Quebec, should the wronged workers have chosen to do so.

In some cases, wronged workers – teachers, police officers, firefighters, provincial civil servants – have indeed set up organizations separate from their unions to defend their rights (Brunelle 2002). Initiatives of this kind, which are highly unusual, raise serious questions for the union movement, since in contrast with status of women committees, racial committees, or other equity-based groups that have been able to establish themselves within the union movement, this type of organization is intent upon organizing itself independently and has no qualms about expressing deep disagreement with the union, or defending its own interests to the exclusion of all others'.

Recent Developments

An initiative to contest the legitimacy of two-tiered wage scales managed to achieve limited but recognized success in 2004, when the Supreme Court of Canada acknowledged that these wage scales segmented the unionized workforce. The background is as follows.

In 1998, the Association de défense des jeunes enseignants et enseignantes du Québec (ADJEQ, or the Association for the Defence of Quebec's Young Teachers) challenged some wage clauses in a collective agreement that had been in effect from 1997 to 2000. The parties to the agreement were the Comité patronal de négociation pour les commissions scolaires francophones du Québec, primaire et secondaire, or CPN (management), and the Centrale de l'enseignement du Québec, or CEQ (union). The contested clauses held that for the purposes of promotion in the salary scale, experience gained as a teacher during the academic year 1996-97 would not be taken into account. ADJEQ's position was that teachers who had reached grades 1 to 15 in the salary scale were the ones affected by these clauses, that most of them were among the youngest in the bargaining unit, and that therefore they were being discriminated against.

All the respondent parties in this case, which consisted of the attorney-general of Quebec, the employer negotiating committee for the French-language school boards, the CEQ, and the Fédération des syndicats de l'enseignement, contested the jurisdictional authority of Quebec's Tribunal des droits de la personne (TDPQ) (the Quebec Human Rights Tribunal) to hear the case in May 2000. All these parties were of the view that the case should be addressed through the filing of a grievance under the collective agreement, or the filing of a complaint under Section 47.2 of the Labour Code of Quebec, but in any event, in accordance with the rules of labour law whereby, among other things, the wronged workers would be represented by their union executives. TDPQ dismissed this motion, so the respondent parties submitted the TDPQ decision to the Quebec Court of Appeal, which ruled in their favour on 28 February 2002. Under the ruling, the complaint was to be handled through the grievance procedure, but only the employer would be held responsible for the situation and required to face the plaintiffs, even though the union had also negotiated the agreement being challenged.

TDPQ subsequently appealed this decision to the Supreme Court,[5] which rendered its decision on 11 June 2004 in what is known as the Morin ruling.[6] The Supreme Court upheld the jurisdictional authority of TDPQ to hear the case, acknowledging that if grievance arbitration was the ADJEQ's sole avenue of appeal, which was the main item in contention, the young teachers' interests would not be properly represented. The judges, in doing so,[7] insisted on quoting a well-known earlier ruling: "In an arbitration under a collective agreement, only the employer and union have party status. The unionized employee's interests are advanced by and through the union, which necessarily decides how the allegations should be represented or defended. Applying Weber so as to assign exclusive jurisdiction to labour arbitrators could therefore render chimerical the rights of individual unionized employees"[8] (Abella J.A. in *Ford Motor Co. of Canada Ltd. v. Ontario (Human Rights Commission)* [2001] 209 D.L.R. (4th) 465 (Ont. C.A.) (leave to appeal refused, [2002] 3 S.C.R. x), at paras. 61-62).

The Supreme Court's ruling is highly significant in that it acknowledges that 13,400 "young teachers," organized into an association other than their union, the ADJEQ, have interests distinct from those of their union with respect to the working conditions negotiated in a collective agreement, and that these interests are based on age. As a result, those teachers affected by the two-tiered wage scales could legitimately take their case to TDPQ as a distinct party, and they did, instead of being compelled to use the grievance procedure, as the Court of Appeal ordered them to do in 2002. This ruling could well have had a significant impact on young firefighters, such as those in Sherbrooke who filed a complaint with the Human Rights Commission on 29 August 2003, and on young police officers who are the victims of similar discriminatory clauses (Brunelle 2002), who finally went for out-of-court negotiated agreements with the municipal government or hearings before Quebec's Commission of Labour Standards.

The Supreme Court decision implicitly acknowledges that the executive committees of local unions may be placed in the difficult situation of representing the interests of employees who claim to be the victims of discrimination as a result of clauses the unions themselves have negotiated or applied, while at the same time representing what they consider to be the collective interest of all the members of the certification unit, as expressed at a general meeting. The teachers' case has not yet been heard before TDPQ, but a joint request by union and management to ratify an out-of-court settlement has been denied. This settlement was first offered to ADJEQ on 18 June 2007. The association has recommended its members not agree to it. Both parties to the collective agreement – union and management – then asked TDPQ to ratify the settlement to put an end to the case, which TDPQ refused to do, on 13 September 2007. Union and management, on the one hand, and ADJEQ, on the other, carried on negotiating the proposal to try to come to an agreement, but failed. The proposal was withdrawn on 18 February 2008; on the same day, both TDPQ and ADJEQ withdrew from the case. For the wronged workers, the set of options now comes down to individually asking TDPQ to be heard.[9] At the end of the day, the political split between union and management on the one hand, and ADJEQ on the other, remains.

As these discriminatory two-tiered clauses have now been ruled out, a legitimate question is whether it is still relevant to discuss them. I believe the answer is yes, because two conflicting conceptions of equality are at stake. One focuses on formal equality, or equality of rights, which dictates that all union members be treated equally. The other focuses on equity, or equality of results, which is rooted in human rights, that in turn prevail over all other rights, laws, politics, or agreements, regardless of the union members' majority opinion. I discuss these conceptions of equality and their outcomes below.

Two Conflicting Concepts of Equality

The logic of local union operation is founded on the legal concept of formal equality between members, according to which each individual enjoys a vote of equal weight in any decision process. In practice, in a working context, such formal equality comes down to an equality of treatment, which is obtained by a neutrality of decisions and practices, that is, by treating everyone scrupulously in the same way, applying the same criteria, even if outcomes differ. The democratic nature of unions' decisions is based, in this context, on respect for the wishes of the majority, deemed to be the aggregate of the wishes of individuals who are equal in rights.

This concept of equality is consistent with the traditional concept of citizenship, as described by Marshall (1964, 92): "Citizenship is a status bestowed on those who are full members of a community. All who possess the status are equal with respect to the rights and duties with which the status is endowed." Citizens thus defined form the basis of political democracy as we have known it since the eighteenth century. Moreover, this view of equality is in keeping with the republican ideal that provides the basis for formal, though abstract, equality between citizens within predominantly deliberative democratic institutions (Duchastel 2003, 73).

In a unionized setting, two-tiered wage systems and the struggles around them bring to the fore a deep tension between two dimensions of the formal equality of all union members. On the one hand, decisions are supposed to be based on the primacy of a majority vote taken in a general meeting; in these voting processes, a minority group may see its claims systematically dismissed. On the other hand, unions are also supposed to treat all members the same or, if differentiating, apply the same rules to everyone in doing so, including while bargaining collective agreements. This makes the systematic dismissal of minority group claims problematic.

In addition, the concept of formal equality does not satisfy the equity requirements set out in the Quebec and Canadian charters and human rights laws as they relate to targeted or designated groups. Legislators, as I have noted, recognize that it is sometimes necessary to treat the members of certain groups differently, for instance, to temporarily give preferential treatment until a situation of equality of results (e.g., in representation) has been established. Preferential treatment in a unionized environment may extend, for example, to temporarily suspending seniority as the basis upon which to award promotions, training opportunities, and the like, if it is shown that seniority-based decisions produce systemic discriminatory effects (Killenbeck 1999; Koggel 1994; Legault 2005; Lepofsky 1995; MacLeod 1994).

In the case of the teachers, I mentioned that the shared will of the union executive and management was that the dispute be handled in accordance with the rules of labour law. One of these rules, the majority rule, allows for many union decisions that can be damaging to some particular members' interests, as long as the vote is handled in accordance with the rules in a democratic general meeting, and these decisions respect the laws. Traditionally, labour courts have granted union executives a great freedom of manoeuvre in negotiating matters, since collective agreements are said to be "the parties' law" (Legault 2005; Legault and Bergeron 2007). But since the existence of the charter of rights, under the equity principle, union executives are also required to avoid discrimination and, if needed, treat individuals from different groups differently in order to give them equal chances of arriving at the finish line. It may entail invalidating a majority vote for certain decisions, if those decisions are declared discriminatory.

This latter focus, for example, on results, runs counter to the union egalitarian tradition; in that tradition, it is not that individual disagreements and differences are ignored but that the approach provided for by virtue of the duty of fair representation (in the Quebec Labour Code, s. 47.2) is supposed to take care of them. This approach may be sufficient for a group that perceives itself as being homogeneous. But when the group splinters because of profoundly different collective interests, a gap opens up between a system of union democracy dominated by the rule of formal equality and the responsibility for accommodating groups or minorities, which is essential to the achievement of real equality, the equality of results. (A very interesting reading in this regard is Brunelle 2001.)

When the victims of two-tiered wage scales say that they, as a group, are suffering the effects of systemic discrimination as a result of an action ratified by the majority of their peers, they form a group having distinct interests within their union. They base their stance on the Quebec charter and demand equity, for example, equality of results. As Brunelle (2002) puts it, the principle, well established by the charters whereby an individual (or a group, I would add) is entitled to be treated according to his or her own characteristics if they differ from those of the group of which he or she is a part, may not be reconcilable, under all circumstances, with the postulate that a union must take the collective interest of the entire bargaining unit into account when exercising its discretionary powers, and that it is bound by the decision of the majority as expressed at a general meeting.

The new demands coming from so-called minority groups in unions call into question the concept of union democracy and, in doing so, the whole concept of republican democracy that is based on the expressed will of a majority of equal individuals in a general meeting. These demands deeply upset an important political premise within unions, for instance, that all union members are equal, each has equal weight in collective decision making, and the voice of the majority rules. Such a rationale cannot continue to prevail, since the Quebec charter, implemented in 1975, states that "no one may practise discrimination in respect of the admission, enjoyment of benefits, suspension or expulsion of a person to, of or from an association of employers or employees or any professional corporation or association of persons carrying on the same occupation" (Quebec charter, R.S.Q., C-12, s. 17).

It may seem paradoxical to speak of union activists subscribing to the notion of formal equality, since union ideology in general is not terribly compatible with the presumed equality of all political subjects in a republican democracy, in terms of both rights and obligations. Too aware of the real inequalities in so-called democratic societies, very few union activists actually believe in equality in society in general. But that does not prevent them from quite consistently postulating formal equality within their ranks for the purposes of internal governance, premised on a similarity of class interests among their members.

Social segmentation challenges this basic premise of formal equality and makes the balancing of the legitimate interests of definable groups within a union bargaining unit in the negotiation process more difficult. Submerging individual group interests into the collective interests of the larger group, a process that used to be allowed "a wide range of reasonableness" (Liggett 1987, 237), is no longer as simple as taking a vote in a general meeting, not even after a long democratic debate. Now the Quebec human rights court offers a different forum for certain labour disputes that, moreover, is governed by a very different set of rules. This is a challenging forum for unions' representatives, as dissatisfied members can put in their claims to this competing authority. In addition, the existence of this new forum echoes another wider social debate concerning citizenship, arising from Canada's and Quebec's charters of rights: What does respect for differences really mean in our institutions?

What seems to be emerging is a demand for a new kind of citizenship, one that has a social dimension. Edelson and Wall (chapters, this volume) are right in pointing out that workers from equity groups seek support from grassroots organizations representing their own people, even when they are members of a union, and sometimes do so to defend themselves when they feel their union does not do it adequately, including in supporting a claim in front of the human rights commission. This new type of citizenship claim raises serious problems for unions, in part because it promotes the rights of minorities in a milieu where democracy is a question of majority rule, and also because it is based on an equity argument promoted in the Quebec and Canadian charters of rights that breaks with the tradition of formal equality that characterizes the traditional logic of organized labour.

A Citizenship Claim with a Social Dimension

As Robert Castel (1995) has pointed out, the typical Fordist wage system kept the various labour groups in uniform subordination, but at the same time allowed solidarities among workers to be built and strengthened. That does not mean that unity could be taken for granted, nor that· it did not require any effort, but historically the primary objective of the trade union movement has been to fight against competition between individual workers in order to build a common front for dealing with employers (Offe and Wiesenthal 1980). Unions have therefore historically had a tendency to try as hard as they can to play down socio-professional differences and to deny the importance of generational, sexual, and ethnocultural gaps (Gagnon 1998; Lévesque, Murray, and Le Queux 1998).

Recently, however, new union members' practices have brought organized labour into competition with new social movements, which seem better suited to supporting the claims of special-interest groups such as women, young people (Force jeunesse and Le pont entre les générations are groups known for their opposition to two-tiered wage scales), and people from ethnic communities, to name a few (Offe and Weisenthal 1980; Zoll 1998). This competition brings about a segmentation of social relations and fosters the development of centrifugal forces within unions that make it more difficult for them to maintain unity, even though this unity is crucial (Hyman 1992; Segrestin 1981).

This development challenges union executive committees: it divides the wage-earning group, adds new intra-union conflict, reduces some workers' support of both the local union and the general unionization principle (Castel 1995; Hyman 1992), and raises human rights concerns. This situation is really challenging unions' practices, as Edelson (this volume) points out, in bringing in new options and new forums to support some workers' claims. Also contributing to this challenge is that newly hired workers may share interests with women in traditionally male job categories, as well as immigrants, persons with disabilities, the gay community, and so on, in that they all may feel they have been denied representation in traditional political decision-making processes that are based on majority vote. They also have in common the fact that they are demanding (and I am exaggerating only slightly here) a new type of "union citizenship" for marginal workers such as women (in what are non-traditionally female job categories), young people, victims of two-tiered wage scales, immigrants, persons with disabilities, and so forth (Bich 1999; Collectif 1999; Commission des droits de la personne et des droits de la jeunesse du Québec 1990, 1998; Coutu 2000; Legault 2005; Lepage 1989; Liggett 1987).

Hitherto, the tendency has been to recognize "industrial citizenship" only of aggregates that exist in law, that is, unions and management (Arthurs 1967; Marshall 1964; taken up more recently by Béland and Hansen 1998; Birnbaum 1996; and by Bulmer and Rees 1996). But as a result of the new demands mentioned above, organized labour, the strength of which has traditionally been based on the solidarity of the group, is seeing its legitimacy challenged by these new categories of workers and is faced with demands for profound change (Dufour and Hege 1994a, 1994b; Hege and Dufour 1998; Kochan, Katz, and McKersie 1986; Laplante 2000; Rosanvallon 1988; Zoll 1998). Union decision making is therefore being faced with two contradictory demands: to disregard intra-union differences at the price of an internal weakening of the organization, or to acknowledge such differences at the price of weakening the organization in its dealings with the employer (Regini 1992).

People whose condition is protected from discrimination in compliance with Section 10 of the Quebec charter now can – and do – aggregate in organized groups. These people have come to exist socially but are theoretically not yet social or industrial citizens because they have no existence as groups in law. Ironically, as these people do not yet exist as collective actors in the legal corpus, they can draw only on their rights as individuals under the law. This is largely because the Quebec charter, unlike the Quebec Pay Equity Act, for instance, does not set out universal, precise obligations for employers and social institutions to implement equality in all their decisions and practices, but simply allows individuals and groups to file complaints. In other words, the Quebec charter is a less proactive law in the working environment than is the Employment Equity Act (L.C., 1995, c. 44). Although the labour relations laws do acknowledge explicit collective rights, they do so only for certified unions.

Yet, legislators have inevitably recognized that groups can hold collective interests, if only by virtue of the systemic discrimination they are acknowledged to have suffered, or might suffer, as a group. Even when not targeted by equity programs, those who have the characteristics set out in Section 10 of the Quebec charter – particularly young people, to go back to the example of two-tiered wage scales – are recognized as having collective interests on the sole basis that age is one of the prohibited grounds for discrimination. An association such as ADJEQ that was founded to fight against two-tiered wage scales and brought its case before the Human Rights Commissions is evidence of this.

Despite that in theory no groups other than unions exist to represent workers as "industrial citizens," the Supreme Court's recent ruling in Morin nonetheless constitutes a step in this direction by recognizing that workers have rights distinct from those of their unions.[10] In fact, are these groups of unionized workers not saying that, from at least one standpoint – the representation of their material interests (of significant importance in collective bargaining) – membership in their union does not guarantee them a form of "industrial citizenship" that they are recognized as having under the charter? This situation gives rise to strained relationships between competing interest groups within unions.

Strained Relationship between Interest Groups within Unions

By proposing that strained relationships arise from the opposition between the principles of equality and equity, I am not suggesting that that opposition constitutes the essence of these conflicts. A supplementary materialist reading is also necessary. By making the equality of results the objective of legislation (quasi-constitutional as for the Quebec charter and the Canadian Human Rights Act (R.S., 1985, c. H-6)) and by giving legal recognition to positive discrimination measures to benefit target groups, legislators have upset the social order for awarding "places," in which I include jobs, thereby impinging on the interests of the majority by forcing members to share a territory according to a new set of rules. As a result, outcomes of equity policies are assessed not in terms of their impact on the minority groups for whom they were originally intended but in terms of their harmful effects on the majority group, thus distorting the objective of such policies and leading to accusations of "reverse discrimination" (Pietrantonio 2002, 70).

Admittedly, the two-tiered wage example discussed here took place in a general context of cost cutting and negotiation of concessions by unions, which constituted the backdrop of workers' positions. Nonetheless, deciding where concessions are to be made will necessarily involve tackling the question of equality. In the case of the teachers, if TDPQ rules that discrimination is indeed being exercised jointly by the two parties to the collective agreement, the majority union decision in support of the signing of the agreement can only point to a deep split within the union membership, with new hires on one side and senior colleagues and their union representatives on the other. Indeed, according to Liggett (1987, 237-39), with such a decision, these representatives will be held responsible for discrimination against their own members: "Discrimination charges can ... arise when a union's activities, intended to protect the interests of one group in a bargaining unit, adversely affect the interests of other groups, e.g. employees who recently became members of the bargaining unit" (ibid., 237). Using date of hire in the two-tiered contract separates employees into classes. Historically, competitive seniority has ranked employees on an individual basis; but the two-tiered system divides workers into classes, raising the issue of the duty of fair representation. It is unlikely that the seniority principle can be stretched that far. Where the burden of proof falls on the labour organization, the two-tiered concept based on date of hire cannot be used as a defence under the general standard of relevant differences.

It will be difficult not to notice the cohesion of material interests in each of the groups on either side of the fault line, majority versus minority. Regardless of whatever legal arguments were raised by TDPQ and of the fact that the labour conflict is still unresolved, there is an intra-union political conflict that will have to be addressed, too. Indeed, union officials' "trade-off of the new hires to preserve things for our existing people" (Liggett 1987, 236) will no longer be acknowledged as legitimate. It is sad, though, that the actions of union executives have brought them to this, given that two-tiered clauses, whether wage clauses or other, already disturb internal solidarity and reduce cohesion in unions' bargaining units (Cappelli and Sherer 1990; Lepage 1989; Levine 1989).

Conclusion
It will be increasingly difficult to preserve the uniformity of the unionized workforce that attempts to justify the legitimacy of majority rule, since the Quebec and Canadian charters now recognize that minority groups have potential interests distinct from those of the group of workers to which they belong, and have held that, where those interests are not served, minority groups can appeal to the appropriate bodies, for example, they can file complaints with the relevant human rights commissions. Minority groups' demands existed before; specific women's demands – for maternity leaves or a shorter working day, for instance – have been common. But unions used to manage those demands internally, within the framework of the deliberative

process ruling the general meetings. In a context wherein the majority's vote prevailed, minority interests were likely to be set aside, if not forgotten. Compromises and sacrifices required from the minorities were traditionally said to be made in the name of the collective interest. For we must not delude ourselves: intra-union divisions are not new, and maintaining unity has always presented a challenge for unions.

Feminist research has already condemned a "consensus" within unions that in actual fact was nothing more than an expression of the interests of white male workers (Briskin and McDermott 1993; Cockburn 1995; Creese 1999). The principle of formal equality and the primacy of the majority vote that is a corollary of it were once sufficient to settle divisive intra-union disputes. But with the advent of the human rights charters and the remedies that stem from them, the primacy of the majority vote is no longer sufficient to bring an end to the debate, since another parallel legal arena has been created. Its creation marks the end of a certain degree of union independence in the arbitration of internal conflicts of interest, one that goes hand in hand with the end of a certain degree of independence in collective labour relations. We are only now, with the existence of this parallel arena, beginning to gauge just how often there may be a failure to reconcile these interests locally. There is not necessarily any reason to be unduly surprised about this, since it is a huge task.

Only the future will tell whether unions are able to develop the necessary modes of arbitration between these divergent intra-union interests that would make such extra-union remedies superfluous. Unionism and the principle of equity are not contradictory terms. Unions do not contest the essence of the equity principle, and many have explored some very fertile avenues for union action to promote equity within unions. Collective agreements can protect or ensure a certain form of equity, prohibit discrimination and harassment, and provide for redress; they can provide for maternity and adoption leave and a variety of measures for reconciling private and professional life (Briskin 1999; Briskin and Bernardo 2005). So, hopefully, union representatives will work to close the "gap between what is said and what is actually done about racism and other inequities in the labour movement" (see Clarke Walker, this volume) instead of widening it.

Union representatives can make all the difference when any of the problems I have mentioned so far arise. When it comes to negotiating two-tiered wage scales, many unions have refused these proposals, restricting themselves to other initiatives whose adverse effects were better distributed throughout the union membership. For instance, since these conflicts took place in the public sector where reducing the public budget deficit was often at stake, the alternative was all too often to accept limited wage raises that were distributed more evenly, such as decreases in hourly wages or wage increases in percentage terms across the board, covering all members of the bargaining unit; reductions in employers' costs for insurance or social plans; reduction of overtime rates of compensation; and so forth. In a way, the elimination of orphan clauses narrows the range of alternatives available to parties seeking to solve a problem, possibly causing working conditions to deteriorate for the majority, as compared with what could be gained for the senior employees under orphan clauses. When such clauses were prohibited, some even contended that discrimination against one group was replaced with precariousness for everyone, as employers used to lay down a simple alternative between two-tiered wage clauses on the one hand and layoffs and outsourcing on the other. This is a poor understanding of the rules of equity, surely at least in part because of inadequate member training and communication about equity, as Foley (Chapter 7, this volume) emphasizes.

In the past, unions stressed all too often that they were forced by circumstances to negotiate two-tiered wage clauses, since they were required to protect the rights of the majority of their members. But when local union representatives adhere strictly to the principle of formal equality between workers (tightly linked to the majority rule), it leads them too often to deny the socio-historic gains that have led to the recognition of the effects of systemic discrimination, to differential treatment, and to the resulting approach toward equity that is supported by the Quebec and Canadian charters. As Wall (this volume) points out, this is a real challenge of our times for unions.

Notes

1   *Charter of Human Rights and Freedoms* of Quebec (R.S.Q., 1977, c. C-12); *Canadian Charter of Rights and Freedoms* (Part 1 of the Constitution Act, 1982, enacted as Schedule B of the Canada Act, 1982 [U.K.], 1982, c. 11); *Canadian Human Rights Act* (R.S.C., 1985, c. H-6); *Act to secure the handicapped in the exercise of their rights* (R.S.Q., 1977, c. E-20.1); *Employment Equity Act* (S.C., 1995, c. 44); *General Regulation respecting the conditions of contracts of government departments and public bodies*, O.C. 1166-93, 1993, 125 G.O. 2, 6191; *Regulation respecting Affirmative Action Programs*, O.C. 1172-86, 118 G.O. 2, 3416. For the purposes of this chapter's discussion, the expression "human rights charters" includes legislation that plays the same role.
2   Readers interested in the content of this out-of-court settlement can find more details at http://www.adjeq.qc.ca/sgc.
3   *Charter of Human Rights and Freedoms* of Quebec (R.S.Q., 1977, c. C-12). Bear in mind that the *Canadian Human Rights Act* (R.S.C., 1985, c. H-6) affects employers under federal jurisdiction in the same manner as does the Quebec legislation.
4   The banning was included in an amendment of the *Act respecting labour standards*, Quebec's employment standards legislation, in 1999, called Differences in treatment (ss. 87.1 to 87.3).
5   The facts are well summarized in the brief (file no. 29188), submitted by the Commission des droits de la personne et des droits de la jeunesse du Québec to the Supreme Court of Canada, to request permission to appeal the earlier decision of the Court of Appeal; http://www.cdpdj.qc.ca/fr/dossiers/dossier-enseignant.htm.
6   Morin ruling, Quebec's employment standards legislation *Quebec (Commission des droits de la personne et des droits de la jeunesse) v. Quebec (Attorney General)*, [2004] 2 S.C.R. 185, 2004 SCC 39, file no. 29188, rendered 11 June 2004.

7 Quebec *(Commission des droits de la personne et des droits de la jeunesse) v. Quebec (Attorney General)*, [2004] 2 S.C.R. 185, para. 28.
8 Available on the ADJEQ website, at http://www.adjeq.qc.ca.
9 See http://www.adjeq.qc.ca for more details.
10 See Note 6.

References

Arthurs, H.W. 1967. Developing industrial citizenship: A challenge for Canada's second century. *Canadian Bar Review* 45, 4: 786-830.
Béland, D., and R.A. Hansen. 1998. La question de la citoyenneté sociale au Royaume-Uni: Vers une réflexion européenne? *Droit Social* 11: 1-9.
Bich, M-F. 1999. Clauses orphelins et devoir de juste représentation. In *Actes du Forum Droits et Libertés [Proceedings of the Forum of Rights and Freedoms]: L'equité entre générations et les clauses "orphelin"; Des droits à défendre,* ed. Human Rights Commission (Québec), 47-70. Montreal: Human Rights Commission. http://142.213.87.17/fr/publications/docs/actes_ forum_orphelins.pdf.
Birnbaum, P. 1996. Sur la citoyenneté. *L'Année Sociologique* 46, 1: 57-85.
Briskin, L. 1999. Feminisms, feminization and democratization in Canadian unions. In *Feminist Success Stories,* ed. K. Blackford, M-L. Garceau, and S. Kirby, 73-92. Ottawa: University of Ottawa Press.
–. 2006. Equity bargaining/bargaining equity. Series Paper 1, Centre for Research on Work and Society, York University.
Briskin, L., and P. McDermott. 1993. The feminist challenge to unions. In *Women Challenging Unions,* ed. L. Briskin and P. McDermott, 3-22. Toronto: University of Toronto Press.
Brunelle, C. 2001. *Discrimination et obligation d'accommodement en milieu de travail syndiqué.* Cowansville, QC: Éditions Yvon Blais.
–. 2002. L'émergence des associations parallèles dans les rapports collectifs de travail. *Relations industrielles/Industrial Relations* 57, 2: 282-308.
Bulmer, M., and A.M. Rees. 1996. *Citizenship Today: The Contemporary Relevance of T.H. Marshall.* London: UCL Press.
Cappelli, P., and P.D. Sherer. 1990. Assessing worker attitudes under a two-tiered wage plan. *Industrial and Labor Relations Review* 43, 2: 225-44.
Castel, R. 1995. *Les métamorphoses de la question sociale: Une chronique du salariat.* Paris: Fayard.
Cockburn, C. 1995. Redrawing the boundaries: Trade unions, women and Europe. In *Gender, Culture and Organizational Change: Putting Theory into Practice,* ed. C. Itzin, 211-31. London: Routledge.
Collectif. 1999. *Les enjeux des clauses "orphelin."* Montreal: Les intouchables.
Commission des droits de la personne et des droits de la jeunesse du Québec. 1990. *Conformité avec la Charte des droits et libertés de la personne du projet de loi modifiant la Loi sur les normes du travail.* Resolution COM-350-9.1.4.
–. 1998. *La rémunération à double palier et les autres clauses dites "orphelin" dans les conventions collectives: Conformité au principe de non-discrimination.* Resolution COM-428-5.1.4.
Coutu, M. 1998. *Mémoire à la Commission de l'économie et du travail sur la rémunération à double palier et les autres clauses dites "orphelin" dans les conventions collectives.* Montreal: Commission des droits de la personne et des droits de la jeunesse du Québec.
–. 2000. Les clauses dites "orphelins" et la notion de discrimination dans la Charte des droits et libertés de la personne. *Relations industrielles/Industrial Relations* 55, 2: 308-31.
Creese, G. 1996. Gendering collective bargaining: From men's rights to women's issues. *Canadian Review of Sociology and Anthropology/Revue canadienne de sociologie et d'anthropologie* 33, 4: 437-56.
–. 1999. *Contracting Masculinity: Gender, Class and Race in a White-Collar Union, 1944-1994.* Don Mills, ON: Oxford University Press.
Crever, C.B. 1993. *Can Unions Survive? The Rejuvenation of the American Labor Movement.* New York: New York University Press.

–. 1998. Why labour unions must [and can] survive. *University of Pennsylvania Journal of Labour and Employment Law* 1: 15.

Duchastel, J. 2003. La citoyenneté dans les sociétés contemporaines: Nouvelles formes de médiation entre l'individu et le politique. In *Reconnaissance et citoyenneté: Au carrefour de l'ethique et du politique*, ed. J-M. Larouche, 57-78. Sainte-Foy: Presses de l'Université Laval.

Dufour, C., and A. Hege. 1994a. *La hiérarchie des rôles représentatifs.* Paris: Institut de recherche économique et sociale.

–. 1994b. *Comment la légitimité vient-elle aux représentants?* Paris: Institut de recherche économique et sociale.

Edwards, R. 1986. Unions in crisis and beyond: Introduction. In *Unions in Crisis and Beyond: Perspectives from Six Countries*, ed. R. Edwards, P. Garonna, and F. Tödling, 1-13. Dover: Auburn House.

Fudge, J. 1996. Rights on the labour law ladder: Using gender to challenge hierarchy. *Saskatchewan Law Review* 60, 1: 237-63.

Gagnon, M-J. 1998. La "modernisation" du syndicalisme québécois ou la mise à l'épreuve d'une logique représentative. *Sociologie et Sociétés* 30, 2: 213-30.

Hege, A., and C. Dufour. 1998. Légitimité syndicale et identité locale: Une comparaison international. *Sociologie et Sociétés* 30, 2: 31-48.

Hyman, R. 1992. Trade unions and the disaggregation of the working class. In *The Future of Labour Movements: Proceedings of International Sociological Association Conference*, ed. M. Regini, 150-68. London: Sage.

–. 1997. La géométrie du syndicalisme: Une analyse comparative des identités et des idéologies. *Relations industrielles/Industrial Relations* 52, 1: 7-38.

Killenbeck, M.R. 1999. Pushing things up to their first principles: Reflections on the values of affirmative action. *California Law Review* 87, 6: 1299-380.

Kochan, T., H. Katz, and R.B. McKersie. 1986. *The Transformation of American Industrial Relations.* New York: Basic Books.

Koggel, C.M. 1994. A feminist view of equality and its implications for affirmative action. *Canadian Journal of Jurisprudence* 7: 43-59.

Kumar, P., G. Murray, and S. Schetagne. 1998. L'adaptation au changement: Les priorités des syndicats dans les années 1990. *Répertoire des Organisations de Travailleurs et Travailleuses au Canada 1998.* Ottawa: Government of Canada, Human Resources Development Department, Labor and Workplace Information, 25.

Laplante, L. 2000. Réveil des relais infidèles? In *L'utopie des droits universels: L'ONU à la lumière de Seattle*, ed. L. Laplante, chap. 28. Montreal: Écosociété.

Legault, M.J. 2005. Droits de la personne, relations de travail et défis pour les syndicats contemporains. *Relations industrielles/Industrial Relations* 60, 4: 683-708.

Legault, M.J., and P. Bergeron. 2007. La promotion des droits de la personne influe-t-elle sur l'évolution des plaintes portant sur le devoir syndical de juste représentation au Québec? (1978-2005). *Les Cahiers du Droit* 48, 2: 249-80.

Lepage, S. 1989. Les pratiques défavorables au nouveau salarié dans la convention collective: Le cas de la double échelle. *Les Cahiers du Droit* 30, 2: 525-42.

Lepofsky, M.D. 1995. Understanding the concept of employment equity: Myths and misconceptions. *Canadian Labor Law Journal* 2: 1-15.

Lévesque, C., G. Murray, and S. Le Queux. 1998. Transformations sociales et identités syndicales: L'institution syndicale à l'épreuve de la différenciation sociale contemporaine. *Sociologie et Sociétés* 30, 2: 131-54.

Levine, M.J. 1989. The evolution of two-tiered wage agreements: Bane or panacea in labor-intensive industries. *Labor Law Journal* 40, 1 (January): 12-20.

Liggett, M.H. 1987. The two-tiered labor-management agreement and the duty of fair representation. *Labor Law Journal* 38, 4: 236-42.

MacLeod, C.M. 1994. The market, preferences and equality. *Canadian Journal of Jurisprudence* 7: 97-110.

Marshall, T.H. 1964. Citizenship and social class. In *Class, Citizenship and Social Development*, ed. T.H. Marshall, 65-122. Garden City, NY: Doubleday.

Müller-Jentsch, W. 1988. Industrial relations theory and trade union strategy. *International Journal of Comparative Labour Law and Industrial Relations* 4, 3: 177-90.

Offe, C., and H. Wiesenthal. 1980. Two logics of collective action: Theoretical notes on social class and organisational form. *Political Power and Social Theory* 1: 67-115.

Pietrantonio, L. 2002. Le débat scientifique sur l'action positive: L'occasion d'une analyse sociologique de l'égalité. *Études Ethniques au Canada* 34, 1: 64-84.

Regini, M. 1992. Introduction: The past and future of social studies of labour movement. In *The Future of Labour Movements: Proceedings of International Sociological Association Conference*, ed. M. Regini, 1-16. London: Sage.

Rosanvallon, P. 1988. *La Question Syndicale*. Paris: Calmann-Levy.

Segrestin D. 1981. Les communautés pertinentes de l'action collective. *Revue Française de Sociologie* 31, 2: 171-203.

White, J. 1990. *Mail and Female: Women and the Canadian Union of Postal Workers*. Toronto: Thompson Educational.

Zeytinoglu, I.U., and J.K. Muteshi. 2000. Gender, race and class dimensions of nonstandard work. *Relations industrielles/Industrial Relations* 55, 1: 133-68.

Zoll, R. 1998. Le défi de la solidarité organique: Avons-nous besoin de nouvelles institutions pour préserver la cohésion sociale? *Sociologie et Sociétés* 30, 2: 49-59.

Part 2
The Equity Struggle – Black Trade Unionists Speak Out

3
Confronting Racism in the Canadian Labour Movement: An Intergenerational Assessment
Miriam Edelson

This chapter captures a series of conversations between Beverley Johnson and Marie Clarke Walker, her daughter, about systemic racism, racist behaviour and anti-racist strategies employed in the Canadian labour movement.

Marie was first elected executive vice-president of the Canadian Labour Congress (CLC) in 2002. She is the youngest person and first woman of colour to hold a top CLC leadership position. She is an executive member of the Coalition of Black Trade Unionists (CBTU), Ontario chapter.

Beverley recently retired from her position as the first human rights officer for the Ontario Public Service Employees Union. She is a lifelong labour advocate for human rights. She has been involved in social justice work through many struggles and organizations, including as a founding member and, later, president of the CBTU, Ontario chapter.

In the conversation below, several themes come to light: how the success of anti-racist initiatives relies upon nurturing a sustainable link between racialized workers and their communities; what it means when racialized workers encounter white privilege in surprising places, and what it takes, in strategic terms, to develop a constituency that will challenge entrenched practices.

Beverley and Marie are both leaders; both have broken new ground in community and union spheres. Both remain true to the goal of creating a more inclusive labour movement and society. It is their practice that is particularly noteworthy. The insights that emerge below have the potential to recast a vital, relevant, and dynamic labour movement.

Miriam Edelson (ME): *Bev, how did you become involved in the labour movement?*

Beverley Johnson (BJ): I first became involved in the labour movement when I worked as a civil servant in Jamaica. It seemed to me that having an organization concerned about the rights of workers made sense. In fact, I was interested in people's rights from a fairly young age. I remember going to political meetings at the street corner with my father as a ten- or eleven-year-old. I have this image of him standing with his arms folded, taking it all in. At home in Jamaica, I learned about party politics and social issues, about oppression, unfairness, and inequity. The issues were always familiar but it was when I came to Canada that I developed the language, the vocabulary to express it.

In the Caribbean context, the issues of race and class dominate. There you don't talk about race, you talk about class – and when you begin to look at who is in what class, it is crystal clear. It's all about skin pigmentation, set in the context of the region's colonization and the multi-faceted impact of slavery. And then one comes here and the issues are cast somewhat differently.

When I started working in the Ontario Public Service in 1973, I felt it necessary to find out about the union. The union didn't come to me. I went to the union, and it was evident to me that I needed to get involved. Not only was I paying dues, there were things happening around me that I felt needed to be addressed. There was no steward at the Ontario Human Rights Commission, where I was working, and I thought this was ridiculous. Somebody needed to do something, so although I was not officially elected as steward until later, I became the de facto steward ... and it kind of took off from there.

At the Human Rights Commission, as with any other employer, people faced a variety of problems in the workplace. Issues of fairness and differential treatment arose, as did health and safety concerns. We were housed in a building where the temperature was always out of whack. Some people were freezing, others were too hot. In the building as a whole, all kinds of issues came to the floor. Individuals were having problems with their supervisors, for example, and not getting opportunities for training and advancement.

ME: *Marie, what are some of the challenges you face as a woman of colour in a senior position in the labour movement?*

Marie Clarke Walker (MCW): I've had to confront comments that suggest I'm inexperienced and that I was in too junior a position to seek or be elected to the position that I currently hold. I come from the grassroots and as a result I think that I understand where people are at, what they are thinking ... not just about everyday life, but what they think about the Canadian Labour Congress [CLC] and its affiliates. My belief going into this position was that I would be able to give those people – in which I include myself – a voice.

BJ: Marie ran for the post because her union president – another woman – thought she was the right person for the job. I think the establishment in the labour movement had the shock of their lives when she not only won, but [won] by a significant margin.

MCW: In some instances the treatment I receive is definitely different. But when I raise this explicitly I'm told that I "don't have the experience." I believe that racism and other forms of discrimination are couched in the word "experience."

BJ: I take a much harsher position. There is an assumption that because you come from the grassroots, you don't have the requisite knowledge or experience. The assumption is that only people who have been in certain positions know enough to be leaders. So, what happens when a young black woman full of promise, full of energy, with a vision for the movement is elected? When the rest of the movement isn't ready and doesn't want to see innovation or greater inclusion, people in leadership frustrate the opportunities to move forward.

ME: *Activists from racialized groups frequently speak of the link between work in their communities and the struggles in their unions. Why is that?*

MCW: A person of colour who is active and wants to hold a leadership position – at any level in the labour movement – needs a support base *outside* labour as well as inside. The challenge for me, and others like me in leadership, is to not allow oneself to be silenced. You need your community because it understands and identifies with what you're going through and can validate your vision of what the movement needs. It's about working against racism in all sorts of arenas – including our unions.

BJ: It's the community that nurtures you, it's your community that grounds you, and it is the community that provides you with the space to rest if you need it, to recover, to recharge. The labour movement has no such space. For the most part, many of the white women around the table have difficulty recognizing that it *is* different for a woman of colour. They have no understanding of what this added dimension means for that person of colour.

MCW: Sometimes this is very difficult because, even though there are instances where labour-community coalitions are supported and make gains around specific issues, the labour movement really doesn't like it when you go outside. It tends to be seen as a betrayal of the movement, rather than something that has the potential to strengthen us all.

BJ: While there are exceptions, the labour movement tends to step into (racialized) communities only when it wants something. In reality the community is always relevant. Our goal must be to build partnerships; community people have lots to contribute. Being full partners means making decisions together.

Labour's use of the community does not build trust, and trust is important in building successful coalitions. Instead of seeing communities as a threat, labour needs to recognize that a relationship is built when one representative from a community is talking to another person from that community.

The labour movement is very hierarchical; it counts on keeping control of the established system, the status quo. For any improvement to happen, unions must be more respectful, listen to what the community needs, and then work with them to support those goals. Attempting to work in coalitions also means labour must share its power and make space for new ways of doing business.

MCW: I agree. Labour has certainly not yet arrived at the stage where people of colour are welcomed into the fold. One challenge I face – and I know I'm not alone in this – is that my community is not just workers of colour within the labour movement or here in Toronto. It's a much broader community that includes the Caribbean, in which I also have strong roots and a history of involvement.

When I was first elected to the CLC, there were invitations from everywhere under the sun ... people I knew and people I didn't know wanted me to come and speak on a variety of topics. Strangely, when these invitations arrived, *they* became an issue. I was told that I couldn't accept these speaking engagements because they were not part of my "file" – my set of responsibilities as one of the four table officers of the congress.

I tried to explain that my community was responding the same way female activists and leaders had when more women were elected to executive positions of the central labour bodies. These women leaders received a flurry of invitations to speak at conferences and meetings. My community was simply responding enthusiastically to my election. As it had been for my union sisters, black men and *women* and other people of colour were proud of what we had accomplished. They were proud that I came from their community.

One of the best illustrations of this, sadly, was that soon after I was elected, I received an invitation to address the British Trades Union Congress (TUC) annual conference of black workers. The theme of the conference was "Black Women – Struggles and Successes." It seemed appropriate.

When the issue came up for discussion by the CLC officers, they did not agree with me; someone else already carried the race portfolio. In their wisdom, my colleagues identified this particular conference as one dealing with racism, never mind that it was actually double-barrelled and explicitly about black women's struggles. In the end, the officer responsible for anti-racist work (who happened to be a man) was asked to attend but did not.

BJ: This, despite the fact that the theme of the conference highlighted the experience of black women and Marie carried the file for women's issues.

ME: *Couldn't that simply be called a typical bureaucratic response?*

BJ: Of course it was bureaucratic. But it also shows how bureaucracy can be used as a cover for decisions that are discriminatory. I see this as an example of how the systems and structures in place support the networks that hold power. When decisions are made strictly according to "who is responsible for what," I think we make mistakes and miss opportunities. In truth, I believe it comes down to how power and privilege operate in the labour movement and how a person of colour – in this case, a woman of colour – runs up against systemic discrimination.

ME: *The various equity seats and human rights committees were set up, ostensibly, to counter systemic discrimination in the labour movement. What is your experience and assessment of these?*

MCW: The human rights positions and committees were set up initially because people felt they needed a voice. They needed to have a space to talk about their concerns and how best to deal with those issues from their perspective, as well as from the labour movement's perspective. Human rights activists in the movement are also strong trade unionists – although people in power sometimes miss that common ground and commitment. Most leaders do not like to be challenged. And because human rights issues are value-based, they are often unpopular.

When the first affirmative action positions on labour executive bodies were created in the early 1980s, women were elected in positions instituted for women. I often ask myself, when those women became board members, executive members, did anyone try to shut them up or shut them down? And if so, what happened? It's my understanding that when that happened, the women joined ranks and tried to support each other. That worked because there were a number of them around the table.

As people of colour, it's much more difficult. Most of the time you're the only one around that table; a lot of the time you feel threatened. As a black woman there, I'm not just representing women, I'm there representing black women, women of colour, and I'm there representing my community inside and outside the labour movement. This has been very difficult for many people to understand.

In talking with sisters and brothers from several affiliates, I know that we view trying to represent our communities as a significant part of our mandate. Maybe we feel this more acutely than other labour leaders since our positions were created explicitly to represent particular communities and, in many cases, we are elected by those caucus bodies at convention.

BJ: That's a good point. Further, while elected and staff positions now exist in many federations and affiliates, it is not because the leadership decided it was a good idea. Prior to the creation of the human rights director staff position at the Ontario Federation of Labour [OFL] in the late 1980s and, subsequently, the vice-president position on the federation executive board, community and rank-and-file members organized, met in people's homes, debated strategy, and lobbied. Frankly, we embarrassed the labour movement to create that seat on the federation executive board. In my experience, most of the equity positions and committees came about in this way.

MCW: The problem today is that although the elected committees are in place, positive outcomes are sparse. The fact that there is no ongoing mechanism for consultation with and feedback from the constituencies they represent is one problem.

Furthermore, few committees possess enough actual power to kick-start the changes necessary to create a more vibrant, inclusive movement. The individuals in these positions are also under considerable pressure not to stray from their own union's perspective on issues. They have to toe the line because they are reliant on their affiliate for support. And yet, despite the odds, some representatives still manage to keep in touch with their caucus base.

More often than not, the committees, working groups, or people in the representative positions are not assigned a budget – or it is a token amount. Without a budget and an action plan – that includes material support from the affiliate – their ability to move the equity agenda forward is seriously thwarted. In short, there is no real representation and the status quo is maintained.

BJ: In effect, the positions and people are there, but they are not in power. They are in positions that *appear* to have power. The movement doesn't analyze how to make the committees more productive and effective. It is completely patronizing – without an adequate budget and infrastructure, it is window dressing, pure and simple. The point is to build the voices of workers of colour and Aboriginal peoples in our organizations. Instead we hear, "We've given you the opportunity, we've allowed you to have committees."

MCW: I think this comes partly from a lack of understanding as to what genuine self-determination means. The original purpose of these committees and positions was to enhance marginalized groups in the labour movement to achieve self-determination. I do not see that happening.

We have the ability to make it happen, but first, the political will is needed. Those people in power need to recognize – and I know that I am now one of those in power – that they/we don't always know what's best for marginalized groups of people.

It should be for the elected committee members to identify needs and decide how best to conduct their business. I think we (and I mean leadership) should sit and listen and then put their recommendations and action plans in place. We, and again I mean leadership in all the affiliates, have to stop being so arrogant as to think that we know what's best for everyone. Until that shift occurs, until genuine listening begins, I don't think we're going to move forward. Racism will continue to plague the labour movement just as it does outside.

The worst thing that could transpire in the labour movement now, however, would be to allow the equality rights positions and committee structures to morph into *entirely* token bodies. It took years to organize around these structures as a way of dealing with existing power imbalances, and to strengthen solidarity within our movement. Although we have learned that they are imperfect vehicles, they are still worth defending and, moreover, improving.

ME: *Bev, how would you characterize racism in the movement earlier on and how has it changed?*

BJ: It is both the same and different. When in 1990, for example, Fred Upshaw became the first black person to head a major Canadian union, many of us thought this was a great breakthrough. And it was! He had risen through the ranks to become president of the Ontario Public Service Employees Union [OPSEU]. But although he was the only elected leader of colour at that level, he could not get elected as a visible minority representative to the CLC executive board. Why? In my opinion, Fred was not beholden to anyone on the issue of equity; he spoke his mind and was not afraid to confront people on issues. The board did not want to have that voice at the table because they knew that he would challenge them on race and gender. As Marie has mentioned, these perspectives are not always welcomed – even today.

In my assessment, racism was, has been, and continues to be alive and well in the labour movement. In some instances it is well hidden, in other instances it is just below the surface, and in others it's right up front in your face.

Some union sisters and brothers find it difficult to accept when some of us say that not a whole lot has changed. When they see people of colour – male and female – in leadership positions, the inclination is to say we've made progress and things are so much better. I would argue that we have not really made any progress. Workers of colour in the labour movement are, in my opinion, still almost voiceless and, with a few exceptions, invisible. There is still resistance to having us in positions where we can actually speak freely, be heard respectfully, [be] listened to, and have our contributions taken seriously and acted upon.

Just like in the community when black people get together in a group, white people – whether they are in the labour movement or in the community – get nervous. They want to know what we are up to, what we are planning. We couldn't just be having a conversation about our issues, how we want to deal with them, and how we want others of like mind to work with us to tackle our issues. Instead, there is always some suspicion that we're engaged in a conspiracy.

MCW: I think we need to say something here about how important the Coalition of Black Trade Unionists (CBTU) has been in providing a space for our community to come together, to speak to our issues, and develop strategy in anti-racist work. I'm certainly a product of the mentoring CBTU has offered many of us. Unlike in Canada, in the United States, African-American union leaders are not a rare commodity. The CBTU is a significant force *within* the American labour movement that maximizes the strength and influence of black workers – and other workers of colour.

Many black labour leaders in the United States recognized that, by participating in the labour movement, significant steps toward achieving economic, social, and political equality could be made. They also realized that to be really effective in this endeavour, the labour movement also had to change from within. At its founding convention in 1972, delegates passed a statement of purpose to call for more black leadership in local unions and to increase black and female representation on the AFL-CIO [American Federation of Labor and Congress of Industrial Organizations] executive council.

BJ: In the US political arena, CBTU has been very successful in its effort to have unions allocate considerable resources to mobilize black voters to influence elections and public policy at every level of government. It was the first labour organization to adopt and act on resolutions regarding South Africa, Namibia, and Zimbabwe.

The coalition has held conventions annually, including a women's conference. Now, more than fifty international and national unions are represented in the coalition, with fifty-seven chapters in the United States and one in Canada.

The chapter in Ontario applied for its charter in 1996, but the coalition in Canada was born out of a struggle for more than ten years by labour activists to position issues of racism and discrimination higher on labour's agenda. We made a concerted effort calling for affirmative action seats for racially visible activists on the boards of the CLC and the OFL.

In the late 1980s and into the 1990s, this network of activists had supported black candidates for leadership positions in many labour organizations. By 1992, the CLC was considering one seat for a racially visible representative.

The coalition had been advocating for two seats. In the end, two racially visible representatives were elected on the CLC board. As Marie mentioned, the CBTU holds an annual convention. Each year the Ontario chapter sends delegates to both the main convention and the one-day women's conference that is part of it. Throngs of people attend; the agenda in 2007 included speeches from Democratic Party presidential candidates, as well as other public figures and international guests.

In 2003, Marie was invited to be the keynote speaker at the women's conference luncheon. This was a huge honour – the luncheon is a centrepiece of the CBTU annual convention. It celebrates the contributions of African-American women in the United States and internationally and, frankly, the list of women who have spoken over the years is quite impressive. It was the very first time that an elected CBTU member from Canada had ever been invited to address this group. And, of course, unlike what our community experiences at most Canadian labour gatherings, our delegation is barely visible among the sea of US trade unionists.

MCW: I was very honoured to be asked and also appreciated the historic moment such an invitation captured; it was a tribute to the maturity and successes of the CBTU Ontario chapter, of my community, and our contribution to the Canadian labour movement. Our leadership and anti-racist programs were suddenly on the map!

Unfortunately, my colleagues did not share my enthusiasm. I was barred from representing the CLC at this event. Was this a discriminatory decision? In a word, yes. I was elected because I bring a particular perspective to our movement and I was, in effect, silenced. People in positions of power were reluctant to share that power – even when it was an opportunity to make room for a new, different voice to be heard speaking on behalf of Canadian workers.

After considerable thought, I decided to accept the invitation anyway. I booked a week's vacation, paid my own way and, other than my accommodation, which CBTU International graciously assumed, covered my own expenses. I delivered my official remarks as a CBTU sister from Canada and was well received.

BJ: The coalition in Canada also challenged the under-representation of blacks and racially visible peoples on the staff of unions. To highlight this systemic exclusion, the coalition began a report card on the hiring practices of unions.

CBTU's work extends beyond the labour movement and into the broader community. Some of the Ontario chapter's activities, for example, include providing scholarships and educational grants to African-Canadian students. We also honour community activists through an annual awards dinner that is sponsored by unions and labour organizations.

MCW: CBTU Ontario links with others to monitor major issues which families in our community are grappling with. Along with many African-Canadian community organizations, we formed a coalition to meet directly with the prime minister, Ontario premier, and mayor of Toronto to discuss systemic responses to gun violence. This involvement is part of building the CBTU's profile in the community and is very positive for the labour movement.

ME: *Bev, you have always mentored young people. You have expressed publicly that the labour movement's hope for the future lies with young workers. How do youth and equity issues intersect?*

BJ: Certainly today the labour movement is focused on getting more young workers active, and I support that wholeheartedly. In OPSEU, as young workers became active as a caucus and subsequently matured to a provincial committee, we always made an effort to include them in our equity unit planning, strategies, and events. One thing that soon became clear to me is that the youth may well decide to do things differently from how we have always done [them]. Now that will shake things up! Just look at some young people's critique of globalization and environmental challenges – for young activists, the world is a much smaller place.

At the same time, when the movement approaches young workers, an equity perspective must be part of the approach. *Our Times* recently did an article on youth in the labour movement. Where were black youth? While it was a good article – the content dealt with important issues for youth – black workers, workers of colour were absent. Even in the accompanying graphics – I didn't see anyone who looks like me. It is that kind of thinking that makes me question whether the workers in the equity positions are given adequate opportunity to help build the movement. I think lip service is paid to that, quite frankly.

In many situations we have people in leadership positions in the labour movement who, in my view, are anti-union in their thinking and behaviour. They have no working-class analysis. The reality is, most of the people in those leadership positions are so far removed and have removed themselves from the average working person's situation that they are not able to adequately or correctly articulate the issues, the aspirations, the feelings, or the concerns of the folks who they claim to represent. It is my opinion that the rank-and-file membership of the labour movement is way ahead of their leaders on many, many issues.

MCW: The labour movement is supposed to be a place where there is respect and equality. Our job is to look out for working families and communities. We say that we believe in [the] tenets of justice, equality, respect, and fairness. We tend to forget that the labour movement – like any other organization – is a microcosm of society. In mainstream society there are racists, people who discriminate, people who are prejudiced, homophobes, Islamaphobes, and so on ... It's no different within the labour movement.

When I – and many others – acknowledge that dilemma, [we are] automatically labelled as "bashing" the labour movement. As a leader, I am seen by some as not supporting my own movement. If we are going to make change, however, and truly address issues of racism ... we have to first acknowledge that they exist.

Acknowledging the problem doesn't just mean creating special seats and committees, it means giving people the tools to do things and to effect change. So, I think that between the 1970s and now, there has been some shift. The change is that committees have been set up, we have people in positions, not that many. We have affiliates that have recognized that there are marginalized people in the membership and have set aside seats for equity-seeking groups.

We have all kinds of anti-racism policies, anti-harassment policies, training, and in some cases training that leadership must take before they actually get into a leadership role. What people in those positions and on committees have done between the 1970s and now is considerable; I don't in any way want to diminish the important work accomplished. But it is also true that in terms of racism very little of substance has been achieved.

BJ: In 1994, the CLC set up an anti-racism task force. It was an excellent process; the task force went right across the country in 1996, meeting with members to hear about and discuss what racism looked like in the movement, how it operated in the community, in housing, in education, and in the workplace. The task force report *Challenging Racism: Going Beyond Recommendations* came out in October 1997.

I worked with OPSEU members to prepare a brief to the task force and attended the sessions in Toronto. I had hoped that the recommendations would have an accountability component attached and that there would be pressure put on affiliates and central labour bodies to comply. I hoped that there would be *real* change!

MCW: No question, the report is a far-reaching document. The Anti-Racism and Human Rights Department was established by the CLC officers in 1998, a key response to recommendations set out.

Nonetheless, almost ten years later, where are we? If you look closely at the recommendations, we are in exactly the same place – in some instances worse [off]. I know this may sound contradictory because there has been some change, but it is minimal.

Some people in the movement express the view that we've come a long way because – and I've heard it said – we have a woman of colour – in fact, two workers of colour – at the helm of the CLC. We have a woman of colour who is one of the top officers at the OFL. But when we take a closer look, how many presidents, general secretaries, vice-presidents are people of colour?

Leaders – all members – have to first acknowledge that racism permeates the movement and, having taken that step, take concrete action to make change. It is no longer sufficient to simply recognize the problem.

People who have power don't want to relinquish power – not just in the labour movement but also in society as a whole. It's how white privilege works. Until we as a movement acknowledge that we are caught up in the same dynamic, nothing we do will meet the challenge. We have to be serious about wanting to make our unions more inclusive. There has to be a willingness to share and sometimes concede power.

One challenge is that mainstream society has gotten better at disguising what it really thinks and feels about racialized peoples. I have heard many people of colour here in Canada say, "I wish we were living in the United States because at least there you know it – it's in your face – you know how to deal with it."

It's worse since September 11, 2001. Since 9/11, lots of people worldwide have been given licence to make certain statements, to question others, to look differently at people who have particular names or ethnic backgrounds. These individuals are not called to task in the same way they would have been on the 9th of September 2001.

On that day, if a co-worker had said, "I don't want that person around me because they may be tied to a terrorist organization," there are people who would have taken them to task, who would have insisted, "You're being discriminatory; you cannot pre-judge anyone like that."

BJ: Today, the climate is filled with fear and heightened suspicion. It's people of colour who experience the brunt of it, and this is reflected in the labour movement just like anywhere else. In Canada, it's still more covert than in the United States, but since 2001, it is much worse – right in your face. For black people, racist behaviour was always there. In the mainstream, at some union meetings, in the newspaper, the message that "Canada is not a racist country, we don't have racism here" resonated. But black people and other people of colour could always see it, feel it, and [they] lived with the repercussions.

We have to first acknowledge that race and race-based incidents exist. We have to find ways as a community, as a society, as a movement to acknowledge what people experience – people who look like me – and be prepared to take responsibility for one's role, or lack of role, in confronting racism and helping to eradicate it.

MCW: This points again to the gap between principles espoused and what actually happens on the ground. We still do not have equitable representation. While the CLC indicates that we want members from equity-seeking groups appointed to all committees, we still rely on the affiliates to make the appointments. We are still struggling; the health and safety and the environment committees, for example, have women but no workers of colour. The women's committee has no workers of colour on it. As the anti-racism task force recommended, it is important that we look at the causes and effects of multiple oppressions. We need as many perspectives at the table as possible if equity-seeking groups are to have voice.

ME: *Can you give some specific examples of how systemic discrimination impacts racialized workers and how it affects their involvement in the labour movement?*

MCW: Many people who come to Canada with foreign credentials are unable to get them recognized here. Those with early childhood education or accounting degrees, for example, are often told they are not qualified for positions, as they have no Canadian experience. This applies mainly to the professional categories but not exclusively.

This has three impacts in terms of systemic exclusion. First, these workers cannot obtain employment, which keeps them out of the workforce and from becoming workers in unionized workplaces. That barrier means these workers of colour cannot contribute their talents and experience to the movement.

Second, respected members of the black community are often invisible to their own unions. Long-time activists involved in various ethnic and racial organizations, advocacy-based or service-oriented, are often more influential and connected to the lives of our members than trade union officials.

Third, if such a person *is* in the union but their previous labour experience is not recognized or respected, what is the point of coming to meetings? Again, it is the labour movement that loses out – we miss diverse, credible contributions and the solidarity that would bring.

ME: *Marie, given the challenges that diversity poses, do you think solidarity can be built in the large unions of 2007?*

MCW: I've certainly observed a differential impact on workers of colour when unions merge and amalgamate. We definitely gain bargaining strength at the table, but there is a flip side. In Ontario, with the amalgamations of cities and school districts, several locals chose (and some were forced) to merge. Many of the locals, particularly the school boards, had elected a significant number of workers of colour to their executive committees. Once merged into a single local with only one executive committee, many of those workers of colour lost their positions.

My own local is a perfect example. We went from more than twenty amalgamated locals – many with representation from communities of colour on their executives – to one local with none. It was not until an equity seat was inserted into the structure via the constitution that we got someone there. And it didn't happen the first time we tried. We were an amalgamated local for two years before we had a person of colour on the executive committee. While mergers and amalgamations were good in terms of strengthening bargaining sectors, they also led to a decrease in the numbers of racialized local leaders.

We need to build strong unions to counter the globalization of capital. At the same time, we need to be aware of how these mergers affect the day-to-day life in our locals. Along with the systemic nature of racism in our unions and the fact that it is expressed in more subtle ways, many workers of colour feel that their concerns are not being heard. And that affects our ability to build local capacity for taking on employers at any level.

ME: *How does an anti-racist agenda link the Canadian labour movement to global struggles for social justice?*

BJ: The diversity of the labour movement is growing and we need to be aware of issues such as housing and education that affect new immigrants. Large numbers of contingent and part-time workers, for example, are people of colour and women – although, of course, many are not new Canadians. We need to be aware that what is happening in members' countries of origin has political and economic impacts in Canada.

MCW: Yes. I was fortunate to participate in the CUPE [Canadian Union of Public Employees]/CLC delegation to the United Nations' World Conference against Racism (WCAR) in late summer 2001. The conference was held in Durban, South Africa. At the time, I was the CUPE national diversity vice-president and also a board member of CUPE Ontario Division.

At the World Conference there were Asian descendants caucuses, African descendants caucuses, indigenous caucuses, and so on. I participated in the African descendants group. It was decided that each of these particular groups would hold their own conference a year or two down the road.

Through extensive negotiations, the Durban Declaration and Programme of Action from the August 2001 United Nations' World Conference against Racism was subsequently agreed upon officially and ratified by 168 nation states.

For my caucus, the greatest victory was that the final declaration recognized the trans-Atlantic slave trade as a crime against humanity. In October 2002, a follow-up conference, the African and African Descendants World Conference against Racism, was scheduled [to take place] in Barbados. The purpose of the conference was to address anti-racist strategic objectives and future work aimed specifically at the nations and peoples of Africa and the African Diaspora.

When the issue came up for discussion among the CLC officers, we had a rather fractious debate. My position was clear. I argued that a person of African descent had to attend, even though the person responsible for the anti-racism portfolio was also a worker of colour. My colleagues looked at me like I was crazy. They didn't understand the dynamics; just because we're all from the Caribbean region, we're not all of African descent.

These labour leaders wouldn't do the same thing to women. They would not send a non-Aboriginal woman to a First Nations' conference when an Aboriginal woman had been invited. They wouldn't do that. They would look and find an Aboriginal woman to represent the congress. In retrospect, I firmly believe that decision was disrespectful; worse, thinly veiled racist behaviour was allowed to hide behind bureaucratic rigidity.

ME: *Are you saying that racism is thwarting the unions' efforts to be more relevant to their members?*

MCW: Yes. The labour movement is a microcosm of society. We live in a racist society and the movement reflects this. To be clear, I'm not saying the entire movement is racist – I do believe there has been some progress.

BJ: I don't agree. There have been *advances;* there has *not* been progress. An advance is that we have these committees; we have some people in positions. For me, progress is when we are invited to the table. We sit at the table; we speak and are heard in a respectful manner. What we say is valued and acted upon. That, for me, is progress.

MCW: Okay, I agree there is a difference between "advances" and "progress." A few of the anti-racism task force's recommendations have been implemented, although far fewer than what's needed. The congress has hired more workers of colour and Aboriginal workers. We also now have a national Anti-Racism Department. We organized Days of Action and make public statements targeting employers who engage in discriminatory practices. But I would argue that these are just superficial changes – we scrutinize employers, not ourselves. I do not know of any affiliate that has implemented an internal employment equity plan. Notwithstanding the comprehensive recommendations in the task force report, few have been acted upon in a meaningful way. Without the political will, we cannot make the great strides the situation demands.

BJ: In order for the movement – and it's not just about the labour movement, the same is true for the community – to really function in a way that is just and fair and has some semblance of equity, not only do we have to be included but we have to be valued in that inclusion, respected in that inclusion, and given the credibility by having our recommendations about ourselves accepted and acted upon. If that is not happening, like I said before, we are not making progress.

The leadership need to understand how oppressions are linked. From my perspective, there is still little understanding of the issue of intersectionality or, for that matter, the absolute need for equity-seeking groups to have their own space in caucuses. Where union structures allow for equity caucuses but then schedule them as part of convention and conference agendas, members are invariably forced to choose identities. Schedules don't contemplate the reality that members are packaged in diverse ways, and this inhibits their ability to participate in a manner that is respectful of the totality of their beings. An Aboriginal woman who is a lesbian or has a disability, for example, must make a choice about when and where she locates herself.

ME: *Did Labour get anything right?*

MCW: I believe there are some – not many – examples of a shift toward greater inclusion of marginalized, equity-seeking groups. In coordinating support for the resolution that established a national diversity seat in CUPE in 1999, for example, we took the issue of linking of oppressions seriously. It was working with other equity-seeking groups that ensured the resolution's success. I am confident that we can only make progress if we work together in this fashion.

BJ: Yes, it is critical that equity-seeking groups seek to understand and respect each other's issues and concerns. They also need to understand that they may not always agree on the solutions; they may need to take diverse routes to accomplish genuine equality and inclusiveness. Ensuring that understanding and respect exists makes the groups stronger and more empowered to act collectively – and individually – because they are assured of support. That cohesion makes it more difficult for the establishment to divide and conquer to keep the status quo intact – or to play groups off against each other and thereby distract them from their goals. It also helps to make leadership more accountable.

MCW: I agree. I can think of a few instances where we have tried to work together to link oppressions. In the 2002 Medicare campaign, for example, we made sure that materials were produced that linked trade union and health care issues to the different communities within our membership. It was a more effective campaign in that we included equity-seeking groups in our outreach to the public. I am currently leading a similar exercise [for] health and safety.

We still have a very long way to go. This inclusive approach is not consistently utilized; it depends a great deal on the particular affiliate and leadership at all levels. I am convinced, however, that this work cannot be successful if we do not involve the different groups of people both inside and outside the labour movement.

It's the *only* way to appeal to what really matters to our members and resonates with their communities. For the labour movement to grow and become more relevant to the people we represent – and want to represent in future – we need to take a good hard look at our practices and structures and retool them.

Including voices of workers of colour and Aboriginal peoples in decision-making processes and bodies, and encouraging inclusion in all aspects of union leadership and activity, would go a long way toward building genuine solidarity and strength. The labour movement will never flourish without them.

4
Equity in Unions: Political Correctness or Necessity for Survival?
Carol Wall

> When spider webs unite, they can tie up a lion.
>
> – Ethiopian proverb

If the title of this chapter pulled you in, you may feel that political correctness has run amok, or you may simply be curious about why I would use the term "political correctness." I will explain. Not so long ago, it was considered acceptable within the labour movement to make derogatory comments about various equity-seeking groups, or, in social circles, to make jokes about various ethnic or racial groups. Those who challenged this behaviour were silenced with comments like, "Can't you take a joke?" Then, as a result of workshops on harassment, racism, and oppression that promoted greater understanding and respect, we started to make progress in this area. Those who previously lacked the courage to do so began to challenge racial or ethnic jokes and inappropriate comments, and felt they were on safe ground in doing so. Those who had previously told such jokes began to think twice before making racist, sexist, homophobic, and other, similar comments because it was now deemed politically incorrect.

However, what is disturbing is that over the last several years, folks who I consider progressives and allies in the fight for social justice have started using the phrase "political correctness" as a silencing, negative term. To me, "political correctness" means that before I say something that may be offensive, ignorant, degrading, or intolerant, I check myself to think about the effect it will have on others. I happen to believe that this is the way everyone should always have conducted themselves, especially those in organizations fighting for social justice and dignity for all such as the labour movement. It was encouraging, especially to equity-seeking groups, that we had started this exercise as a community of caring people living the solidarity that is the backbone of the labour movement. So just to set the record straight, language does matter. We must embrace "political correctness" as a positive, rather than a negative, term and be diligent in refusing to adopt the language and ways of any oppressive force, because integrating and thinking about equity in a meaningful way is a necessity for the survival and growth of the labour movement.

In this chapter I explore the changing demographics that support my assertion that in order to have a vibrant, strong labour movement, we must view the issues we face through an equity lens, rather than from what can be considered the dominant view of straight, white, Anglo-Saxon, male protestants. I also discuss where I think we are as a movement – from my perspective as an African-Canadian woman – and where we need to go for our survival and growth.

Before we can address what it means to integrate equity to ensure union renewal, we need to get the true picture of the current and potential future labour force, and of existing unionization levels. Approximately 17 million people were employed in Canada in January 2009 (Statistics Canada 2009a), 48 percent of them women (Statistics Canada 2009b). According to the 2006 Census data (Statistics Canada 2008a), 16.2 percent of the labour force is part of a visible minority group.[1] The majority of women and minority group members works part-time or in temporary jobs in the service sector, which accounts for 77 percent of employment overall (Statistics Canada 2009a).

The Conference Board of Canada (2007) indicates that the labour force is aging and that massive numbers of baby boomers are due to begin retiring in 2010. As the retirements occur, labour force characteristics are expected to change dramatically. Population growth trends indicate that by 2017 one in five people in Canada could be a member of a visible minority group (Statistics Canada 2005), and Aboriginals could constitute 3.4 percent of the working age population, compared with 2.7 percent in 2001 (Luffman and Sussman 2007). Studies have shown that both visible minorities and Aboriginals experience discrimination and unfair treatment at work because of ethno-cultural characteristics (Canada 2005; Statistics Canada 2003, 18, 21). In addition, immigrants and Aboriginals tend to be over-represented within low-income groups (Palameta 2004) and to experience higher unemployment rates: for Aboriginals, the unemployment rate (12.1 percent) in 2005 was two and a half times that of non-Aboriginals (Statistics Canada 2007).

Less than one-third of the labour force (approximately 4.2 million workers) is currently unionized (Statistics Canada 2008b), and although the number of unionized workers increased 43 percent between 1977 and 2004, unionization has not kept pace with job creation. Unionization rates for males between the ages of twenty-five and thirty-four have declined precipitously (from 43 percent in 1981 to 24 percent in 2004) (Statistics Canada 2006). Since 2004, unionization rates for women have exceeded those of men (Statistics Canada 2008b). They currently hover around 30 percent and overall are much higher in the public than in the private sector (71 percent versus 16 percent). Close to 600,000 unionized employees work part-time (Statistics Canada 2008b).

These labour force statistics and projections suggest that the labour movement could be doing a better job of keeping up with the changing demographics of the labour force. Unionization is weak in the service sector where Aboriginals, visible minorities, and women are increasingly likely to be employed, despite the real disadvantages these workers face in the form of low wages, poor working hours, minimal benefit entitlements, racism, and discrimination. It could also be doing a better job of representing "the dispossessed, the despised, the neglected, the downtrodden, the poor," as the late, famous labour activist A. Philip Randolph exhorted the labour movement to do. Workers who are experiencing the most precarious of employment conditions today, often immigrants, women, and workers of colour, are not turning to unions for help, but rather to worker advocacy centres such as the Workers' Action Centre in Toronto (formerly the Toronto Organization for Fair Employment, or TOFFE). These centres represent workers in low-wage, unstable, unfair employment situations and provide a forum that allows people not represented by unions to join together to fight for their dignity at work.[2]

In light of the above, there is an obvious need for the labour movement to re-evaluate its strategies if it is to regain a secure spot in the minds and hearts of workers. This will be difficult because the movement is currently facing a number of internal and external challenges (Kumar and Schenk 2006). Global competition, the ability to outsource manufacturing jobs, and the decentralized industrial relations system are some of the external challenges unions now face, which have made it difficult for unions to deliver much in the way of improved wages and working conditions. Rising member expectations and reduced member willingness to get involved in union campaigns or activities are some of the internal challenges. In addition, unions have lacked a vision that would enable them to once again become an effective institution for workers (ibid.).

It seems appropriate that those who are directly affected by poor working conditions should be the ones to lead the struggle for change. But the labour movement should work in solidarity and strategic partnership with grassroots organizations such as the Workers' Action Centre, and with disadvantaged groups such as immigrants, visible minorities, and Aboriginals who are in precarious employment situations, to challenge a global agenda that embraces a race to the bottom with wages, benefits, and any protections for workers. If the union leadership wishes to reach the generation of Canadians coming of age, it needs to embrace them.

To broaden and put an equity lens to what has been said to this point, the leadership must reflect the future membership. The past and present leadership has sacrificed and worked hard to bring the labour movement to where it is. But to move forward, leaders must engage members in a lively, perhaps difficult debate, to arrive at an action plan for the future. Yet, our current leaders fear open debate and constructive criticism, preferring to come to agreements behind closed doors with a handful of their mostly white male brothers, in a patronizing way of "they know best." They simply tell the members what the issues are and expect them to blindly follow. When demonstrations are shelved for fear of very poor attendance, they console themselves by blaming members for being apathetic. If leaders did some soul-searching they might find that these tactics have contributed to the rise of apathy and the disconnect that exists between them and their members. It is now time to turn over the baton and unleash the potential of new leadership and ideas from people who look and think differently. The perspectives of equity-seeking groups must be sought out because they are the future of the labour movement. They also have a vested interest in the outcome of the debate because they are at the bottom of the economic and social order.

The road to equality within the labour movement for workers of colour and, more recently, Aboriginal workers, continues to be too long, with far too many detours. The current state of affairs reminds me of a quotation by Bella Abzug, the US feminist, who said, "First they gave us a day for women. Then they gave us a year. Then they gave us a decade. Now we're hoping for a century – and maybe then they'll let us in for the whole show." The Canadian Labour Congress established an anti-racism task force in 1994 that heard presentations from members from across Canada who were Aboriginal, people of colour, and community anti-racist activists. The task force report (Canadian Labour Congress 1997) revealed the extent to which racism pervades Canadian society, including the labour movement, and set out many recommendations for change.

When the report was released, great hope existed that its findings would be a catalyst for change. But although some changes have been made, the labour movement appears to have gone as far as it intends to on the issue of equity. Without adequate funding, resources, and authority to reach out to their constituencies, the various equity positions that have been created within affiliate unions and labour centrals are virtually ineffective, viewed only as token roles. More recently, the Canadian Labour Congress postponed the Aboriginal and Workers of Colour Conference because of low numbers, bringing into question its commitment to equity, despite the growing numbers of these groups within the ranks of labour. The questions labour must ask are, as an institution, can it recreate itself to be representative of a larger movement, can it confront the growing inequalities of today, or will it remain unfocused, stuck in the past and doomed to suffer the decline we see south of the border?

In the midst of crisis, windows of opportunities may open up for a short period; therefore there is no time for inaction. Members are looking to the leadership for effective short- and long-term strategies that they can embrace and be hopeful about. Given the demographic shifts that are happening in Canada with the growing numbers of Aboriginals and people of colour, I would suggest that an opportunity now exists. The labour movement will be able to make headway in the battle for equality, dignity, and justice for all if it is willing to join with other groups seeking the same things. To be successful, labour has to have the courage to identify and remove the barriers to full membership participation that are embedded in the existing ways of doing things. As Barb Thomas, Labour Educator, stated at a workshop held as part of the December 2005 conference of the Australian Council of Trade Unions, "Few Canadian unionists would argue that the demographics of the Canadian workforce is multi-racial and diverse; that the next wave of leadership needs to reflect the workforce; that organizing and mobilizing young workers is key; in short that building a powerful worker and social movement must have an equity agenda. We agree on the big ideas. We face challenges in the daily default to inequity in our workplaces and unions."

It is a new era, and today's younger generation of Aboriginals and people of colour is not asking but demanding to be included in a meaningful way. It is no longer willing to be over-represented on human rights committees and under-represented on finance committees and within the leadership of the labour movement. It wants to be part of the "whole show" to which Bella Abzug alluded. The irony is that if labour does not let equity-seeking groups in for the whole show, those groups will put their energies into their community, side-stepping the labour movement completely. The show will continue to stall, and the future of the labour movement will be greatly imperilled.

The labour movement needs to dust off the 1997 anti-racism report and annually communicate the progress or lack of progress achieved on the various recommendations. The report provided the blueprint for equity. What is now needed is the political will and commitment to roll up our sleeves and do the very hard, ongoing work of tackling the many important issues that are still unresolved. Advancing equity within unions is the only way to give the labour movement the strong, unshakeable foundation it needs to weather the storms that will inevitably arise in a global world.

Notes

1   The 2006 Census provides information on the characteristics of people in Canada who are members of a visible minority, as defined in the Employment Equity Act. The act defines visible minorities as "persons, other than Aboriginal peoples, who are non-Caucasian in race or non-white in colour." Under this definition, regulations specify the following groups as visible minorities: Chinese, South Asians, Blacks, Arabs, West Asians, Filipinos, Southeast Asians, Latin Americans, Japanese, Koreans, and other visible minority groups such as Pacific Islanders.

2   The Workers' Action Centre's website at http://www.workersactioncentre.org describes the workers the centre represents: "Thousands of workers in Toronto are struggling to make ends meet. We are recent immigrants, workers of colour, women, youth and workers in precarious jobs. Most of us don't belong to unions because we work in small workplaces, work as temps, are on contract, independent contractors or unemployed. One week we

may be juggling 2 or 3 jobs while next month there is no work or income. When we are able to find full-time work, there is little protection on the job if we are facing unfair conditions or not being paid what we are entitled to."

References

Canada. Department of Canadian Heritage. 2005. *A Canada for All: Canada's Action Plan Against Racism.* Ottawa: Government of Canada.

Canadian Labour Congress. 1997. *Challenging Racism: Going Beyond Recommendations. Report of the CLC National Anti-Racism Task Force.* Ottawa: CLC.

Conference Board of Canada. 2007. *Industrial Relations Outlook: Finding Common Ground through the War for Workers.* Ottawa: Conference Board of Canada.

Kumar, P., and C. Schenk. 2006. Union renewal and organizational change: A review of the literature. In *Paths to Union Renewal: Canadian Experiences,* ed. P. Kumar and C. Schenk, 29-60. Peterborough, ON: Broadview Press.

Luffman, J., and D. Sussman. 2007. The Aboriginal labour force in western Canada. *Perspectives on Labour and Income* (January). Statistics Canada catalogue no. 75-001-XIE, 13-27.

Palameta, B. 2004. Low income among immigrants and visible minorities. *Perspectives on Labour and Income* (Summer). Statistics Canada catalogue no. 75-001-XIE.

Statistics Canada. 2003. *Ethnic Diversity Survey: Portrait of a Multicultural Society.* Statistics Canada catalogue no. 89-593-XIE.

–. 2005. Study: Canada's visible minority population in 2017. *The Daily.* 22 March. http://www.statcan.gc.ca/Daily-quotidien/050322/dq050322b-eng.htm.

–. 2006. Changing patterns of unionization. http://www41.statcan.ca/2006/2621/ceb2621_001-eng.htm.

–. 2007. Study: The Aboriginal labour force in western Canada 2001-2005. *The Daily.* 25 January. http://www.statcan.gc.ca/Daily-quotidien/070125/dq070125c-eng.htm.

–. 2008a. Ethnic origin and visible minorities. http://www12.statcan.ca/census-rencensement/2006/rt-td/eth-eng.cfm.

–. 2008b. Unionization. *Perspectives on Labour and Income* (August). Statistics Canada catalogue no. 75-001-X, 17-26.

–. 2009a. Latest release from the Labour Force Survey. 6 February. http://www.statcan.gc.ca/subjects-sujets/labour-travail/lfs-epa-eng.htm.

–. 2009b. Employment by age, sex, type of work, class of worker and province (monthly) (Canada). http://www40.statcan.gc.ca/101/cst01/labr66a-eng.htm.

5
Are We There Yet? The Struggle for Equity in Canadian Unions
Marie Clarke Walker

The Canadian labour movement has experienced many changes in policy, structure, leadership, and culture over the years. Many of these changes came as a result of pressure from within the movement, but our country's changing demographics have also been a factor. For one, the number of workers of colour in the Canadian labour force has significantly increased in the last twenty to thirty years. But these workers have never been part of the culture and structure of the labour movement. I believe that if the labour movement is to survive and maintain relevance and vibrancy, many more changes of substance and meaning are required.

In this chapter, I demonstrate how the changes the labour movement has experienced to date have affected it, and provide recommendations for its renewal among all sectors of our diverse population. In places, I am critical of the labour movement because I believe that unless we acknowledge our shortcomings it will be difficult to make the systemic changes necessary for the movement's survival. Although my comments may apply across the board, in this chapter I focus on racialized workers and draw upon my own experiences in the labour movement at the national level and in Ontario, the province with the majority of racialized workers.

Racism and discrimination have long been an issue within the trade union movement. Although the workforce has always been diverse, there have been times when women, Aboriginal, and racialized workers were not welcome in the movement. In the late 1800s and early 1900s, Chinese and black workers faced a great deal of racism. The predecessor of today's Canadian Labour Congress, the Trades and Labour Congress, actively campaigned for years to increase the head tax on Chinese and other Asian workers and to have the Chinese Immigration Act passed, in order to bar people of Chinese origin from entering Canada.

Workers of African descent, although part of the Canadian labour force since the seventeenth century, were not welcomed into existing white unions. These unions were mainly internationals, based in the United States, and hostile to black workers because of the segregationist thinking of the time. In 1918, when the black porters at the Canadian National Railway applied for a union charter, they were rejected and told to join one of the existing railway labour groups. When they tried to do so, they were told that membership was restricted to whites (Winks 1997). This caused workers of both African descent and Chinese origin to form their own unions early in the 1900s.

It was not until the Second World War that organized labour began to welcome workers of colour and women, most of whom worked in munitions plants and on the railway, into the unionized workforce, and to actively fight for equity for all workers (Winks 1997, 423). Through the efforts of many, the Ontario Fair Employment Practices Act was passed in 1951, and the Ontario Human Rights Code in 1962. Since then, many others have taken on the fight for equity and fairness, both outside and inside the labour movement, and have done much to force necessary changes within the Canadian movement. (See Appendix 1 for a partial list of these anti-racism and equity advocates.)

Workers of colour have organized outside as well as inside the movement. The trade union movement in the United States was shaken up when, in response to the American Federation of Labor and Congress of Industrial Organizations leadership's refusal to take a stand during the 1972 presidential election, five black trade union leaders founded the Coalition of Black Trade Unionists. It was to be an independent organization within the trade union movement to represent the views of black workers and to increase their representation at all levels of the political decision-making process.

Black workers' organizing, according to Roger McKenzie (2003, 13) of the British Trades Union Congress, "is distinct from the many individual responses to racism that are played out daily in workplaces throughout the country and which are sometimes given an identity by employment tribunal cases. The collective means of black resistance to racism has been born from necessity. The existing structures of the labour movement have not ... always been particularly welcome to either black workers specifically or, more widely, the fight against racism in the workplace or beyond. Black workers have had little choice other than to organize together to ensure that their voices would be heard in an unfiltered and undiluted way."

In the late 1980s, the Canadian Union of Public Employees' Ontario Black Workers' Caucus and the Ontario Coalition of Black Trade Unionists (OCBTU) were formed. The OCBTU included black workers from both public and private sector unions who wanted a forum in which to voice their concerns about racism in workplaces and in unions, as well as about discrimination and the need for support systems, and who wanted to develop strategies for change. Because existing unions provided no space for that kind of caucus and felt some discomfort with racialized workers, strategy meetings were held in basements, living rooms, and hotel rooms. The OCBTU wanted to ensure that blacks were represented on executive boards, that designated equity seats were created, and that the under-representation of blacks and other workers of colour on the staffs of unions was corrected.

The tireless efforts of the OCBTU and of people of colour to gain respect and recognition did bring results. Delegates to the 1987 Ontario Federation of Labour convention elected Brother Herman Stewart of the International Ladies Garment Workers Union to the federation's executive committee. He was the first person of colour to achieve such a post. In the mid-1980s, Fred Upshaw, another person of colour, was elected first vice-president and treasurer of the Ontario Public Service Employees Union, one of Ontario's largest public sector unions. He then became acting president, later serving two terms as president of that union. Other than the leadership of the sleeping car porters, Brother Upshaw was the first person of colour to lead a major union.

Subsequently, the OCBTU targeted change at the national level. Brother Dory Smith, a member of the Carpenters' Union and a founding member of the Coalition of Black Trade Unionists (CBTU) Ontario chapter, challenged the leadership candidate list proposed by the Canadian Labour Congress' (CLC) executive committee at its 1990 convention and secured over 1,000 votes from among the 2,300 voting delegates. Although that was not sufficient to gain him a seat on the CLC executive, it did indicate that many of the delegates were ready for change.

Brother Smith's success was a wake-up call for the CLC. Following that convention, the CLC established a task force on representation. Then, in 1992, after much pressure from black trade unionists, the CLC added two vice-presidential seats for visible minorities to its executive council, the main decision-making body of the labour movement. Hassan Yussuff and Lynn Jones were elected to those seats. This was a major victory, as the CLC had been considering the addition of only one seat. The CLC also established two working groups, one for workers of colour and the other for Aboriginal workers. In 1994, the CLC formed an anti-racism task force that went across Canada holding forums to assess the presence of racism and strengthen the network of Aboriginal peoples and people of colour within the labour movement and the community. Following the CLC's example, other unions began to add racialized and Aboriginal workers to their executive bodies and human rights committees, and the Ontario Federation of Labour hired its first director of human rights.

The successes achieved by people of colour working together to ensure equity in their organizations were achieved through struggle, but backlash occurred. By 1997, the anti-racism task force had reported that racism permeated all facets of Canadian life, including unions (CLC 1997). This finding was not surprising to many who had been doing anti-racism work. But any initial hopes that the report's recommendations would be embraced by the CLC and its affiliates, and implemented in their entirety, were eventually dashed. Only about two of the thirty-two recommendations were fully implemented. White members and leaders chose to justify the existing systemic barriers facing racialized workers rather than take concrete action to remove them. They attempted to find common ground with workers of colour, making comments like, "I have nothing against black people but ..." or "My neighbour is black," or "I have friends who are black." Black workers and other equity-seeking groups became increasingly frustrated with this reaction. Many of them gave up on elected positions, some left the labour movement, and others focused their energies on working in community organizations to challenge inequities and, in Ontario, to work for the passage of employment equity legislation.

As I look at the equity situation in Canadian unions today, there seems to have been little advancement. With the exception of numbers as they relate to gender, there are no accurate or reliable statistics on current equity demographics or the number of workers of colour in leadership positions at the local level. But minimal gains and tokenism are the reality even where committees and designated seats exist. Although the 1997 anti-racism report indicated that members wanted labour to close the gap between what is said and what is actually done about racism and other inequities in the labour movement and our communities, in reality the gap has widened. Many of the 1997 recommendations remain outstanding, and there are no mechanisms in place to ensure that corrective action is taken on those outstanding recommendations.

To place the lack of progress made with respect to workers of colour and other equity groups into perspective, it is informative to look at what has been achieved for women since the 1970s. The evolution of women's rights within the labour movement, and the manner in which women pushed their way onto executive committees, was both similar to and different from the experiences of workers of colour. Women in the labour movement were supported by the larger women's movement, which pressured labour to ensure women's equality inside and outside the movement. As a result, the Ontario Federation of Labour became the first labour organization to designate seats for women when, in 1983, it created five affirmative action positions on its executive board. The CLC followed suit, creating six vice-president positions for women the following year. While it took some time, many other labour bodies created positions and committees for women. This allowed women to strategize and create an environment within unions that was less hostile to their perspectives. Other equity-seeking groups, which lacked a critical mass within the labour movement, did not have the same ability to make their presence felt. Where there were usually at least five or six women on union executive bodies, there was generally only one worker of colour. That made caucusing and strategizing at that level somewhat difficult.

Nevertheless, the addition of women to executive boards opened the door to other designated seats for equity groups. By 2002, the CLC had seats at its executive council, and working groups, set up for workers of colour, Aboriginal workers, disabled workers, gay/lesbian/bisexual/trans workers, as well as young workers. However, the creation of affirmative action seats was not really a full step forward. Although women could now voice their concerns and bring their perspective on issues to executive boards, they could not challenge dominant male views without jeopardizing their futures within the union.

In terms of other equity groups, there are many at both provincial and national levels who believe that designated seat holders, although elected by their equity constituencies, merely give the unions they represent an extra vote on the executive, rather than their constituents a stronger voice. The prevailing view is that these members do not really have constituencies, that their purpose is to simply say their "piece" at the executive board level, and that they have no real power to create change or, for that matter, make decisions that would effect change for the workers who elected them. Moreover, very few of the equity committees, working groups, or designated positions created have budgets or action plans and therefore have no real ability to bring about necessary change to encourage equity in unions, despite the best efforts of the individuals involved. Consequently, regardless of the existence of new equity structures, the people in charge are still mostly middle-aged white men, and although they talk about equity and equality on a regular basis, in most cases they are not willing to give up, or share, power.

There are those who would disagree with the above perceptions, and who believe that things have significantly improved in the Canadian labour movement. For instance, in 2002, the CLC issued a report card for elected and staff positions within some of its affiliates. It showed that the representation problems that the OCBTU had identified in 1994 had been somewhat addressed. The faces of union staff representatives today are more diverse than previously. The CLC presently has two full-time officers and three vice-presidents who are workers of colour. There is also an Aboriginal vice-president and an Anti-Racism and Human Rights Department, two Aboriginal national representatives, and four national representatives who are workers of colour. At the Ontario Federation of Labour, there is one person of colour in a leadership position. In addition, there are some progressive male allies at the executive board level who do speak up on equity issues and take action whenever possible. But these changes have been minimal, given that there has been federal employment equity legislation in place since 1987, that Ontario unions have been working on employment equity issues since the early 1990s, and that there has been a dramatic increase in the number of workers who are recent immigrants, whose first language is not English or French, and who, for the most part, are workers of colour (see Wall, this volume).

It is not difficult to see that racism continues to exist in Canadian society, although those in privileged positions often refuse to see or acknowledge it. In some instances it still takes the form of overt racism, once commonplace. Generally, though, it takes more subtle forms, akin to the sexism experienced by women upon their arrival on executive boards, such that men's opinions are acknowledged but similar suggestions or comments by women are ignored, or in their omission from some committees and relegation to non-leadership roles. Workers of colour encounter similar types of behaviour on an ongoing basis. For instance, despite constant discussion and claims of inclusiveness, they are still more likely to be seen on human rights and anti-racism committees and working groups than on health and safety, bargaining, or pension committees. Equity has not yet been fully integrated into the work of unions in Canada.

The Canadian labour movement has been good at identifying the problem of racism to employers and has made cosmetic changes within many of its labour organizations by establishing positions and committees and anti-racism departments. But comments such as "There is already one there, why do we need another one?" which suggest that unions have done their duty by having a designated seat or one minority representative on a committee or board are still all too common. The reality is that, although the labour movement considers itself a beacon of justice, equity, and fairness, it is a microcosm of society and, similar to other organizations, unions reflect the society in which they exist. Therefore, the behaviours and comments seen and heard inside and outside the movement are often the same. Racism manifests itself in the union movement – for instance, in its refusal or un-willingness to deal with employment equity; its treatment of racism as a side issue; its willingness to cover up incidents of racism; its refusal to rec-ognize racism when it exists; and its omission of an anti-racist analysis as it deals with issues such as privatization, globalization, bargaining, health care, child care, and environmental issues on a daily basis. Needless to say, the movement could be doing so much better.

If we are serious about addressing equity issues, it must be acknowledged that racism differs from ethnic discrimination or racial discrimination and sexual discrimination from sexism, in that one can behave in ways that have racist and sexist overtones or impacts without having the intent to be racist or sexist. Racism and sexism does not just lie in words and overt actions but in the attitudes, perceptions, silences, and subtle messages that say "You don't count."

The actions needed to redress the situation today are the same as those needed a decade ago, when the CLC anti-racism task force made its recommendations. Ten years is too long to wait for all the recommendations to be implemented. The first step is for all, particularly those in positions of power, to first acknowledge that the problem of inequity exists. Then we can work on finding solutions.

There are many things the labour movement could do. First, a greater respect needs to be given to the experiences and knowledge that newcomers to the Canadian labour force, for the most part workers of colour, bring with them from their countries of origin. They may have found successful ways to organize and mobilize workers, to get governments to listen and make change, and to mount campaigns on a variety of issues that could be applied to a Canadian context. The labour movement does not avail itself of that information when it excludes those members from the discussion table.

Second, labour must continue to build coalitions with communities, working with them in an inclusive way, and taking an interest in what is happening in these communities. Our members spend the majority of their time in communities, so they belong to communities first, unions second. It is no longer acceptable to utilize communities solely when we need their support, or to speak solely for our members. Labour should take on issues such as the $10 Minimum Wage campaign, designed by various labour councils in conjunction with community organizations. In Toronto, the Toronto and York Region Labour Council work with their community partners to raise the minimum wage for all workers to a living wage, particularly for workers in large urban centres. Minimum wages and poverty are issues with which all workers can identify, and communities need to be involved in discussions about how to address them. By linking what is happening in communities with what is happening in workplaces, and vice versa, we can show our true concern for the rights of all workers, not just those of our members. This will help the labour movement gain support for the majority of its campaigns, build capacity for growth, and attract new members.

Third, equity-based labour organizations such as the CBTU, the Asian Canadian Labour Alliance, and Workers' Action Centre must be given the respect they deserve, must be included in union activities, and must be consulted on all union issues, as their members also benefit from the work of the broader labour movement. These organizations will ensure that the labour movement does not become complacent with the progress achieved thus far but continue to put forward issues of importance to workers of colour. The push for equity needs to come from both inside and outside the labour movement if the necessary changes are to be made.

Fourth, we must do a better job of communicating with our members. The movement will not be successful in attracting new members and community support if we are unable to effectively communicate with diverse groups. The CLC has adopted a policy that requires all resolutions, constitutional language, policies, and documents to be clearly written, and other unions have begun to implement this policy as well. Some have started to make campaign material available in various languages. This initiative must be expanded to cover policy papers, constitutions, bylaws, and so on, as the majority of new union members does not speak English or French as their first language.

Fifth, we must embrace the energies that young people bring to the movement and make a greater effort to reach out to young workers of colour. Many of them have limited labour experience but extensive community experience, and what better place to learn about the movement than inside the movement itself. Reaching out to youth will build and revitalize the labour movement.

Sixth, an ongoing campaign is necessary to educate leaders, staff members, and union members about the importance of giving space to equity groups to allow their issues to emerge, and about the existence of multiple oppressions. Union conferences should not schedule caucuses for women, workers of colour, and gay/lesbian/bisexual/trans members at the same time, because one person can belong to all of those groups and should not be forced to choose between them. Ensuring that all members of an executive get equity training, once elected, would promote a better understanding of workers' issues and needs and the ways in which the movement could address equity challenges at the leadership level. Even members of equity-seeking groups require this education because oppression is frequently internalized and manifests itself when it is least expected. Adequate time must be allowed for this education.

Seventh, if there is to be sustainable change and renewal among unions in Canada, the labour movement must canvass the perspectives of all its constituents and ensure that marginalized workers and workers from all equity-seeking groups are an integral part of all union structures, discussions, campaigns, and solutions. Therefore, there is a need for the movement to find new ways to allow marginalized members to participate. Existing constitutions, by-laws, meeting times, and structures must be changed because they prevent many women and racialized members from participating. In addition, all policies, policy papers, programs, hiring, promotions, and practices must be reviewed to ensure they are, and remain, inclusive, and that an anti-racism perspective and anti-oppression principles are applied in all cases. Other barriers to participation, both structural and psychological, must be removed.

Eighth, structures that are created must be adequately resourced to do the tasks they have been set up to do. The issues of racism and inequity are just as serious within the labour movement as are bargaining or health and safety, but anti-racism and equity initiatives have not been given the financial and human resources necessary to be effective. This is not acceptable.

Ninth, it is critical that, in making its decisions, labour practices what it preaches. We must demand of ourselves the same equitable practices, inclusion, and anti-racist practices we demand of employers and governments on a daily basis. It is no longer good enough to indicate on a job posting that a union is an equal-opportunity employer. Many affiliates have policy papers on employment equity but very few have action plans to ensure equitable hiring. Concrete action must be taken, and leaders must have the political will to ensure it is. The current power holders and decision makers within the movement must also recognize that they hold their positions largely as a result of white privilege and power. They must be willing to give up or share power.

Finally, there is still a need for self-organization of constituency groups such as the CBTU and the Asian Canadian Labour Alliance, since the labour movement still has not come to terms with the fact that representation of equity groups within unions is still a major issue, and that racism and sexism still occur within the movement.

In the United Kingdom, the Trades Union Congress worked with government to pass anti-racist legislation. Affiliated unions are now required to put anti-racist practices in place because they must report on equity progress to the government and the Trades Union Congress every two years. This policy does not just target employers – it holds the labour movement accountable for outcomes. The Canadian labour movement needs to have a similar accountability system, one that applies to unions as well as employers. The status quo is not an option.

Appendix 1

A Partial List of Anti-Racism and Equity Advocates

Bromley Armstrong – former member of the United Auto Workers and commissioner of the Ontario Human Rights Commission.

Peter Birmingham – Canadian auto worker, member of the Ontario Federation of Labour Human Rights Committee, and member of the Ontario Coalition of Black Trade Unionists.

Muriel Collins – First woman of colour elected to the CUPE Ontario executive board.

Stan Grizzle – member of the Brotherhood of Sleeping Car Porters and author of the 1998 book *My Name Is Not George: The Story of the Brotherhood of Sleeping Car Porter in Canada.*

Carmen Henry – Staff representative for the Canadian Union of Public Employees, founding member of the CUPE Ontario Black Caucus, and long-time community activist.

Livingston Holder – Now deceased, former board member and activist for the Canadian Union of Public Employees, Ontario Division; member of the CUPE Human Rights Committee and of both the National and Ontario Division Rainbow committees.

Beverley Johnson – now retired; first human rights officer for the Ontario Public Service Employees Union; founding member and former president of the Coalition of Black Trade Unionists, Ontario chapter; and member of the Ontario Federation of Labour Human Rights Committee.

Peter Marcelline – now retired, former CUPE member and member of the CUPE Human Rights Committee and of both the National and Ontario Division Rainbow committees.

Jay Nair – anti-apartheid activist, founding member of the Coalition of Black Trade Unionists, Ontario chapter, and human rights staff for the United Food and Commercial Workers International Union.

Ann Newman – retired Communications, Energy and Paperworkers Union of Canada member; active with the Bell telephone workers' pay equity case; founding and executive member of the Coalition of Black Trade Unionists, Ontario chapter, and of Ontario Coalition of Black Trade Unionists; member of the Ontario Federation of Labour Human Rights Committee; and member of the Labour Hall of Fame.

Winnie Ng – Former Ontario Region director for the Canadian Labour Congress, community activist, and former member of the International Ladies Garment Workers Union.

Dory Smith – founding member of the Coalition of Black Trade Unionists, member of the Carpenters' Union, and member of the Ontario Coalition of Black Trade Unionists.

June Veecock – retired human rights director for the Ontario Federation of Labour, and first president and founding member of the Coalition of Black Trade Unionists, Ontario chapter, and Ontario Coalition of Black Trade Unionists.

St. Clair Wharton – member of the Ontario Federation of Labour's Human Rights Committee, member of the Ontario Coalition of Black Trade Unionists, commissioner on the Ontario Human Rights Commission, and member of the United Steelworkers.

George Williams – activist, one of the first racialized staff at CUPE, and member of the Canadian Union Of Public Employees Ontario Black Caucus.

References

Canadian Labour Congress. 1997. *Challenging Racism: Going Beyond Recommendations*. Ottawa: CLC.

McKenzie, R. 2003. Some key influences on the development of black self-organisation in the UK labour movement. Paper presented at the London Metropolitan University Working Lives Institute Lunchtime Seminar Series, 12 November, London.

Winks, R. 1997. *The Blacks in Canada: A History*. Montreal: McGill-Queen's University Press.

Part 3
Equity, Solidarity, and Union Renewal

6
Bargaining for Economic Equality: A Path to Union Renewal, Then and Now
Anne Forrest

The issue of women and union renewal, from the 1950s to the present, is an important one for the future of organized labour. I begin with the observation that unions in Canada have been most active and most engaged both in the workplace and in the larger community when they self-consciously adopted what Flanders (1970, 15) evocatively called their "sword of justice" face. I take this to be one of the lessons of the post-Second World War years. Two twenty-year periods – the mid-1930s to mid-1950s and the 1970s to 1980s – stand out as times during which organized labour actively sought a fairer and more just distribution of power and wealth in the workplace and in Canadian society at large. In so doing, unions reversed their slide toward irrelevance and repositioned themselves at the centre of economic and employment growth, and public debate.

Contemporary discussions of the challenges facing unions tend to frame union renewal as a problem of strategies. From their review of the literature, Kumar and Schenk (2006, 36) identify seven major strategies used or discussed by unions to rebuild themselves: organizational restructuring internally or through mergers; organizing the unorganized; grassroots political action to expand rank-and-file activism; coalition building and alliances with social and community groups; inter-union cooperation and solidarity networks, nationally and internationally; partnerships with employers and governments on issues of mutual interest; and education, training, and research for leadership development and rank-and-file awareness. Less discussed is the overarching purpose that these strategies articulate. The word "strategy" implies a vision of the future different from the present, which raises the question, what is it that union renewal moves us toward? The answer offered often appears to be backward- rather than forward-looking: renewal is necessary for unions to recover their lost power and influence. Such an answer positions unionism as self-evidently a good thing. Certainly, there is a lot of evidence to support this conclusion: in every country, unions have improved the living conditions of the working class and enhanced social and economic equality. But this is not their only impact. The sword of justice face of unionism has vested interest as its obverse.

The tension between these two faces of unionism is historic (Hyman 2002) and central to the union renewal dynamic. I argue that periods of union renewal are those in which organized labour self-consciously acts as an equality-seeking movement; concomitantly, renewal stalls when this vision fades and unions focus their energy on protecting the relatively privileged position of the already organized. My argument parallels Flanders' belief (1970, 15) that unions grow in numbers and power – "deepen their grip on public life" – when they have a clear social purpose and become vulnerable when motivated by materialism. When organized labour acts for its members only, when it turns its vested-interest face to the public, it can "no longer count on anything but its own power to withstand assault" (ibid.).

The mid-1930s to mid-1950s and the 1970s to 1980s were periods of union renewal because union leaders and activists on the progressive wing of the labour movement knew that organizing the unorganized was prerequisite to industrial and social democracy, and that success in this project required a more egalitarian vision of unionism, attractive to new groups of workers. In the 1930s, 1940s, and 1950s, this new group consisted of unskilled and semi-skilled industrial workers; in the 1970s and 1980s, unionism expanded to embrace public sector workers – blue-collar, white-collar, and professional – and women workers. All brought with them their own particular needs and expectations related to (paid and unpaid) work – needs and expectations that were both similar to and different from those that informed the established structure and practice of organized labour then in place. Embracing these new groups was an active, not a passive process, and it was divisive. Each of these new groups joined a labour movement that prioritized other workers' needs and expectations: the un/semi-skilled joined a movement that put the needs of the skilled at the centre; public sector workers joined a movement attuned to the needs of blue-collar, goods-producing workers; and women joined a movement organized by and for men. To grow, unions had to modify or abandon the structures and practices that until then had defined their purpose and function. That the emergent models challenged the privileged position of the already organized helps explain why these periods of renewal were also periods of conflict and division within the union movement.

I call this process of union growth and renewal "bargaining for equality." I choose the term "equality" rather than the more traditional labour relations language of fairness and justice to draw attention to the gendered dimensions of this dynamic. Unions have long employed the language of fairness and justice to legitimate their demands at the bargaining table and in the public sphere. What unions mean by fairness and justice has changed over time (as I demonstrate); however, that meaning has always had the breadwinner ideal at its base. The belief that blue-collar working-class men should earn enough to support their families in comfort and that unions are the means to that end is a central, if little discussed, tenet of union thinking, structure, and practice in North America, past and present. In the hands of unions, this ideal has been both a sword of justice and a vested interest: both a demand for economic equality and a justification for economic inequality between and among women and men.

I use the lens of women and gender relations purposefully. Too often, analyses of union structures and practices marginalize women because gender is thought to be the property of women alone. This way of thinking, which early feminist academics called "add women and stir," is evident in the union renewal literature. Most authors continue to see women/gender as one aspect of diversity, which in itself is but one of many challenges facing unions today. This approach is inadequate from a left-feminist perspective because it obscures the extent to which labour relations systems and union activity within those systems institutionalize privilege and disadvantage (Kainer 2006). The analysis offered in this chapter demonstrates that gender in/equality discourses – by which I mean ways of thinking about gender relations evident in union structure and practice – have been and continue to be integral to union growth and renewal. I argue that unions are more likely to act as a vested interest when their high-wage members are encouraged to see themselves as legitimately at the top of the wage hierarchy rather than as the beneficiaries of institutionalized privilege. When conservative discourses of hard work, high productivity, education, or militancy are used to explain and justify why some union workers are consistently better off than others, systemic forms of gender and race dis/advantage such as collective agreements, union constitutions, bargaining structures, and labour laws are ignored. By contrast, periods of union renewal are those in which established structure and practice are seen as mechanisms of privilege and so actively contested by those for whom the sword of justice and equality vision is paramount.

In the next two sections, "Bargaining for Industrial Workers: Men during the 1930s, 1940s, and 1950s" and "Bargaining for Gender Equality during the 1970s and 1980s," I examine the sword of justice and vested-interest faces of the equality discourses adopted during these periods by describing and analyzing the impact of the structures and practices created for the purpose. I then conclude by arguing that we need a new equality discourse that breaks, firmly and finally, from the breadwinner ideal, which is out of touch with the realities of the labour market and the working class household. My focus throughout is the economic dimensions of the bargaining for equality agenda. I analyze the impact of the changes in structure and practice in unions on gender equality, leaving the analysis of the political processes that facilitated these changes to others.

Bargaining for Industrial Workers: Men during the 1930s, 1940s, and 1950s

Union renewal during the 1930s, 1940s, and 1950s took its energy from the Congress of Industrial Organizations' (CIO) commitment to industrial and political democracy. The CIO and its affiliated unions, which organized under the umbrella of the Canadian Congress of Labour (CCL) in Canada, exemplified what is now called social movement unionism. In alliance with like-minded social justice organizations, the CCL and its affiliates pressed employers and government for the right to bargain collectively, a higher standard of living, and social security. Its message of a living wage for industrial workers articulated the moral sensibility of working-class families who were frustrated and exhausted by the deprivations imposed by the Depression and prolonged by the Second World War (Ursel 1992, 179-227). "Everyman" – skilled and un/semi-skilled, white and racialized, Canadian-born and immigrant – was entitled to a wage sufficient to support his family in dignity, these thinkers and activists argued, because all were equal as workers, family heads, and men.

This egalitarian vision challenged head-on established trade union structures and practices that, in that era, identified craft and skilled workers as uniquely entitled to a living wage. In Canada, these ideas informed the thinking and practice of the Trades and Labour Congress (TLC), whose affiliates included the Canadian sections of American Federation of Labor (AFL) unions and the railway brotherhoods. All were organized along craft principles with a clear purpose of advancing and protecting the relatively privileged position of their skilled members, most of whom were Canadian-born whites or British immigrants. In the hands of the TLC, the importance of skill went well beyond the workplace: skilled men organized into craft unions were responsible citizen-consumers and family heads. This uniqueness entitled skilled men to higher wages than immigrant men from eastern and southern Europe or Asia, whose "naturally" low style of living was satisfied by substandard wages; to higher wages than black men, whose supposedly frivolous and dissipated lifestyles were an irresponsible use of high wages; and to higher wages than women, who were socially constructed as the economic dependents of fathers and husbands with no need to support anyone but themselves (Glickman 1997, 55-91).

This sense of privilege was articulated by craft unions' lack of concern for the working and living conditions of anyone other than their members. The TLC had no large vision of social justice and was averse to government intervention in the economy on principle (Pentland 1979). In the workplace, craft unions claimed broad jurisdiction, yet refused to embrace the un/semi-skilled, racialized men, and all women. This was a unionism that would "neither organize the army of non-craft wage-earners itself, nor let anybody else do it," Pentland (1979, 16) observed. Sangster (1978) offers a clear example of this dynamic at work in the International Brotherhood of Electrical Workers (IBEW), which asserted jurisdiction over telephone operators but was totally uninterested in organizing them because they were unskilled and women. In 1907, the IBEW failed to support the women's strike, repeatedly refusing their requests for financial support. Clarke Walker (this volume) provides examples of men excluded from membership because they were black or Chinese. These attitudes and practices, honed to a fine point in the United States, found plenty of support in Canada.

The CIO took up the cause of these neglected workers. The result was a new model of unionism suited to a mass-production, mass-consumption economy. Industrial unionism was fundamentally different from the model of unionism that preceded it. Workers were organized into inclusive, single-industry unions – appropriately named the United Packinghouse Workers of America, the United Rubber Workers of America, the United Clothing Workers of America, and so on – in which the social and economic glue was these workers' long-term, continuous, on-site, and full-time commitment to a single employer rather than a shared occupation (Cobble 1994, 286). Organizers argued that this all-in structure was powerful. Gone was the Depression-era image of the working man cowering under the boss's thumb. Acting together, in plant-wide bargaining units of hundreds, even thousands, industrial workers could "beat the boss" because they had the potential to stop production. Solidarity meant equality: the skilled mixed with the unskilled, decisions were made collectively and by majority, and racial and ethnic discrimination was actively discouraged. (For an example of this dynamic in the United Steelworkers of America, see Crawley 1997.)

Another bridge across difference, less discussed in the literature, was a shared sense of frustrated male pride. Industrial workers were encouraged to see themselves and their unions as tough and manly, and to back up this image with aggressive tactics such as mass picketing, sympathy strikes, blockades, and sit-down strikes (Faue 1993). Everyman's claim to a wage sufficient to support an at-home wife and children in comfort became the hallmark of industrial unionism: organized labour's assertion of the working man's right to a full share of the postwar abundance (Christie 2000, 249-309).

At the bargaining table, CCL unions vigorously pursued their equality agenda. The immediate goal was union recognition and a substantial increase in wages, much needed by the thousands of families who could not afford the most basic requirements of adequate food, housing, and health care despite wartime price controls (Ursel 1992, 213). To this end, CCL unions insisted on significant, uniform cents-per-hour add-ons to the base wage (popularly known as across-the-board increases). Employers dismissed both demands. In this they were backed by the federal government whose central wartime labour relations policy was wage controls. It temporized on the issue of bargaining rights and held fast to its policy of permitting wage increases only when wages were low by community standards (MacDowell 1987). These issues were eventually resolved on the back of the 1943 and 1945-46 strike waves that secured both union recognition and the basis on which collective bargaining would proceed. A breadwinner wage for unskilled industrial workers was central to this postwar compromise; it was a non-negotiable demand. Absent this critical government-employer concession, there would have been no chance of industrial peace (Forrest 1997).

The bottom-up bargaining strategy of the 1930s, 1940s, and 1950s was egalitarian because it significantly and disproportionately raised wages for the lowest paid. Industrial unionists were not opposed to higher wages for workers with apprenticeship-based (male) skills but demanded that they reflect the relative value of the work performed, not skill privilege. Popular slogans such as "Pay the job, not the worker" and "Equal pay for equal work" (neither fully applied to women, as I explain below) required employers to pay every man the same wage for a given job and regularize pay differentials above the minimum, on the one hand, and revalue upward physically difficult (hot and dirty) unskilled jobs, on the other. Some unions – the United Steelworkers of America and the International Woodworkers of America are examples – negotiated job evaluation schemes that arranged jobs into a formal pay hierarchy based on the relative skill, effort, responsibility, and working conditions of jobs in relationship to each other; other unions – the United Automobile, Aerospace and Agricultural Implement Workers of America (UAW) is an example – rejected job evaluation and preferred to negotiate directly over perceived anomalies (Slichter, Healy, and Livernash 1960, 559-64). In most workplaces, access to higher paying jobs was regulated by seniority systems that required employers to promote from within. Typically, this hard-won cap on managerial discretion gave preference to longer service workers in cases of promotion, layoff, and recall when other factors such as ability and physical fitness were relatively equal.

Equality for industrial unions meant equal pay for equal work between, as well as within, establishments of the same employer and industry. Solidarity and fairness required workers who performed the same jobs to be paid the same wage no matter where they worked. Negotiators sought to take wages out of competition by creating company-wide or industry-wide bargaining structures. This was another non-negotiable element of the postwar compromise that directly challenged the federal government's vision of Canada as a federation of distinct local economies. Again, organized labour prevailed. Industry-wide agreements were negotiated by the International Woodworkers of America and the British Columbia logging and paper industry (Lembcke 1980), and by the United Packinghouse Workers of American and the national meatpacking firms; company-wide agreements were negotiated by the UAW and each of the major automobile firms. In all, two-thirds of organized workers were covered by multi-establishment collective agreements in the 1950s and 1960s (Craig and Waisglass 1968), despite legislation favouring decentralized wage bargaining (Woods and Ostry 1962, 270), and the wages of many others were determined by key settlements or pattern bargaining that effectively took wages out of competition.

In these ways, industrial unions were true to their vision of equality. Commitment to the breadwinner wage and the bottom-up bargaining strategy used to achieve it paid off. Every study of the impact of unions on men's wages reports a sizable wage premium for unionization, with the largest premium paid to unskilled, blue-collar workers (Benjamin, Gunderson, and Riddell 1998, 553-62). Unskilled blue-collar men benefited the most, particularly those employed in capital-intensive resource, transportation, utilities, and manufacturing industries, where industry- or company-wide bargaining added to the size of the union/non-union wage differential (ibid., 556). Without doubt, unionization offered these workers the prototypical, much coveted "good job" characteristic of the primary labour market. By the mid-1950s, union membership was a ticket to a middle-class lifestyle with house, car, and consumer durables, augmented by an impressive array of fringe benefits. The decade saw the adoption of employer-paid sick pay; life, medical, and hospital insurance; and retirement pensions (Taylor and Dow 1988, 38), which magnified the wage differential between union and non-union workers (Benjamin, Gunderson, and Riddell 1998, 566-69).

The 1930s, 1940s, and 1950s bargaining agenda increased wages and reduced wage inequality among men (but not women) both within and between establishments of the same industry. This was the main finding of Freeman and Medoff's innovative study (1984) of the impact of collective bargaining on the distribution of wages in the United States, and others have found the same for Canada. In general, skill premiums are smaller and wages less influenced by personal characteristics in the union sector. In two-thirds of the industries studied by Meng (1990), wages were more equitably distributed in the union sector, even though union workers displayed a wider range of wage-related characteristics, such as education and experience, than their non-union counterparts. This flattening of the wage distribution is a common outcome of collective bargaining, according to Benjamin, Gunderson, and Riddell (1998, 563-64).

For immigrants, black, Chinese, and Aboriginal workers who suffered severe labour market discrimination, union representation marked a notable improvement.[1] Black men interviewed by Sugiman (2001) reported that life in the auto plants in Windsor, Ontario, was comparatively free of racial discrimination: they earned the same wages as whites and had the same access to better paying jobs. This was not always the case, however, as many unions failed to enact their own policies and so did not contest their employers' discriminatory hiring practices. In other circumstances, unions negotiated seniority systems that confined racialized workers to the hottest and dirtiest departments, for example, steelmaking and coke ovens in the steel industry and foundries in the auto industry. This form of job segregation by race and ethnicity limited both promotional and bumping opportunities of racialized workers to other jobs in the same seniority district or department. Although never investigated in Canada, this practice was found to be a violation of equal opportunity legislation in the United States (Fehn 1993; Kelley 1982).

The egalitarian edge of the CCL vision dulled over the 1950s as more and more energy was directed toward protecting the breadwinner wages of the already organized. Money matters dominated at the bargaining table: cost-of-living allowances, productivity increases, medical and dental insurance, and retirement pensions all widened the wage differential between union and non-union workers. The breadwinner wage was no longer everyman's rightful share of a growing economy. Organized labour was prepared to defend their unskilled members' particularly high earnings as a legitimate return to their hard work, high productivity, and militancy. This shift toward unionism as vested interest began to worry CCL insiders, who decried the rise of what the CCL's Research Department called the "slot machine" mentality among new recruits (Finkel 1995, 59). They feared the vision of equality for all was being transformed into a conservative system of economic privilege for a "sheltered proletariat" (ibid.). Union commitment to improving the living conditions of the poor became token as more and more union members joined the ranks of the middle-income (ibid., 70).

This subversion of the equality agenda was antithetical to union growth and union renewal. I offer two examples. First, union preoccupation with material gains for its relatively small core of members thwarted efforts to expand that core. Union density in the private sector peaked in the mid-1950s, as did union density among men; yet, most unions cooperated with technological change, speed-up, and corporate restructuring, even when the result was cutbacks or layoffs. A middle-class lifestyle for the few rather than jobs for the many was a trade-off unions were prepared to make, so long as employers were prepared to share some of the gains in the form of higher wages – for example, in the form of an annual productivity increase such as that negotiated by the UAW with the major auto companies – and so long as the remaining jobs and wage gains were distributed according to the negotiated seniority rules. Sugiman's account (1994) of restructuring in the auto industry following the Auto Pact is a case in point. General Motors in Oshawa, Ontario, hived off the less profitable, labour-intensive parts jobs into a new division where the workers (in this case, women) were paid less, ostensibly on the grounds that they were less productive than those still employed in the oligopolized, capital-intensive assembly division. This dynamic of winners and losers was repeated again and again: a select group of workers secured a higher and higher standard of living while their co-workers

– men as well as women – lost their jobs or were reassigned to lower paying ones. Alternative solutions such as opposing technological change or sharing the work and the wealth more broadly were interpreted as an attack on unionism or dismissed as "sharing the poverty."

Commitment to the breadwinner ideal has limited union growth in other ways as well. By the mid-1950s, efforts to organize outside the unionized core had clearly failed. These efforts included campaigns to organize medium-sized manufacturing firms, the chartered banks, and Eaton's department store. Many commentators have connected these failures to shortcomings in labour legislation, which put many obstacles in the way of organizing drives, and excluded public sector workers altogether until the mid-1960s. Legal definitions of appropriate bargaining units, the built-in preference for decentralized bargaining, and the many, many opportunities afforded employers who wished to delay the certification process combined to make it very difficult to win certification in small and medium-size manufacturing firms and the service industries (Forrest 2005 summarizes this research).

What is less discussed in the literature is union complacency in the face of these losses. There was no collective response akin to the 1943 and 1945-46 strike waves. It's difficult to believe that organized labour would have accepted failure at Inco, GM, or Goodyear without ongoing protest. On the contrary: post-Second World War labour relations law and policy favoured workers in the industrial core. Had the outcome been different, had the law obstructed organizing in these industries, I believe unions would have responded with industrial unrest until the government produced a labour relations policy that made unionization of this sector possible. Yet, these same unions were not willing to press for the changes to labour relations law and policies required to extend meaningful collective bargaining in the rest of the economy, even within their own jurisdictions. Instead, there emerged a discourse that characterized women, racialized men, and young workers – that is, the workers who predominate in small establishments, in white-collar and service occupations, and in part-time and casual jobs (see Wall, this volume) – as hard to organize, anti-union by nature, and afraid of strikes.

Bargaining for Gender Equality during the 1970s and 1980s

Equality for women was every bit as radical a demand as equality for industrial workers had been, with an equivalent potential for union growth and renewal. Activist women, armed with the sensibilities and alliances of second-wave feminism, challenged organized labour's outdated but deeply embedded male-centredness. Union response was uneven – some unions were quick to act, others followed only when required by changes in legislation – and, uniformly, less than thorough. Whereas unionism reinvented itself in the 1930s, 1940s, and 1950s to put the needs of male blue-collar workers at its centre, this was not true for women. Bargaining for gender equality provoked changes in structure and practice that improved women's earnings but stopped short of putting women and "women's issues" at the centre of the union project. Efforts to apply feminist principles, such as the Service, Office, and Retail Workers of Canada's campaign to organize bank workers, were viewed with suspicion and sidelined by mainstream labour (Bank Book Collective 1979).

The 1970s and 1980s vision of gender equality championed by the women's movement was grounded in the belief that women had a right to work for pay outside the home in "good jobs" in the primary labour market. This root assumption reflected the impact of second-wave feminism, which focused on paid work as an important route to women's equality and independence. The Royal Commission on the Status of Women in Canada put these ideas into broad circulation as it travelled across the country in the late 1960s. The connection between paid work and equality, and the role unions could and should play in making that connection, became the subject of public debate as woman after woman recounted her workplace experiences. These witnesses demanded an end to unfair gender-based wage and fringe benefit differentials, discriminatory policies that required women (but not men) to resign upon marriage or pregnancy, and restrictions that limited their ambitions to undervalued "women's work." The more radical among them called for the adoption of policies to advance women's interests as women, such as fully paid maternity leave, government-funded child care, and pay equity/equal pay for work of equal value.

Union women pursued both approaches. Initially, most took the formal equality route. Men were the benchmark of success, that is to say, women would be equal when they were entitled to what men had. In unionized workplaces, this meant removing discriminatory barriers so that women could perform the same jobs as men when they had the same skills and the same seniority, and earn the same rates of pay as men when they performed the same or similar jobs in the same bargaining units. This was the demand of the UAW women at GM, whose story is told by Sugiman (1994). They marked their success by "the wall's comin' down" between men's work and women's work so that women could take whatever jobs they had the qualifications and seniority to perform. For them, success was access to men's jobs at breadwinner wages.

Other women benefited less from this strategy. By corollary, the formal equality standard legitimated lower pay for women who were not the same or similar to men, for example, women whose seniority was interrupted by child-bearing or whose jobs required a different complement of so-called women's skills and abilities. By the formal equality model of equality, these union women were not entitled to breadwinner jobs or breadwinner wages. The realization that gender equality on this basis marked women's gender "difference" as negative shifted union women's thinking toward substantive equality. In alliance with feminists in the community, and using the Charter of Rights and Freedoms as their backdrop, they began to argue for structure and practice that valued women as women and "women's work" (precision, clerical, cleaning, and caring jobs) for its particular contributions to economic growth and social development. On the brilliant insight that men did not need to be like anyone else to have what they had, union women came to believe they should not need to be like men in order to have the same standard of living as men (MacKinnon 1990).

The claim for gender equality was articulated against a unionism that idealized full-time blue-collar breadwinner jobs and the family men who performed them. Public sector unionism had exposed the blue-collar/industrial bias built into the model inherited from the 1930s, 1940s, and 1950s, but it did nothing to dislodge the male breadwinner model worker. Blue- and white-collar unions were heavily invested in the gendered structure of the labour market. "Good jobs" were the legitimate property of men alone because men, by nature, were more productive workers and family breadwinners. Like other elements of the immediate postwar labour relations system – labour laws, employer policies, even public opinion (see Ursel 1992, 239-52) – unions of all types segregated and excluded women in the name of the working-class family. In the union worldview, women should be the complements, not the competitors of men. They were mothers first and foremost, and should work for pay only when they were single or married to men whose earnings were inadequate to support their families. In the workplace, women should be confined to lower skilled, lower paid "women's work." Both Tillotson (1991) and Sugiman (1994, 42-51) demonstrate that unions demanded equal pay for women only when women's lower wages threatened the job security of their male co-workers.

This understanding of women and the second-class treatment it legitimated were not ad hoc but woven into the structures and practices of Second World War-era unionism, even when women were represented by unions that prided themselves on their social justice principles. Although widely regarded as a highly democratic union, Sugiman (1994, 172) argues that the UAW held to a gendered vision of social justice during the 1940s, 1950s, and 1960s: leaders "adopted a narrow definition of unionism that advanced the general principles of democracy, equality, and worker unity, yet failed to question the blatant sex-based inequalities in employment." Similar dynamics were at work in the United Electrical Workers, according to Guard (1996), despite the union's left-wing politics and public commitment to eliminating discrimination against women. Women represented by the United Electrical Workers fared better than others employed in manufacturing – they kept their jobs after the war ended and earned more in relation to their male co-workers – yet continued to work at women-only jobs and receive lower, women-only wages until well into the 1970s. The union's "principled adherence to gender blindness was mediated by unchallenged assumptions that placed male breadwinners at the centre of union policies," Guard (1996, 167) concludes. ˙

Bargaining for women's economic equality required unions to remove the most egregious barriers to women's full participation. Collective agreements were rewritten in gender-neutral language and the special provisions that applied only to women were deleted. By the end of the 1970s, women remained on the job after marriage and during pregnancy and were on the cusp of winning fully paid maternity leave with seniority and protection from male harassment through union action (White 1993, 61-97). Job postings were no longer designated "male" or "female," and sex-specific, non-interchangeable seniority districts were eliminated, allowing women access to all jobs in the bargaining unit. Also gone were male and female wage scales and lower rates for women simply because they were women. Unions began to apply the pay-the-job, not-the-worker principle to women, with the result that those who worked alongside men started to earn a wage formerly paid only to men. Women also benefited from union application of the equal-pay-for-equal-work standard on their behalf. This modest effort to bridge the gender gap in pay created by job segregation by gender produced pay increases for those employed in jobs that required substantially the same skill, effort, responsibility, and working conditions as jobs traditionally performed by men in the same bargaining unit, for example, female nursing aides whose jobs were deemed similar to those of male orderlies.

In theory, these reforms converted a discriminatory workplace into a gender-neutral one: union women were given equal access to union men's work at union men's wages. But the reality was not so straightforward. The sword of justice face of the gender equality agenda improved women's earnings but did not dislodge the male breadwinner's pride of place. What Guard (1996, 176) says about the United Electrical Workers – "the men saw overt discrimination rather than institutional power as the problem" – applied generally. The most obvious forms of gender discrimination were eliminated but in a way that left men's preferred access to "good jobs" intact. Notwithstanding the reforms, union-influenced pay practices, seniority systems, and bargaining structures continued to entrench male privilege and the gender gap in earnings because they segregated women and women's work from men and men's work. The result was two systems of value: (1) a higher one for "workers" that benchmarked breadwinner wages against men's skills and abilities, men's life cycles, and men's breadwinner responsibilities, and (2) a lower one for women whose generally different skills and abilities, life cycles, and family responsibilities were regarded as workplace liabilities, not assets.

Yet, the positive value attached to masculinity was invisible because the structure and practice introduced by unions to defend un/semi-skilled industrial workers had come to define "good unionism." For many, industrial union-style pay practices, seniority systems, and bargaining structures constituted unionism's expected form, the institutional expression of what unions did and ought to do. Any questioning of these practices was suspect and likely to be dismissed as anti-union. Outspoken and persistent critics risked their union careers (see Clarke Walker, this volume).

Pay practices, past and present, are a case in point. Without exception, the benchmarks of value in the union sector have been those associated with blue-collar production jobs, traditionally performed by men. In workplaces of all sorts – public and private, white collar and blue collar, with and without job evaluation schemes – this male bias is revealed by the higher pay associated with full-time over part-time jobs; formal qualifications and job-specific training over general education; physical effort and strength over dexterity, caring, and endurance; responsibility for capital equipment and product over the demands of working with vulnerable populations; and the dirt and grease of factories, mines, and construction sites over the tears, urine, and feces common in women's work. These norms have protected men, particularly unskilled men, at the expense of women. That this was their purpose is made clear by Creese (1999, 56-133). She describes in great detail the contortions of logic and distortions of process adopted by the union at BC Hydro to ensure that low-skilled men in jobs traditionally performed by men earned more than better skilled women in the office. Other examples abound; for instance, where I worked in 1980, just-hired male parking lot attendants earned as much as mid-career clerical workers (women) responsible for a major data management system.

The lived reality of this unfairness pushed women to demand pay equity. In theory, pay equity/equal pay for work of equal value has the potential to close the gender gap in wages because it requires workers employed in female-dominated jobs to be paid the same wage as workers in male-dominated jobs of equivalent skill, effort, responsibility, and working conditions in the same workplace, whether or not the jobs are the same or similar to each other. Full application of this principle means developing a new gender-inclusive job evaluation scheme appropriate for the workplace as a whole, and applying it across the gender divide. In practice, however, pay equity has modified but not displaced the male bias in pay systems. Its acceptance by unions has been limited: as a rule, pay equity is integrated into pay bargaining only where and to the extent that legislation requires. Voluntary adoption is rare and subject to union politics driven by the male breadwinner norm. Hunt and Haiven (2006) describe a successful application of pay equity in a Saskatchewan school board that was resisted by male caretakers who simply would not accept the finding that their jobs were less skilled than those of teacher assistants and secretaries. The men could not overturn the reformed wage structure but they did win Canadian Union of Public Employees support for creating a separate male-dominated local union. This story of intense male resistance helps explain Baker and Fortin's finding (2004, 587) that non-compliance with Ontario's pay equity legislation, which was widespread, was more acute in unionized workplaces.

Another dimension of the hidden male bias in union structure and practice is seniority systems, which continued to give men preferential access to better paying, more secure jobs even after the elimination of sex-specific seniority districts. Although fair on its face – seniority links workplace benefits such as pensions, vacation, promotion, and job security to length of service – in most workplaces these systems perpetuate gender inequality because unions have been slow to challenge employers who hire only men into jobs traditionally performed by men. In mines, auto factories, steel mills, universities, and municipalities, women were all but excluded from "good jobs" until the late 1970s and early 1980s, and once hired found themselves especially vulnerable to restructuring because of their low seniority.

A similar dynamic continues to match men with men's work and women with women's work in gender-mixed workplaces, with the result that job segregation by gender is as widespread in the union as in the non-union sector (Currie and Chaykowski 1995).[2] Typically, the gender division of labour that results from discriminatory hiring practices is frozen in place by promotion, layoff, and recall rights delimited by departmental seniority districts. Workers who wish to move from lower paying, women-dominated departments or seniority districts to better paying, male-dominated ones are commonly required to take the lowest seniority job (e.g., the lowest paying, least secure job) in the new district. The complications are even more profound for workers seeking to move from one bargaining unit to another – for example, from a part-time to a full-time unit in the same union – in the same workplace. In these situations, the seniority of full-time workers is usually worth more than that of part-time workers who are blocked from all but entry-level positions in the full-time unit, regardless of their seniority and qualifications.

Economic inequality in the union sector is also produced and reproduced by gender-segregated bargaining structures. These originate from the confluence of union jurisdictional claims and labour relations policies that, together, institutionalize job segregation by gender. On the one hand, unions have tended to organize jobs traditionally performed by women into different unions or different locals and bargaining units of the same union; on the other hand, labour relations boards certify unions according to outdated and sexist ideas about workers' "community of interest" that divides workers along gender lines. Depending on the jurisdiction, one or all of blue-collar/manual, office/clerical, professional, sales, security, part-time, casual, contractually limited, self-employed, and home workers are routinely separated from each other. The overall effect of these overlapping and varying practices is a highly decentralized, gender-segregated bargaining structure that almost ensures lower pay for women and women's work (Forrest 2005).[3] Gender-inclusive broader-based bargaining – for example, company- or industry-wide bargaining that links the pay scale for jobs traditionally performed by women with the pay scale for jobs traditionally performed by men – can narrow the gender gap in wages (Kidd and Shannon 1996). However, cross-gender bargaining structures are rare in Canada (outside of government employment), both because of the long-standing public policy preference for decentralized bargaining and because of union preference for broader-based bargaining structures that link like with like, that is, men's work with men's work and women's with women's (Forrest 2007).

This complex of reformed and unreformed structure and practice reveals both the sword of justice and the vested-interest aspects of union engagement with gender equality. The changes introduced during the 1970s and 1980s improved women's earnings and likely narrowed the gender gap in wages in the union sector.[4] Organized women of all sorts earn significantly more than their non-union counterparts (Card, Lemieux, and Riddell 2003), and this advantage was larger post-reform than earlier (Shamsuddin 1996), but unevenly distributed.[5] The main beneficiaries were the women most "like men," that is, those employed in traditional men's work, and the women whose "different" jobs were most obviously comparable to men's, that is, those with post-secondary education.

Women who work primarily with other women in traditional women's work have not fared as well, nor have racialized women. This conclusion is supported by Elvira and Saporta's analysis (2001) of the gender gap in wages in American manufacturing industries from 1975 to 1985. In all but one industry, union women earned a wage premium; however, only those employed in male-dominated industries (e.g., paint and varnishes and non-ferrous foundries) or gender-balanced industries (e.g., wool and cotton fibre textiles) narrowed the gender gap in wages. By contrast, union women employed in men's and boys' shirts manufacturing experienced a larger gender gap; that is to say, union women in the women-dominated industry earned more than their non-union counterparts in the same industry but less in relation to union men than did non-union women in relation to non-union men in that industry.

My claim is also supported by the finding that the union pay advantage is as large or larger for women with post-secondary education than for other women. Because the reverse is true for men – skilled union men benefit less than the unskilled – unions have likely narrowed the gender gap in wages between highly skilled or educated women and men in the union sector. But this success has come at the price of increasing wage inequality among women (Card, Lemieux, and Riddell 2003). Union women who are employed in less-skilled women's work in female-dominated workplaces earn more than their non-union counterparts; yet many are worse off, both in relation to highly skilled union women and in relation to equivalently qualified union men, than women in the non-union sector. And this relatively disadvantaged position is compounded when the women are racialized. A recent study by Reitz and Verma (2004) discovered that racialized women (both immigrant and Canadian-born) earn no union premium at all because they are more likely to be employed in less-skilled jobs, notwithstanding their generally high educational qualification. Also startling is the finding that these outcomes hold despite pay equity. Baker and Fortin (2004) could detect no general increase in women's wages (with the exception of non-union clerical workers employed in women-dominate job classifications) and no across-the-board narrowing of the gender gap in pay from Ontario's province-wide pay equity exercise.

These findings illustrate the continued centrality of the breadwinner ideal in the union sector and its power to constrain progress toward gender equality and union renewal, even in the context of pay equity. Without question, the elimination of overtly discriminatory structure and practice has been positive for women. However, these reforms did not go far enough. They left intact the many mechanisms that ensured pride of place for the male breadwinner, now applied to the advantage of his female – disproportionately white – look-alikes. It is women who work alongside men or women whose jobs require post-secondary education who have benefited most from union representation because it is they who best fit the parameters set by the industrial union model. Other women have benefited less or not at all because organized labour has adopted few women-friendly changes in structure and practice – changes that would have decentred men and men's work.

Calling this success would be perverse. Union defence of the male breadwinner has cut short the growth and change that could have resulted from an unreserved commitment to gender equality. I offer two examples. In my view, it is the vested interest of the male breadwinner that drives the retrogressive union policy toward part-time (and other forms of so-called non-standard) work and workers. Part-time workers do benefit from union representation – organized part-timers earn more than their unorganized counterparts (Jackson and Schellenberg 1999) – however, their interests are subordinate to those of full-time workers. These attitudes are changing – some unions have come to see part-time work as integral to the new economy or as a legitimate "women's issue" – but the discourse of difference remains predominant: part-time is less than "real" work and part-time workers are less than "real" workers. One result is that organized part-timers do not get "real" union protection. Commonly, unions do not fully apply basic union principles such as pay the job, not the worker; equal pay for equal work; or seniority on their behalf.

Consequently, the norm for part-time workers is inferior terms and conditions of employment in relation to their full-time counterparts in the same establishment. Part-time workers have less job security, lower wages for performing the same jobs, fewer fringe benefits, and less access to better paying jobs than their full-time co-workers. Indeed, part-time work is considered so different that not even pay equity has bridged the divide, as Kainer (2002) discovered from her analysis of pay equity bargaining in the Ontario retail food industry. Because union leaders consistently acted in the interests of a small number of full-time workers, mostly men, they failed to apply Ontario's pay equity legislation on behalf of the majority, who were part-time and mostly women. This attitude is counterproductive in an economy in which part-time work is more and more the entry point to the labour market, or the way to balance paid work and family responsibilities or education for women, youth, and racialized men. It also stands in the way of union growth and union renewal. The model of difference and inferiority makes it is all too easy to explain lower rates of pay and lower rates of unionization on part-timers' supposed lack of job commitment, low skill, newness to Canada, anti-union bias, or other blame-the-victim arguments, rather than on union structure and practice that institutionalize their disadvantaged place.

My second example is organized labour's response to pay equity. In the case of Ontario, where pay equity legislation covering both the public and private sectors was introduced in 1986, union protection of male privilege undercut the potential benefits to women and, perversely, legitimated higher pay for traditional men's work. Baker and Fortin (2004) discovered that many unions failed to hold their employers accountable to the law, while others attempted to keep the process at arm's length. Overall, pay equity was added onto rather than fully integrated into union structure and practice. I draw this conclusion from union commitment to the two tables model (Canada 2004), in which regular (read "real") pay bargaining was followed by the pay equity exercise, on the one hand, and union preference for negotiating pay equity bargaining unit by bargaining unit, on the other (Baker and Fortin 2004, 858). Together, these defences of existing structure and practice eviscerated much of the good that could have come from the introduction of gender inclusive job evaluation schemes. The two tables model allowed unions to ignore the extent to which pay bargaining as usual – for example, pay differentials linked to seniority or bargaining power – contributed to the gender gap in wages that pay equity was needed to correct. Union insistence that pay equity bargaining adhere to the existing pattern of union representation had a similar effect. Given the fragmentation of union representation and widespread job segregation by gender in the union sector, the decision to implement pay equity on a bargaining unit by bargaining unit basis left the highly decentralized system of wage determination in place. This disadvantaged women more than men because it limited the range of male-dominated job classifications available to workers in female-dominated jobs for wage comparison (McDermott 1991). No surprise, then, that Ontario's pay equity exercise had no perceptible impact on the gender gap in wages, although it may have exacerbated wage disparities among women in the union sector. Having survived the process, the pre-existing wage hierarchy that favoured men's work over women's now has the pay equity stamp of approval. If so, this is another subversion of the gender equality agenda on behalf of the male breadwinner, and one of the reasons why the Pay Equity Task Force (Canada 2004, 469) concluded that collective bargaining on its own could not produce wage equality for women.

Conclusion

Commitment to social equality, both for and within the working class, is an organizing and bargaining agenda that has generated union growth and union renewal in Canada. Organized labour repositioned itself at the leading edge of the social justice movement in the 1930s, 1940s, and 1950s and again in the 1970s and 1980s because it pursued an equality agenda on behalf of un/semi-skilled industrial workers and women workers whose fairness claims were widely acknowledged in society at large. But equality has not been the sole union purpose. Protecting and advancing the interests of the already organized – a purpose that, at times, has exacerbated inequality among workers – has also defined union structure and practice. Both faces of unionism – the sword of justice and the vested interest – are evident in the cases discussed here. The former brought new groups, energy, ideas, and leadership to the movement at points in time when it was in danger of losing its broad social purpose; the latter focus has generally had the opposite effect. Bargaining on behalf of the male breadwinner has preserved hard-won gains for a relatively small number of workers but choked off membership growth and organizational change in the process.

Today, an equality agenda would mean directing union energy and resources to organizing the largely non-union workers employed in service sector and part-time and other "non-standard" jobs. These workers are at the centre of economic and employment growth; yet, they are commonly underpaid, have minimal job or income security, and have little control over their working hours or conditions. They are also disproportionately women, racialized, and young.

There is nothing new in this proposal. Union insiders (see Clarke Walker; Edelson; Wall; this volume) and academic commentators alike believe the future of unionism lies with these groups; indeed, many argue that the necessary shift in focus is well underway. Examples of union efforts to engage these under-organized groups are the centre of Kumar and Schenk (2006) and other collections on the theme of union growth and renewal. Yates (2003) argues that unions in Canada both understand the need for and are well positioned to do this work. In her view, serious engagement with the growth and renewal project has pushed unions to adapt to changing economic conditions and workforce demographics. As well, she holds that the industrial union model is "proving resilient due to the relative success of industrial union structures and practices in defending and representing workers in the previously unorganized private sector" (ibid., 229).

The analysis offered in this chapter leads me to a different conclusion. In my view, industrial unionism is more resilient than adaptive and as much an obstacle to union growth and renewal as a means to those ends. The needs of the unorganized – that is, of women, youth, racialized men, service sector and part-time and other "non-standard" workers – are in tension with the established industrial union model. To serve these groups well would require unions to modify or abandon long-standing structures and practices that for many members define the meaning and purpose of unionism. Significantly, these changes would decentre the blue-collar, industrial, male breadwinner who many believe is unionism's core member.

Industrial unionism was a powerful force for equality in the mid-twentieth century. It broke open a small, self-privileging union movement, raised the standard of living for all working-class families, and reinvigorated working-class political demands for justice and equality. Yet, within this progressive, inclusive vision there was a particular commitment to the male breadwinner that limited the ability of unions to adapt and fully embrace women, white-collar, and service workers. Consequently, the modifications of structure and practice demanded by women workers in the 1970s and 1980s failed to displace the breadwinner ethos. Accordingly, the women who benefited most from this period of reform were those most "like" breadwinner men.

Union focus on the breadwinner is out of step with an economy that produces few breadwinner jobs, and with the modern family that relies on two earners by choice as well as necessity. Industrial unionism in its present form cannot meet the needs of the unorganized whose labour power and jobs are systematically undervalued by both employer and union measures of worth. Organized into existing union structures and represented by existing union practices, service sector and part-time and other so-called non-standard workers find themselves positioned as "naturally" low-wage workers by virtue of their labour-intensive jobs or other-than-full-time status, despite their often high level of education, skill, and effort. As such, they are often seen as threats rather than allies by unions, whose vision of work and worker is informed by the breadwinner ideal.

A labour movement that stubbornly adheres to what is, that is reluctant to fight for structure and practice that would advance the interests of the unorganized, turns its vested-interest face to the public. The re-emergence of its sword of justice face would require unions to purposefully put equality for the under-organized at the centre of the renewal project. This would be a bold assertion by organized labour: that unions belong at the centre of the social justice movement because they are prepared to take the difficult decisions and actions needed to embrace women, youth, and racialized men as the equals of unionism's core membership. What this reorganization and reorientation would look like cannot be prescribed; it must emerge in the process of struggle.

Notes

1 In some cases, labour market discrimination was compounded by union discrimination. See Mathieu (2001) for an analysis of the discrimination faced by sleeping car porters. See also Clarke Walker (this volume).
2 Using collective agreement data from Ontario for the years 1980-90, Currie and Chaykowski (1995) estimated that almost two-thirds of women workers would have to change jobs in order to eliminate gender segregation. This is higher than the Duncan indexes estimated for the economy as a whole (Fortin and Huberman 2002, S23).
3 Examining collective agreements covering more than two hundred workers in Ontario, Currie and Chaykowski (1995) found that average wages were highest in male-dominated bargaining units and lowest in female-dominated units in both the public and private sectors.
4 This is implied by the fact that the union wage advantage for women is larger than for men on average. Remarkably, I could find no study that analyzes the impact of collective bargaining on the size or composition of the gender gap in pay for the economy as a whole in Canada or elsewhere.
5 Card, Lemieux, and Riddell (2003) report a falling off of the size of the union wage premium for women post-1985.

References

Baker, M., and N. Fortin. 2004. Comparable worth in a decentralized labour market: The case of Ontario. *Canadian Journal of Economics* 37, 4: 850-78.
Bank Book Collective. 1979. *An Account to Settle: The Story of the United Bank Workers (SORWUC)*. Vancouver: Press Gang.
Benjamin, D., M. Gunderson, and W.C. Riddell. 1998. *Labour Market Economics: Theory, Evidence, and Policy in Canada*, 4th ed. Toronto: McGraw-Hill Ryerson.
Canada. 2004. *Pay Equity: A New Approach*. Ottawa: Pay Equity Task Force.
Card, D., T. Lemieux, and W.C. Riddell. 2003. Unionization and wage inequality: A comparative study of the U.S., the U.K., and Canada. NBER Working Paper Series 9473, National Bureau of Economic Research, Cambridge, MA.
Christie, N. 2000. *Engendering the State: Family, Work, and Welfare in Canada*. Toronto: University of Toronto Press.
Cobble, D. 1994. Making postindustrial unionism possible. In *Restoring the Promise of American Labor Law*, ed. S. Friedman, R.W. Hurd, R.A. Oswald, and R.L. Seeber, 285-302. Ithaca, NY: ILR Press.
Craig, A., and H.J. Waisglass. 1968. Collective bargaining perspectives. *Relations industrielles/ Industrial Relations* 23, 4: 570-89.
Crawley, R. 1997. What kind of unionism? Struggles among Sydney steel workers in the SWOC years, 1936-1942. *Labour/Le Travail* 39 (Spring): 99-123.
Creese, G. 1999. *Contracting Masculinity: Gender, Class, and Race in a White-Collar Union, 1944-1994*. Don Mills, ON: Oxford University Press.
Currie, J., and R. Chaykowski. 1995. Male jobs, female jobs, and gender gaps in benefits coverage in Canada. In *Research in Labour Economics*, ed. S.W. Polachek, 171-210. Greenwich, CT: JAI Press.
Elvira, M., and I. Saporta. 2001. How does collective bargaining affect the gender pay gap? *Work and Occupations* 28, 4: 469-90.
Faue, E. 1993. Gender and the reconstruction of labour history: An introduction. *Labor History* 34, 2: 169-77.

Fehn, B. 1993. "Chickens come home to roost": Industrial reorganization, seniority, and gender conflict in the United Packinghouse Workers of America, 1956-1966. *Labor History* 34, 2/3: 324-41.

Finkel, A. 1995. Trade unions and the welfare state in Canada, 1945-90. In *Labour gains, labour pains: 50 years of PC 1003*, ed. C. Gonick, P. Phillips, and J. Vorst, 59-77. Winnipeg and Halifax: Fernwood.

Flanders, A. 1970. *Management and Unions: The Theory and Reform of Industrial Relations.* London: Faber and Faber.

Forrest, A. 1997. Securing the male breadwinner: A feminist interpretation of P.C. 1003. *Relations industrielles/Industrial Relations* 52, 1: 91-113.

–. 2005. Hidden in the past: How labour relations law and policy perpetuate women's inequality. In *Canadian Woman Studies: A Reader,* 2nd ed., ed. A. Medovaski and B. Cranney, 287-96. Toronto: INANNA Publications and Education.

–. 2007. Bargaining against the past: Fair pay, union practice, and the gender gap in pay. In *Equity, Diversity, and Canadian Labour,* ed. G. Hunt and D. Rayside, 49-74. Toronto: University of Toronto Press.

Fortin, N., and M. Huberman. 2002. Occupational gender segregation and women's wages in Canada: An historical perspective. *Canadian Public Policy* 28 (Supplement): S11-39.

Freeman, R., and J. Medoff. 1984. *What Do Unions Do?* New York: Basic Books.

Glickman, L. 1997. *A Living Wage: American Workers and the Making of Consumer Society.* Ithaca, NY, and London: Cornell University Press.

Guard, J. 1996. Fair play of fair pay? Gender relations, class consciousness, and union solidarity in the Canadian UE. *Labour/Le Travail* 37 (Spring): 149-77.

Hunt, G., and J. Haiven. 2006. Building democracy of women and sexual minorities: Union embrace of diversity. *Relations industrielles/Industrial Relations* 61, 4: 666-83.

Hyman, R. 2002. The future of unions. *Just Labour* 1: 7-15.

Jackson, A., and G. Schellenberg. 1999. Unions, collective bargaining, and labour market outcomes for Canadian working women: Past gains and future challenges. Research Paper No. 11, Canadian Labour Congress.

Kainer, J. 2002. *Cashing in on Pay Equity? Supermarket Restructuring and Gender Equality.* Toronto: Sumach Press.

–. 2006. *Gendering union renewal: Women's contributions to labour movement revitalization.* Gender and Work Database, Union Module. http://www.genderwork.ca.

Kelley, M. 1982. Discrimination in seniority systems: A case study. *Industrial and Labor Relations Review* 36, 1: 40-55.

Kidd, M., and M. Shannon. 1996. The gender wage gap: A comparison of Australia and Canada. *Industrial and Labor Relations Review* 49: 729-46.

Kumar, P., and C. Schenk. 2006. Union renewal and organizational change: A review of the literature. In *Paths to Union Renewal: Canadian Experiences,* ed. P. Kumar and C. Schenk, 29-60. Peterborough, ON: Broadview Press.

Lembcke, J. 1980. The International Woodworkers of America in British Columbia, 1942-1951. *Labour/Le Travail* 6 (Autumn): 113-48.

MacDowell, L. 1987. The formation of the Canadian industrial relations system. *Labour/Le Travail* 31: 75-96.

MacKinnon, C. 1990. Breaking new ground. *Leaf Lines* 3, 2.

Mathieu, S. 2001. North of the colour line: Sleeping car porters and the battle against Jim Crow on Canadian rails, 1880-1920. *Labour/Le Travail* 47: 9-41.

McDermott, P. 1991. Pay equity challenge to collective bargaining in Ontario. In *Just Wages: A Feminist Assessment of Pay Equity,* ed. J. Fudge and P. McDermott, 122-37. Toronto: University of Toronto Press.

Meng, R. 1990. Union effects on wage dispersion in Canadian industry. *Economics Letters* 32: 399-403.

Pentland, H. 1979. The Canadian industrial relations system: Some formative factors. *Labour/Le Travail* 4: 9-23.

Reitz, J., and A. Verma. 2004. Immigration, race, and labor: Unionization and wages in the Canadian labor market. *Industrial Relations* 43, 4: 835-54.

Sangster, J. 1978. The 1907 Bell Telephone strike: Organizing women workers. *Labour/Le Travail* 3: 109-30.

Shamsuddin, A. 1996. The effect of unionization on the gender earnings gap in Canada: 1971-1981. *Applied Economics* 28: 1405-13.

Slichter, S.H., J.J. Healy, and E.R. Livernash. 1960. *The Impact of Collective Bargaining on Management*. Washington, DC: Brookings Institute.

Sugiman, P. 1994. *Labour's Dilemma: The Gender Politics of Auto Workers in Canada, 1937-1979*. Toronto: University of Toronto Press.

–. 2001. Privilege and oppression: The configuration of race, gender, and class in southern Ontario auto plants, 1939 to 1949. *Labour/Le Travail* 47: 83-113.

Taylor, D., and B. Dow. 1988. *The Rise of Industrial Unionism in Canada: A History of the CIO*. Kingston, ON: Industrial Relations Centre, Queen's University.

Tillotson, S. 1991. Human rights law as prism: Women's organizations, union, and Ontario's Female Employees Fair Remuneration Act, 1951. *Canadian Historical Review* 72, 4: 532-57.

Ursel, J. 1992. *Private Lives, Public Policy: 100 Years of State Intervention in the Family*. Toronto: Women's Press.

White, J. 1993. *Sisters and Solidarity: Women and Unions in Canada*. Toronto: Thompson Educational.

Woods H.D., and S. Ostry. 1962. *Labour Policy and Labour Economics in Canada*. Toronto: Macmillan.

Yates, C. 2003. The revival of industrial unions in Canada: The extension and adaptation of industrial union practices to the new economy. In *Trade Unions in Renewal: A Comparative Study*, ed. P. Fairbrother and C. Yates, 221-43. London and New York: Continuum.

7
Developing a Conceptual Model of Equity Progress in Unions
Janice Foley

The changing nature of the membership demographics within unions (see Wall, this volume), along with declining union density and myriad other challenges, have made it mandatory for unions to change their traditional ways of doing things. In particular, because the proportion of female and minority group members within unions has grown considerably since the 1970s, equitable membership representation has become an issue of significant concern. The objective of this chapter is to develop a general conceptual model of how to advance equity within unions. As mentioned in the Introduction, the conception of equity utilized here derives from the insight provided by the Abella Commission Report (1984, 3) that "Sometimes equality means treating people the same, despite their differences, and sometimes it means treating them as equals by accommodating their differences." As Briskin (2006a, 13) puts it, "Equity refers ... to what is fair under the circumstances."

Equitable representation of an increasingly diverse union membership has been a matter of some general concern in Canadian unions since the early 1970s, although the original focus was on the female membership as a result of the 1970 Royal Commission on the Status of Women. That report found that significant male-female gaps existed in terms of wages and labour market opportunities. Occupational segregation was the norm at that time, with most women performing low-paid, administrative roles in the workplace. No legislation yet existed that protected women and minority groups from discrimination and harassment in the workplace. Within unions, despite that women had been entering the labour force and joining unions in increasing numbers since the early 1960s, few women held leadership positions, few staff representatives were female, and women's voices were significantly under-represented in all areas of union decision making, including bargaining committees. Union policies and structures to facilitate female participation in unions were rare. For instance, union meetings were often held in the evenings, which made female members' attendance difficult, and lack of child care prevented many women from taking part in educational events.

Not surprisingly, the Royal Commission findings resulted in some agitation among female union activists, who started exerting pressure on union executives to establish women's committees. Their mandates were to (1) improve female representation on union executives and in other leadership positions, (2) develop collective bargaining clauses that would advance the interests of women, (3) make the wording in union constitutions more inclusive, and (4) ensure that constitutions afforded female members protection against harassment and discrimination on the part of their union "brothers." Over time, concerns over the status of women in Canada gave way to more general concerns about achieving those same goals for all non-traditional group members. The need to modify union cultures to accomplish that objective became more apparent. The union equity project also took on international overtones, with union and other social movement activists forming alliances around the world to promote social justice for all.

Looking back thirty years, it is evident that some (perhaps even "dramatic") (Briskin 2007, 244) progress has been made in Canadian unions. The innovative equity structures, including women's and equity committees, equity conferences, and designated seats now in place in most unions, have been noted by many, along with improvements in contract clauses, inclusive language in union constitutions, and the like. However, it is still the case that women and minority group members are under-represented in union leadership positions, not only in Canada but throughout the developed countries. Although this should not be the sole indicator of progress achieved (see Briskin 2006b), it does suggest that the changes to date have not been sufficient. As Rayside (2007, 208, 209) notes, despite Canadian unions having made as much or more progress than unions elsewhere, progress has been uneven and, at least in some cases, change has taken place only at the formal (e.g., policy) level. Much effort is still required to achieve the representational structures and the modified culture of fairness and inclusiveness believed inherent to union renewal because of its expected positive impact on member participation and mobilization (Colgan and Ledwith 2002).

An additional problem is that while much of the mainstream literature suggests that organizing is key to union renewal (Kumar and Schenk 2006), and even identifies the gender bias within unions as an obstacle to organizing (Yates 2006), it is not yet widely acknowledged that achieving equitable outcomes for the rising numbers of non-traditional members within unions is necessary or even desirable, especially now that it is becoming clearer that it may require giving equity group members preferential treatment. The nature of this problem is described well in Legault (this volume). As Wall and Clarke Walker (chapters, this volume) point out, much more needs to be done on the equity front.

To gain a better understanding of what continues to impede progress on equity in unions, two studies were undertaken, one in the early 1990s and another ten years later. Both studies involved interviews with feminists and female activists. They were members of women's and other equity committees, of bargaining committees and local and union executives, or union staff representatives supporting the efforts of these committees, actively participating in efforts to achieve equity within their unions. The equity they envisioned was for non-traditional members to have their interests taken seriously at the bargaining table, to be equitably represented in leadership and on decision-making bodies, and to have appropriate levels of influence in all decision-making forums. From these two studies, a conceptual model of how to advance equity was developed.

Study 1

The first and most extensive study focused on women's committees, and asked how and under what circumstances women's committees in unions were able to secure tangible gains for women, given a context in which they had traditionally been and continued to be at a power disadvantage relative to men (Foley 1995). Gains were defined as securing changes in contract clauses beneficial to women, changes in committee and union structures that would make future gains for women more likely, and increases in female representation on union governing bodies. The literature review revealed many variables of potential significance. The social movement literature in particular afforded useful insights, since the women's movement is a social movement, and provided at least some of the impetus behind the establishment of women's committees.

A social movement is generally defined as "a collectivity acting with some continuity to promote or resist a change in the society or group of which it is a part" (Turner and Killian 1972, 246). Women's committees and other equity committees housed within unions, which seek to promote the interests of women and equity groups in unions and in society as a whole, can be seen as intra-organizational social movement organizations seeking changes to the status quo. That places them in a power struggle with established authorities who are the existing power holders. The outcomes of such conflicts depend largely on how the authorities respond to the social movement, and how well supporters are mobilized (Gamson 1975, 1990; Piven and Cloward 1977; Tilly 1978). Authorities have the power to squash challenger groups and are most likely to do so where the goals of the challenger group and the authority are at odds, where the authority's political interests will not be advanced by forming alliances with the challengers, and where its legitimacy will not be adversely affected by acting against the group (Zald and Berger 1987).

The social movement literature identifies factors that must be present for mass mobilization in support of change to occur. Of utmost importance is the need for a group of individuals to recognize that they share salient characteristics, that their rights are being violated, that the "system" is to blame, and that through collective action they can do something about it (Ferree and Miller 1985; Klandermans 1992; McAdam 1988; Melucci 1995; Nepstad 1997). The small group setting within which this collective identity emerges, known as the micromobilization context, is seen as the actual staging ground for collective action (McAdam, McCarthy, and Zald 1988; Mueller 1992). Social movement leaders play a significant role in mobilization in that they frame the difficulties being experienced in such a way that the sense of injustice, as well as the efficacy of collective action, are reinforced. This is easier to do where the members are homogeneous, interact frequently, and have dense social networks. Once mobilization has been achieved, leaders again play a key role in choosing and communicating strategies and tactics that will maintain mobilization. However, even where the mobilization context is favourable, unless there is also a favourable political opportunity structure (McAdam, McCarthy, and Zald 1988), meaning that the group is able to gain a receptive hearing within the political structure, collective action will not materialize.

This literature, like the organizational, feminist, and industrial relations literatures that were also examined, emphasized the importance of leadership and committee actions, as well as committee characteristics such as homogeneity and the role of membership support, in determining the kinds of outcomes committees were able to achieve. Collectively, the literatures also indicated that formal and informal structures and processes might be significant.

Based on the literature review, a preliminary theoretical model was developed of variables potentially contributing to women's committee power, where power was defined as the ability (as perceived by the committee itself, the membership, and the leadership) to secure the gains it sought (see Figure 7.1). It was initially assumed that committee power was the determinant of outcomes. Internal variables such as union and committee structures, committee characteristics and activities, and support for the committee were identified as potentially significant factors affecting committee power. How these variables interacted with one another was unclear; hence, all relationships were depicted as reciprocal (note the double-headed arrows in Figure 7.1). The external environment was also identified in the literature as a potential influence on all the internal variables.

These variables were defined as follows. Union structures referred to formal structures and procedures regarding the operation of the union as set out in the union constitution, which could only be changed at constitutional conventions. In addition, regularized procedures and processes that were determined by the union leadership, such as practices in the areas of decision

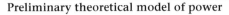

Figure 7.1

Preliminary theoretical model of power

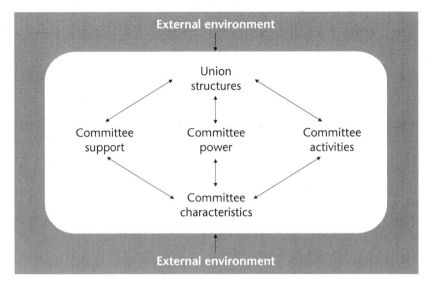

making, resource allocation, and communication, were considered to be union structures.

Committee structures included formal mandates, rules regarding the makeup of the committee, the size of the committee, and the autonomy of the committee. Committee characteristics referred to such things as the calibre of the leadership, its political skill, group cohesiveness, and commitment to change. Committee activities referred to strategies and tactics employed, the kinds of programs the committee sponsored, and so on, as it pursued its mandate. Committee support included both leadership and membership support. Important aspects of the external environment included the economic, legal, and social environment within which the union and the committee operated.

This preliminary theoretical model guided data collection. The methodology involved comparative case studies of two Canadian public sector unions that had both established women's committees in the mid-1970s. Members of one of the unions were organized by occupation, so separate components existed for health care workers, administrative clerks, highway workers, and the like. Data collection began in 1992 and consisted of a review of documents that covered the entire twenty-year history of the two committees to date, followed by intensive semi-structured interviews with thirty-three female activists. The documents reviewed included all minutes from women's committee and executive committee meetings, union constitutions, and convention resolutions and reports prepared by either group.

The documentary analysis generated understanding and quantification of the variables in the theoretical model, a twenty-year history of how membership and union leadership size and composition changed, the numbers and types of resolutions proposed by the women's committees, and a chronology of significant events arising internally and externally that affected the union and the committee over the period. The interviews clarified how women involved in the search for equity found their path either eased or made more difficult, explained issues raised by the documentary analysis, and described, in great depth, what the women's committees had been able to achieve over their twenty-year histories, and why.

Study 1 Findings

Two very different pictures emerged of how these committees operated over time. Both were set up as advisory committees to the union executive and as such had no policy-making authority, yet they both managed to make significant progress on behalf of the female memberships of their unions. One committee started with a very activist, feminist agenda, with the active support of the union leadership and good levels of membership support. It had access to abundant resources that enabled it to set up and maintain communications with a provincial network of committee supporters.

This committee achieved a great deal on behalf of women initially, but as levels of support for the committee eroded over time, so did the resources allocated to its operation. According to informants, the loss of support was due to what were seen by some of the leadership and membership as inappropriate goals being pursued, such as the decriminalization of abortion, and overly aggressive tactics employed by the committee. Eventually, the union leadership introduced a resolution at the 1988 convention that proposed to reduce funding for the women's committee. It passed by a narrow margin, despite the efforts of the feminist lobby that by then constituted the committee's main support base. The committee languished for the next decade and in 1998 was replaced by a social justice committee.

The other committee, right from the start, was less inspired by feminist thinking and more committed to working through existing union structures to achieve its goals. This union was quite concerned that giving women special consideration within the union would lead to conflict, threatening union solidarity; hence, committee resources and activities were restricted. Only when the committee realized after a decade had passed that little progress had materialized for the female membership did it decide to change its strategy. It struck up an alliance with the largest, female-dominated component of the union, which enabled it to get the message across to the

Figure 7.2

Revised power model

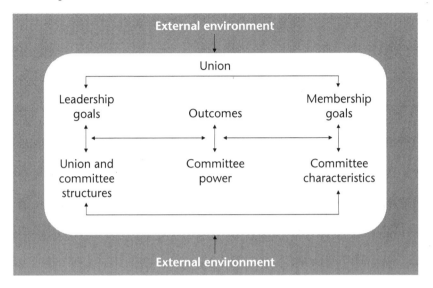

membership that women were not being fairly treated within the union. This partnership was so effective that the union leadership was forced to support efforts advanced to secure major structural reforms. Two of the major successes achieved included the addition of two vice-presidential positions to the union governing body that were reserved for women, and ensuring that the largest, female-dominated components had additional representation on the union executive. After securing these major gains, the alliance lapsed and the committee reverted to once again attending to largely routine matters. Unlike the other committee, however, it still exists.

The data analysis revealed that it had been inappropriate to attribute to committee power all gains achieved on behalf of women. For instance, in the first case, the union leadership's decision to place more women on bargaining committees affected the types of collective bargaining clauses negotiated. Similarly, in the second case, a decision made by the union leadership to hire more female staff representatives directly affected the amount of female representation within the union. Controlling committee funding affected what initiatives the committee could pursue, and restricting committee funding limited the number of times a committee could meet, and therefore how effective it could be. As a result, the preliminary theoretical model was modified (see Figure 7.2).

Modifications to the Preliminary Theoretical Model

In the revised power model, the variable "outcomes," which had not been part of the preliminary model because committee power had been hypothesized to account for them, was added. The new model showed that outcomes and power were related but separate, so that either or both could be affected by the other variables in the model. Modifications were also made to some of the other variables in the preliminary model. For instance, "committee activities" was collapsed into "committee characteristics." Also, "committee support" was replaced with "leadership goals" and "membership goals" because it became apparent that support for the committee depended upon the degree to which it pursued goals aligned with those of either the leadership or the membership.

Goals, in turn, were important because they affected the actions of the leadership and the membership in relation to the committee. Leadership goals were particularly relevant because they determined leadership actions, could affect membership goals and actions, factored into what union and committee structures existed, and affected the characteristics and actions of the women's committees. These goals were somewhat dictated by the membership and could be positively or negatively influenced by the women's committee.

The other variables in the preliminary model remained unchanged. The "structures" variable in the revised model was clarified as referring to union and committee structures, which were found to be significant. How much power the women's committees had was affected by structures that dictated their budgets, their links with the leadership and the membership, and thus the degree to which the committee could influence or align with leadership and membership goals. The external environment was found to have a potential impact on outcomes achieved, by affecting the other variables in the model. For instance, in the first case, the bargaining unit was redefined when the provincial government granted full bargaining rights in 1988, with the result that a substantial number of high-dues-paying members were lost. The loss in revenues resulted in cuts in all advisory committee budgets, including that of the women's committee.

Summary of Major Factors Influencing Outcomes

Overall, analysis suggested that the major factors affecting committee power and outcomes for women were (1) union leadership behaviours in the face of threats to its own or the union's interests; (2) the degree of alignment of committee and membership goals or, less optimally, of committee and leadership goals; (3) union and committee structures, particularly where the membership was not mobilized to change them; and (4) the committee's own character, for example, its activity levels and the tactics it employed, for instance, in choosing to be proactive or submissive to leadership direction as it pursued its mandate.

Insights from the Social Movement Literature

The social movement literature proved to be very helpful in understanding the dynamics affecting how these committees operated, and how, why, and when they were able to make progress toward fulfilling their mandates. It was evident that sometimes progress came less easily, depending on how clear the committees were about what they wanted and how much influence they had with their respective union executives, which bespoke more or less favourable micromobilization contexts and political opportunity structures over time. Power struggles between the committees and the union leadership were also more or less apparent over the twenty-year period of study. The following examples illustrate how these social movement concepts applied.

In the first case, both the micromobilization context and the political opportunity structure were initially highly favourable, allowing the women's committee to make great progress. However, as the union membership and leadership grew somewhat concerned about the ability of the committee and its network of supporters to get resolutions passed that were perceived as rather too progressive, constraints were imposed on the committee by the union executive. This included a reduction in the resources that allowed the committee to maintain its network and hold six meetings per year. The leadership's unwillingness to listen to the committee's protests at that point, and its determination to control the committee's actions for the remaining years of its existence, underlined a change for the worse in the political opportunity structure. The erosion of the network and the reduction in committee meetings to three per year also negatively impacted the micromobilization context. Ultimately, the committee was unable to achieve its goals, and the lack of success disheartened committee members, further impoverishing the micromobilization context. For further examples, see Foley (2003).

In the second case, neither the political opportunity structure nor the micromobilization context were particularly favourable until after the committee had operated for a decade without achieving much success. And neither the constraining structures imposed by the union executive to prevent this committee from posing a threat to union solidarity nor the committee's willingness to operate within the boundaries established for it were conducive to committee effectiveness. Since its funding allowed it to meet only three times per year and the committee itself had more than twenty members, it was never able to develop a collective identity, articulate what it was trying to do, or get organized to achieve its goals. Once it formed an alliance with the largest component in the union, representing thirteen thousand mostly female members, the situation quickly changed for the better. The leaders of the component, who strongly believed that their members were underpaid and undervalued, were able to successfully convey this message to their component's members, and to other female-dominated components within the union. This created an environment within which a collective understanding of female members' underprivileged status and the necessity of correcting it could emerge within the union, along with a strategy to do so.

As this large group of members became mobilized to seek change, the union leadership could no longer ignore it, which improved the political opportunity structure, setting the stage for the gains the alliance was eventually able to achieve. The failure to maintain the alliance negatively impacted both the political opportunity structure and the micromobilization context that subsequently faced the committee, which reduced the probability of future collective action to achieve further gains. Foley (2000) describes this in further detail.

Study 2

One decade later, a second study was undertaken to gain additional insights into what might contribute to or detract from equity advancement within unions, only this time all non-traditional union members, rather than just women, were of interest. Participants for this study were solicited from a group of female union activists in attendance at a spring 2004 educational event sponsored by a provincial labour federation. Interviews were conducted with thirteen of the twenty-one women who volunteered. They were chosen based on their extensive experience with equity initiatives within their unions. All of them had been equity advocates for five to twenty years and active participants in their unions for up to thirty years. The unions represented were the Public Service Alliance of Canada, the Canadian Union of Public Employees, the Service Employees International Union, the Canadian Office and Professional Employees Union, the Saskatchewan Union of Nurses, and an affiliate of the National Union of Provincial and General Employees.

The interview protocol asked the participants what kinds of equity initiatives existed within their unions, what degree of equity for women and other non-traditional members had been achieved to date, how satisfied they were with the progress made, how they explained any progress or lack of progress achieved, and what would have to change, if anything, in order to achieve greater success. The interviews, which lasted from sixty to ninety minutes, were tape-recorded and transcribed. The transcripts were then examined to identify emergent themes and patterns in the data.

Study 2 Findings

Basically, two types of comments were made: those relating to degree of progress achieved and those explaining why progress had or had not materialized. Findings are briefly reviewed here, but further details can be found in Foley (2006).

Progress Reported

The major successes reported related to the equity structures now in place in most unions that made them more welcoming for equity group members. These included equity committees, designated seats on union executives, training seats reserved for equity group members, and equity group conferences. In addition, inclusive language and prohibitions against harassment and discrimination had been written into union constitutions and collective agreements. Expressing lack of support for equity initiatives in public union forums was unacceptable (except see Wall, this volume). Equity members were somewhat represented within the leadership structure, and in some unions equity considerations affected decisions made about committee membership, training eligibility, convention attendance, and the like. Informants believed that the membership was more aware of the issues facing equity group members and less fearful of equity initiatives.

All agreed that equal outcomes for women and minority group members had yet to be achieved, although some portions of the membership believed that the opposite was the case. For example, some members believed that women and other equity group members had no reason to keep agitating for further improvements because equity had been achieved. Informants felt that equity concerns continued to get short shrift at the bargaining table, and that there was continued resistance to electing women and minority group members into leadership positions. They did note, however, that these problems were less pronounced in some unions than in others.

Rationale Provided for Lack of Progress

In general, respondents felt that equity was still not being taken as seriously as it should be within their unions and identified both internal and external factors accounting for that. One of the external factors identified was a perceived backlash against feminists within society as a whole, accompanied by a desire to reverse some of the gains achieved. One interviewee pointed out, for example, that abortion was once again on the table, and queried, "That's a fight we fought in the '70s – why is it back?" She complained that whatever gains were made in one period seemed to erode in later periods, resulting in little net advance.

In regard to internal union factors, four general categories of explanatory factors were identified: (1) shortcomings of equity and other union structures,

(2) resource issues, (3) training issues, and (4) communication issues. Each is discussed below.

Shortcomings of Equity and Other Union Structures
First, it was noted that despite the progress made in terms of equity structures, not all unions had introduced them, and some had done so only quite recently. Where they existed, there were numerous problems with them that limited their utility for advancing equity. For example, the lack of qualifications or commitment to equity advancement of the people occupying equity seats was a matter of some concern. Electoral deficiencies at conventions were held responsible for this in that union constitutions dictated that only those equity activists who were present at constitutional conventions were eligible to run for equity seats. There were no guarantees that the best equity candidates would be in attendance because of the structures dictating who was eligible to attend conventions.

A further issue was that being elected into one equity position could carry obligations to sit on several additional committees. The enormous time pressures this created could make good candidates reluctant to hold these positions or divert them from actually working on initiatives to advance equity. The time commitment required to carry out the duties attached to leadership positions was the most frequently mentioned problem in regard to union structures.

Another problem identified was that the committees' actions in many ways were circumscribed by their advisory status. The executive often appointed some if not all of the committee members, who were therefore not necessarily highly committed activists. Furthermore, in most unions the local executives had to approve resolutions going to convention. The interviewees reported that not all resolutions proposed by equity committees were forwarded, which meant that a non-progressive local leadership or membership could stonewall efforts to advance equity. Some suggested that designating equity positions and establishing equity committees was a highly effective way to marginalize equity issues and equity activists.

Resource Issues
Inadequate funding that constrained how frequently committees could meet and what events they could sponsor, and competition between the various equity and women's groups for funding, were seen as problematic. The resource constraints that limited direct communications to the membership were seen to contribute to membership apathy about unions in general, and about equity.

Training Issues
One special case of resource inadequacy was the lack of resources allocated

to membership equity training. According to these activists, little training on equity was being done, and opportunities to access training were not evenly distributed across the membership. It seemed to many of them that "the same damn bunch," mostly male, went to all the educational events, conferences, and conventions. This was seen as problematic because attending training sessions and going to union events such as conventions were essential means of motivating members' continued involvement in their unions, of securing mentors or sponsors, and of learning about union politics. All of these outcomes were prerequisites to making successful leadership bids. Equity group members who aspired to leadership but could not get into training courses or attend conventions were at a significant disadvantage.

There was some overlap between this category and the one about structural problems because structures were held somewhat responsible for the inequitable access to training and mentoring. The prerequisite for getting to educational events was to attend union meetings, which could be difficult for women because of family responsibilities or even work schedules. One of the interviewees reported that although she had been a union steward for years, her shift schedule precluded her attendance at union meetings. For that reason alone she had been told that she "shouldn't be privy to going to this conference or that convention."

It was generally true that unless members attended meetings they were unlikely to get opportunities to go to conventions or conferences. But even if opportunities existed, issues of timing, location, and daycare remained. Getting to educational events was also difficult because training seats were generally filled on a first-come, first-served basis, and those who were well connected often filled the seats before others even became aware that training was being offered. Little effort was made to ensure that equity candidates received preference in terms of training opportunities. In addition, no formalized procedures existed to identify and groom promising equity group members for leadership positions.

Communication Issues
Another concern was that union stewards and executives did not necessarily convey all information about upcoming equity events and initiatives to the membership, either because they did not keep on top of information circulars or chose not to let their members know about them. In that way, local executives who did not fully support equity advances could ensure that the membership did not support equity events either, whatever the members' personal views might have been. Two other communication issues identified were that equity representatives had an incentive to water down their messages in order to escape potential negative sanctioning by members or leaders for pursuing "special interests" too energetically, and that equity representatives were sometimes not good spokespersons, which detracted from the

importance of the message they were trying to convey. One opinion expressed was, "They're shrill and they're goofy and they're combative ... the second somebody says something they take instant offence ... I think, be quiet because you're making us all look like fools."

A Model of Equity Progress

Based on these interviewees' comments, a model of the route to equity progress was devised (see Figure 7.3). Seemingly, the path begins with members getting involved in their unions by attending local meetings. This increases their knowledge and interest in union affairs, creating chances to secure additional training opportunities, gain a mentor, and perhaps acquire a position on the local executive or a delegate spot at convention. Attending conventions is a significant learning event, particularly where new delegates are matched up with experienced delegates who can show them how things work. Attending conventions provides entrée to committees beyond the local level and additional opportunities to learn and to gain influential patrons, and may lead to a successful leadership bid, resulting in a seat on the union executive. That is where decisions are made about the degree of priority the union will give to equity issues, who will be appointed to bargaining and equity committees, what structures will govern equity and other committees and how well they will be resourced, and what resources will be allocated to training and membership communications, perhaps to pique membership interest in union priorities such as equity. The model proposes that modifying structures and resource allocations, as well as training, communication, and decision-making processes, will encourage progress on equity, which will in turn increase the participation of equity group members in union activities.

Figure 7.3

Factors affecting progress on equity

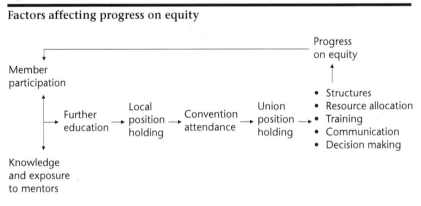

Discussion of Studies 1 and 2

To recap, the first study indicated that leader behaviours along with goal alignment, union and committee structures, and the characteristics of the committee itself affected union women's committee power and outcomes. In the second study, much of the responsibility for lack of progress on equity was attributed to factors directly controlled by the formal union leadership or to decisions made at constitutional conventions where, as a result of delegate selection procedures, delegates were most frequently formal union leaders and rarely women and equity group members.

Many of the obstacles to equity identified in both studies arose from the inability or unwillingness of all members to attend local meetings and other union-sponsored events. Although the timing and venues of local meetings, the lack of child care at union events, and women's primary responsibilities for home and family contributed to this problem, in addition there was a lack of active encouragement of equity group member participation. This may have created an impression that such participation was not really welcome, and resulted in non-attendance at local meetings and union-sponsored events. As mentioned, non-attendance created problems associated with lack of knowledge, lack of profile within the union, and lack of opportunities to find sponsors or to attend conventions, which narrowed the pool from within which equity seat holders could be elected and blocked entry to local leadership positions.

Attempts could have been made to address these problems of non-participation, yet not all unions did so. A possible explanation for this, supported by both of the studies presented and which might also explain why equity progress in unions remains so elusive, can be inferred from social movement theory. For the discussion that follows, some caveats are necessary: first, neither the leadership nor the membership within a given union can be considered a monolithic entity, and second, not all unions are the same. Thus, there may not be a typical reaction of union executives to challenges posed by women's committees and other equity committees. However, the conceptual model of challenger groups struggling with one another and with the authorities to gain permanent power positions is useful, as is the suggestion that unfavourable political opportunity structures or micromobilization contexts can impede collective action.

As with the first study, the obstacles identified by interviewees in the second study can be categorized into deficits in regard to either the micromobilization context or the political opportunity structure.

Problems with the micromobilization context – for example, the ability to instigate collective action by helping individuals develop a collective sense of grievance and a belief in the efficacy of collective action for addressing that grievance – stemmed from many factors. These included the individual equity committees' limited autonomy, for instance, with respect to the need to have the number and type of activities approved in order to have them funded; these committees' restricted ability to get their resolutions forwarded to convention; the failure of the various equity committees to come up with a clear, unified message regarding injustices that must be fixed and that could be conveyed convincingly to the membership; the lack of homogeneity within the individual equity committees because of appointment procedures that made it more difficult for them to generate a sense of collective identity; committee leaders or spokespersons who were not always effective at getting their messages out; and the limited equity training received by the union membership that made members unreceptive to the messages being conveyed and unwilling to give equity candidates preference during leadership races.

Problems with equity advocates' ability to gain a favourable hearing within the union executive committee, that is, with the political opportunity structure, included the deficiencies associated with electing equity seat holders at conventions from within the very small pool of candidates present; requiring them to hold several positions at once, which limited the time they could actually devote to equity activities; the inability of the various equity groups to work together to better influence the actions of the executive committee; less than full support for equity among executive committee members; and no active efforts made to groom or mentor equity candidates for leadership positions, thus limiting their representation on the executive and making them vulnerable and disinclined to push an equity agenda.

In addition, environmental factors present in the second study that had not yet crystallized when the earlier study was done, such as the backlash against feminism that was mentioned in Wall (this volume). The neo-liberal attack on unions that gained momentum in the decade between studies, which was not mentioned but remains relevant, also worsened the political opportunity structure. The backlash delegitimized demands for equity, while the neo-liberal attack focused union attention on survival rather than equity.

Returning to the issue of leadership, social movement theory indicates that how the authorities respond to challenger groups has a significant impact on outcomes. While none of the interviewees in the second study reported instances in which their union leaders had taken active steps to destroy them, the first case in the earlier study provided an example of such an occurrence. In general, the committees were established and funded, but obstacles to their effectiveness were not removed. One plausible explanation for this may be that during periods when the membership was not mobilized in support of equity progress – which, as these studies showed, was the case most of the time – leaders chose to pursue their own goals. It would appear that equity advancement was not among these goals, possibly because it was not seen as central to union survival, or to leaders' own ability to stay in power.

Conclusion

While the foregoing might appear to be a harsh assessment, especially since many union leaders do support equity and the conclusion reached is based on the comments of a relatively small group of activists, the seemingly intractable nature of the equity problem and the disproportionate amount of power that resides within the union leadership and a small cadre of members suggest that the answer to the problem may lie there. Although collective pressure from the membership can force leaders to act, any problems with the political opportunity structure or the micromobilization context can suppress collective action. The leadership is in the best position to ensure that these problems are resolved. It is hard to believe that leaders would not act to remove impediments to mobilization, or merely decree change, if they saw that achieving equitable outcomes for all their members would promote union survival.

To advance equity progress, it is necessary to ensure that the connection between equity and survival is understood. The conceptual model indicates that developing educational programs targeted at the union leadership as well as the membership to get that message across might be the place to start. No less important is convincing members and leaders alike, by similar means, that stonewalling equity group members' attempts to achieve more equitable outcomes for their group members will simply widen the rifts already developing within the membership, articulated by Edelson, Wall, and Clarke Walker (chapters, this volume), and between the membership and the leadership, articulated by Legault (this volume). The picture Legault draws of unions possibly losing their right to represent diverse membership groups if they refuse to accept that equal treatment does not always generate equitable outcomes constitutes a potent threat that will hopefully elicit new, more effective leadership action on equity.

The two studies summarized in this chapter show that one practical step the various equity committees can take to encourage mobilization, echoing Briskin's advice (this volume), is to start developing a joint message that conveys to the membership that *all* members deserve the same opportunity to participate in the union in whatever fashion they desire, that denying them these opportunities based on outmoded structures or exclusionary cultures is unfair, and that the very survival of the labour movement is imperilled unless the current inequities are eliminated. As one of the interviewees so eloquently put it, "In the end we are all individuals with dreams and hopes and desires and abilities ... it isn't up to anyone to say you can't do something because of whoever you are ... encouragement should be there if [becoming a union leader] is what you want to achieve."

References

Abella, R. 1984. *Report of the Commission on Equality in Employment.* Ottawa: Ministry of Supply and Services Canada.

Briskin, L. 2006a. Equity bargaining/bargaining equity. Working Paper Series 2006-01, Centre for Research on Work and Society, York University.

–. 2006b. *Union Leadership and Equity Representation.* Union module of the Gender and Work Database. http://www.genderwork.ca.

–. 2007. Afterword. In *Equity Diversity and Canadian Labour,* ed. G. Hunt and D. Rayside, 244-55. Toronto: University of Toronto Press.

Colgan, F., and S. Ledwith. 2002. *Gender, Diversity and Trade Unions: International Perspectives.* London: Routledge.

Ferree, M., and F. Miller. 1985. Mobilization and meaning: Toward an integration of social psychological and resource perspectives on social movements. *Sociological Inquiry* 55, 1: 38-61.

Foley, J.R. 1995. Redistributing union power to women: The experiences of two women's committees. PhD diss., University of British Columbia.

–. 2000. Developing an explanatory framework for the demise of a women's committee. *Economic and Industrial Democracy* 21, 4: 505-31.

–. 2003. Mobilisation and change in a trade union setting: The role of structures and activism. *Work, Employment and Society* 17, 2: 247-68.

–. 2006. Advancing equity in Canadian unions. In *Proceedings of the 34th Annual Conference of the Administrative Sciences Association of Canada,* ed. H. Kelley, 50-64. Banff, AB: Administrative Sciences Association of Canada.

Gamson, W. 1975. *The Strategy of Social Protest.* Homewood, IL: Dorsey.

–. 1990. *The Strategy of Social Protest,* 2nd ed. Belmont, CA: Wadsworth.

Klandermans, B. 1992. The social construction of protest and multiorganizational fields. In *Frontiers in Social Movement Theory,* ed. A. Morris and C. Mueller, 77-103. New Haven, CT: Yale University Press.

Kumar, P., and C. Schenk. 2006. Union renewal and organizational change. In *Paths to Union Renewal: Canadian Experiences,* ed. P. Kumar and C. Schenk, 29-60. Peterborough, ON: Broadview Press.

McAdam, D. 1988. Micromobilization contexts and recruitment to activism. *International Social Movement Research* 1: 125-54.

McAdam, D., J. McCarthy, and M. Zald. 1988. Social movements. In *Handbook of Sociology,* ed. N. Smelser, 695-737. Newbury Park, CA: Sage.

Melucci, A. 1995. The process of collective identity. In *Social Movements and Culture,* ed. H. Johnston and B. Klandermans, 41-63. Minneapolis: University of Minneapolis Press.

Mueller, C. 1992. Building social movement theory. In *Frontiers in Social Movement Theory,* ed. A. Morris and C. Mueller, 3-25. New Haven, CT: Yale University Press.

Piven, F., and R. Cloward. 1977. *Poor People's Movements: Why They Succeed and How They Fail.* New York: Pantheon Books.

Nepstad, S. 1997. The process of cognitive liberation: Cultural synapses, links, and frame contradictions in the US-Central America peace movement. *Sociological Inquiry* 67, 4: 470-87.

Rayside, D. 2007. Equity, diversity and Canadian labour: A comparative perspective. In *Equity Diversity and Canadian Labour,* ed. G. Hunt and D. Rayside, 208-43. Toronto: University of Toronto Press.

Tilly, C. 1978. *From Mobilization to Revolution.* Reading, MA: Addison-Wesley.

Turner, R., and J. Killian. 1972. *Collective Behavior,* 2nd ed. Englewood Cliffs, NJ: Prentice Hall.

Yates, C. 2006. Women are key to union renewal: Lessons from the Canadian labour movement. In *Paths to Union Renewal: Canadian Experiences,* ed. P. Kumar and C. Schenk, 103-12. Peterborough, ON: Broadview Press.

Zald, M., and M. Berger. 1987. Social movement in organizations: Coup d'etat, bureaucratic insurgency, and mass movements. In *Social Movements in an Organizational Society: Collected Essays,* ed. M. Zald and J. McCarthy, 185-222. New Brunswick, NJ: Transaction Books.

8

Cross-Constituency Organizing: A Vehicle for Union Renewal

Linda Briskin

To survive in the current economic and political context, unions have taken up the challenge of revitalization. Reinventing solidarity through coalition building across unions, with social movements, and across borders – often called social movement unionism – will be critical to successful resistance to corporatization, globalization, workplace restructuring, changing state forms, and the downloading of caring work to families. The union renewal literature emphasizes the importance of coalition building, which "is regarded as one of the most innovative strategies for union revitalization" (Kumar and Schenk 2006, 40).[1]

This chapter explores coalition building *inside* unions between and across equity-seeking groups, what I call "cross-constituency organizing." It considers organizational vehicles for building solidarities and advancing equity organizing inside Canadian unions that support, at one and the same time, union revitalization and the union equity project. In fact, it is my argument that union renewal and equity initiatives are inextricably entwined. The first section of this chapter offers a brief overview of constituency organizing and its contribution to Canadian unions; the second section introduces and discusses cross-constituency organizing and highlights the importance of intersectional practices; the third section describes and analyzes the cross-constituency organizing inside three unions – the Canadian Union of Postal Workers, the Canadian Union of Public Employees, and the British Columbia Teachers Federation – which involve respectively parallel, dual, and integrated structures.

Part One: Constituency Organizing

Over the past thirty years, constituency organizing, also called separate or self-organizing, has brought together members of equity-seeking groups – women, people of colour, Aboriginal peoples, people with disabilities, and lesbian, gay, bisexual, and transgendered peoples – to increase their skills, self-confidence, and political power. Equity-seeking groups have organized in response to male and white domination; patriarchal, racist, and homo-phobic cultures; and hierarchical and undemocratic organizational practices in unions. Such self-organizing, which has politicized equity-seeking groups and produced them as vocal constituencies, is expressed organizationally in both informal caucuses and formal committees (the latter sometimes man-dated by union constitutions), including human rights committees, rainbow committees, Aboriginal circles, women's committees and pink triangle com-mittees. After years of struggle, a growing acceptance of separate and self-organizing, at least in the public statements of unions, is evident (e.g., Hunt and Rayside 2007).

The success of self-organizing by equity-seeking groups has led to a grow-ing awareness in Canadian union discourse of issues of privilege. The last decade has witnessed a remarkable development of union policy on racism, homophobia, sexism, and, recently, ableism and transphobia (a parallel language to homophobia that refers to a fear of transsexuality, and dislike and hatred of transsexual or transgender people). Despite the fact that these policies are not necessarily fully operationalized in the daily life of unions, particularly at the local level, without a doubt the passing of each policy has involved widespread education and mobilization.

Counterintuitively, separate organizing has not led to the ghettoization or marginalization of equity concerns. Evidence suggests the opposite, that is, separate organizing has been a vehicle for mainstreaming equity concerns. For example, through separate organizing, women have promoted women's leadership, challenged traditional leaderships to be more accountable, en-couraged unions to be more democratic and participatory, and forced unions to take up women's concerns as union members and as workers, through policy initiatives and at the negotiating table (Briskin 1999a, 1999b, 2002, 2006a, 2006b). Indeed, as Cobble and Michal (2002, 234) note, "Women are at the forefront of economic change, and they are at the forefront of devising new forms of unionism that will appeal to a new generation of workers."

Union women's organizing has also been instrumental in transforming the Canadian union movement's relationship with other progressive move-ments, and initiating the trend toward social movement unionism that embraces a "wider definition of solidarity" (Murray 2005, 108).[2] Beginning in the 1970s, around issues such as pay equity, affirmative action, sexual harassment, violence against women, child care, and reproductive rights, union women have organized alliances and coalitions across unions and with social movements, contesting the isolationist tendencies within the union movement and legitimizing coalition building with groups outside the union movement. Constituency organizing, then, has offered a strategic bridge into marginalized communities.[3] In recent years, such Canadian coalitions have organized a Quebec women's march against poverty in 1995, and a national march For Bread and Roses, For Jobs and Justice in 1996. The

World March of Women 2000, which was endorsed by over two hundred countries and 2,200 organizations, was modelled on these events; its goals were to eliminate poverty and violence in women's lives (Briskin 2002).

Widespread constituency structures inside unions have provided the foundation for new forms of equity organizing inside unions that facilitate cooperation across various marginalized constituencies, what I call "cross-constituency organizing." The various separate committees and caucuses that have played a critical, if often unacknowledged, role in transforming Canadian unions over the last three decades (Kainer 2006 and this volume) are now beginning to invent new political and organizational ways to work collectively and collaboratively to advance the union equity project and revitalize unions.[4]

Shifting attention from constituency organizing to cross-constituency organizing is not meant to imply a linear or progressive move from the former to the latter; rather, cross-constituency initiatives extend, complexify, and deepen equity organizing and, in so doing, make constituency committees more effective. In unions that are inventing forms of cross-constituency organizing, constituency committees continue to activate specific equity-seeking groups, highlight their concerns, and guarantee that the most marginalized are heard. Such committees provide the basis on which cross-constituency organizing develops. The task, then, is to maintain the delicate balance between addressing the concerns of specific equity-seeking groups and working across these constituencies to develop an intersectional politic and a culture of alliances.

Part Two: Cross-Constituency Organizing

Experience in Canada has demonstrated that taking account of difference can build a stronger union movement. In fact, solidarity is increasingly understood to mean unity in diversity. The 1994 policy statement of the Canadian Labour Congress (CLC),[5] *Confronting the Mean Society,* recognizes that difference can be a source of strength: "Equality seeking groups have strengthened our movement, bringing new ideas and perspectives into the practice of unionism. The diversity that is now present in our unions has not divided the labour movement: on the contrary, it has energized us and brought many more committed people into our activist cadre" (CLC 1994, 4). Further, it is possible to be "unified without uniformity": "The CLC understands that sexism, racism, ableism, and heterosexism share common roots. We acknowledge that we can change attitudes and behaviour if we stand united; we know we will fail if we allow ourselves to be divided. We believe that we can be unified and that we can celebrate our diversity without divisiveness. We will strive to achieve a truly inclusive union movement that is representative of all its members" (ibid.). These statements highlight the link between equity organizing and union renewal; they recognize difference through proactive support for separate organizing and, at the same time, acknowledge the common roots of the equity project for all equity-seeking groups. In so doing, they provide support for cross-constituency organizing inside unions.

New strategies to work across equity-seeking groups in order to achieve a stronger union movement need to take account of the diverse and often marginalized voices of women, immigrants, the racialized, members of sexual minorities, people with disabilities, Aboriginal workers, and young workers. Success will also depend upon deepening understandings of inter-sectionality to appreciate the complexity of lived discrimination.[6] The language of intersectionality recognizes that "intersectional oppression arises out of the combination of various oppressions which, together, pro-duce something unique and distinct from any one form of discrimination standing alone" (Ontario Human Rights Commission 2001, 4). Without an intersectional framework, the differences among women based on race, class, or sexuality can be obscured; for example, sexual harassment experi-enced by women of colour often takes race-specific forms. Without an intersectional practice, women of colour might find themselves torn between participation in women's committees and participation in committees for workers of colour, and experience what Crenshaw (1991) calls "intersectional disempowerment." Beverley Johnson (in Edelson, this volume) comments on this issue: "The [union] leadership need to understand how oppressions are linked. From my perspective, there is still little understanding of the issue of intersectionality ... Where union structures allow for equity caucuses ... members are invariably forced to choose identities. [They] don't contem-plate the reality that members are packaged in diverse ways, and this inhibits their ability to participate in a manner that is respectful of the totality of their beings. An Aboriginal woman who is a lesbian or has a disability, for example, must make a choice about when and where she locates herself."

Cross-constituency work also requires a recognition of the multiple and overlapping realities of privilege and discrimination, so a white woman is both privileged on the basis of her race and oppressed on the basis of her gender. An intersectional practice emphasizes working with and across privileges, in particular accepting and engaging with white privilege. At the same time, those with white skin privilege can be equality allies since a belief in white supremacy is not a necessary outcome of colour privilege (Thompson 2001). The role of white allies is not to help victims but "to speak up against systems of oppression, and to challenge other whites to do the same ... creat-ing the possibility of working together as partners in the establishment of a more just society" (Tatum 1994, 474).

Finally, an intersectional practice can potentially mobilize the political promise of unity in diversity by addressing the interrelationship of equity issues, decreasing the potential polarization among various equity-seeking groups, and making visible the power structures that are at the heart of all forms of discrimination. Yet, simply calling for solidarity among equity-seeking groups will not address the complexities of identities or the realities of power differences and will be no more effective than the traditional exhortations for class solidarity that assumed a *generic* worker with a homogeneous and self-evident set of interests. Like that *mythical* worker, there is no generic equity-seeking worker.

Cross-constituency organizing inside unions is one way to develop institutional and political practices to address multiple and competing identities, and to build inclusive solidarity that takes account of difference, privilege, and power. In her study of the struggles of three clerical workers unions (at Harvard, Columbia, and Yale University), Kurtz (2002, xviii) concludes that "the unavoidable task, then, of each movement is to build internal coalitions" using "a multi-identity politics." The project of this chapter, then, is to deepen understanding of this unavoidable but potentially invigorating task.

This exploration of cross-constituency organizing inside unions offers a consideration of intersectionality in practice. Given the proliferation of constituency committees representing multiple equity-seeking groups, the need for coalition work between and across these groups, and the pragmatic issues of time and resources, how can unions best address the multiple, sometimes overlapping, and sometimes conflicting agendas of various equity-seeking groups? How can unions support the needs of particular equity-seeking groups and simultaneously promote a practice of equity across identities?

Drawing on case studies of three unions – the Canadian Union of Postal Workers (CUPW), the Canadian Union of Public Employees (CUPE), and the British Columbia Teachers' Federation (BCTF), this chapter documents and analyzes three models for cross-constituency work, what I call parallel, dual, and integrated structures. Each of these cases illustrates the complexity, urgency, and contextuality of developing intersectional equity organizing.

Part Three: Parallel, Dual, and Integrated Cross-Constituency Structures

Formalized cross-constituency organizing initiatives are relatively new in Canadian unions, emerging from a heightened awareness of diversity, shifts in union demographics, and the necessity to address the proliferation of equity structures and committees. Drawing on union documentation and interviews, the case studies of cross-constituency organizing in CUPW, CUPE, and BCTF highlight the degree to which structures organically evolve out of the complex political and strategic histories unique to each union. What is evident in all three cases is the ongoing revisioning of equity structures. Despite different trajectories, all three unions struggled over time to find appropriate organizational vehicles to facilitate their equity work. These equity structures have also faced a continuing struggle, especially evident in BCTF, to legitimize and relegitimize their work. Sometimes challenges are couched in the language of financial exigency and efficiency, and sometimes equity work is overtly attacked.

As intersectional theory might anticipate, this research also underscores the contextual nature of equity discourses, the changing profiles of what are deemed equity issues, and the shifting parameters of equity constituencies. For example, whether "youth" can usefully be understood as an equity-seeking group continues to be a matter of discussion. Currently in CUPE Ontario, young workers have asked to be and are represented on the Human Rights Committee, but this is not the case in the equity structure at the national level in CUPE.

Canadian Union of Postal Workers (CUPW)
A majority of the 54,000 members of the Canadian Union of Postal Workers work for Canada Post as rural and suburban mail carriers, letter carriers, mail service couriers, postal clerks, mail handlers, mail dispatchers, technicians, mechanics, electricians, and electronic technicians. CUPW also represents cleaners, couriers, drivers, vehicle mechanics, warehouse workers, mail house workers, emergency medical dispatchers, bicycle couriers, and other workers in more than fifteen private sector bargaining units.[7]

To win the right to set up a national women's committee in CUPW was a ten-year struggle that began in 1980 and culminated successfully in 1990 (White 1990). In 1996, a national human rights committee was established, after many years of informal caucuses at CUPW national conventions. The Human Rights Committee is now composed of four working groups: workers of colour; Aboriginal peoples; lesbians, gays, and transgendered people; and people with disabilities. The committee meets twice a year and spends the first day in a joint meeting and the second day in working groups. There is no working group representing women inside the Human Rights Committee, nor is there a formal representative from the National Women's Committee on that committee. Marion Pollack, a long-time CUPW activist who currently sits on both the Human Rights Committee and the Women's Committee comments: "The national women's committee came first, and as women, we weren't prepared to fold our concerns into another working committee. We felt that our concerns would be weakened and we felt that would be a move back, not a move forward."[8]

CUPW has two parallel structures: a women's committee and a human rights committee, and faces some difficulty finding ways for the committees to collaborate.[9] Reports from the Human Rights Committee and National Women's Committee conventions give almost no indication that any formal work across the two committees has taken place.[10] Pollack reports that in the Human Rights Committee there is little discussion on "the intersection of oppressions" and in the Women's Committee, "We do it but it's in a very *pro forma* way." However, she notes that sometimes individuals cross groups; for example, in the GBLT working group, "the appointed representative from my region is a brother who is deaf" and this crossover "has served to raise people's awareness."

Although intersectional analysis and practice is not highlighted in CUPW, the union has taken some innovative initiatives to ensure representation, although the process on the Human Rights Committee and the National Women's Committee differ. The 2005 CUPW constitution indicates that the Women's Committee "shall be composed of one woman from each region plus all women holding national and regional executive and union representatives positions. The regional representatives shall be elected at the National Convention by women delegates only, assembled in regional caucuses ... In the event that diversity is not achieved through the election process, the National Women's Committee shall select up to four women who are able and willing to represent targeted groups" (4.06).[11] The combination of election and appointment to the Women's Committee ensures both democracy and representation.

In contrast to constituency elections for the National Women's Committee, the four working groups of the national Human Rights Committee are constituted through an appointment procedure: "Each working group shall be comprised of one representative per region to be appointed by the National Executive Board in consultation with the respective National Director after having issued a call to express interest, plus all members holding national and regional executive or union representative positions who belong to one or more of the groups. In the event that transgender inclusion is not met, the National Executive Board shall select up to three transgender members who are able and willing to sit on the National Human Rights Committee" (4.07). The special attention paid to transgender representation underscores the shifting parameters of equity constituencies.

All CUPW members holding national and regional executive or union representative positions who are members of equity-seeking groups are added to the relevant committee, a mechanism that facilitates the bridging of equity work and other union business. However, Pollack points out that this mechanism can create an unevenness among the working groups of the Human Rights Committee, some of which may have three or four "automatic" members from regional executives who bring labour power and experience, and some of which have none, as was the case in 2006 with the Aboriginal and disability working groups. She notes that this disparity reflects the fact that Aboriginal workers and people with disabilities "are much more marginalized ... in the union and the post office and in society."

Canadian Union of Public Employees, Ontario Division (CUPE)
The Canadian Union of Public Employees was formed in 1963 by merging the National Union of Public Employees and the National Union of Public Service Employees. In 2006, CUPE was Canada's largest union, with almost 550,000 members, 60 percent of whom were women. CUPE represents workers in health care, education, municipalities, libraries, universities, social services, public utilities, transportation, emergency services, and airlines. CUPE is decentralized, so each province may operate with different structures. This discussion focuses on the Ontario Division of CUPE, which has a membership of 220,000.

For more than twenty years, CUPE Ontario has had a Women's Issues Committee that was adjoined to a regional women's committee and elected from the Women's Caucus at the convention, and a human rights committee elected from the floor of the convention. Fred Hahn, a long-time activist and currently Secretary Treasurer of CUPE Ontario – a full-time elected position – notes that "as equality seekers organized in various caucuses and made connections with one another, there were resolutions that created other equality-seeking committees," for example, the Pink Triangle Committee, the People with Disabilities Committee, and the Rainbow Committee.[12] And as the number of committees expanded, the demographic of the committees changed, creating a new layer of representational problems, as Hahn explains:

> The women's committee used to be very well mixed. Ten years ago, the women's committee was almost equally made up of women of colour and white women. Lesbians and women with disabilities openly identified in that way on the women's committee as well. But that changed. The women's committee became increasingly a white women's committee, the white, straight, able-bodied women's committee. And that has been identified by them as a problem. Women of colour coming to women's caucuses at conventions were saying, "You guys don't represent us any more, you're all white women." Women of colour feel strongly, at this moment, that the place for them to organize is around anti-racism.

On the one hand, then, the proliferation of equity-seeking committees led to greater representation and voice for marginalized unionists, while on the other hand, it made an intersectional political practice more difficult. Hahn reports that "[around 1998] we realized that the committees were siloed from one another and they were having a challenge coming up with some kind of integrated equality agenda. So in that year, we created a new Equality Steering Committee with one representative from each equality committee, to try and provide cohesion between the equality-seeking committees."

Coming out of a 2003 Task Review of CUPE structures, the Ontario Region disbanded the Equality Steering Committee and, in order to formalize mechanisms for equity-seeking groups to work together, reconfigured its Human Rights Committee as an umbrella committee with representatives from the Pink Triangle Committee, the Women's Committee, the People with Disabilities Committee, the Rainbow Committee, the Youth Committee, and the International Solidarity Committee.

Unlike CUPW's parallel committees, the dual CUPE structure of constituency committees coming together in an umbrella human rights committee may facilitate intersectional analysis and practice. Intersectionality is addressed through structure and representation: first, the Human Rights Committee brings together members of all equity-seeking groups; and second, inside the constituency committees, broad-based representation is also mandated; for example, the CUPE Ontario constitution specifies that "there shall be a Women's Committee elected at each Women's Conference in even numbered years. Five women shall be elected by the Women's Caucus. At least one of these women must be from the North. An additional member of the committee shall be elected by women from each of the following caucuses at the Conference: Aboriginal Workers, Workers with a Disability, Pink Triangle, Workers of Colour, Young Workers" (CUPE Ontario Constitution 2006, Article 8e).[13] This dual structure has the potential to prevent the marginalization of any particular equity-seeking group, highlight the common core to equity concerns, and help demonstrate that solidarity can be built on a foundation of diversity. Hahn notes the advantages and challenges of the new structure:

> The benefit is that people are forced to work together. People are not able to be so silent like they might be. But the challenge is, how do they work together? And how do they identify a joint goal together? I have to tell you, there are debates that happen in individual committees: "I don't know if this is such a good idea after all. It's really hard. How do we do this stuff together?" And we're a part of the society in which we live, we're soaking in it, right? So there is competition between those committees ... We're so used to being on the outside of stuff, and having to fight for attention and fight for resources that part of the big work is to be able to unlearn that culture with each other. People thought we'd all be holding hands and singing "Kumbaya" a lot! But the benefit of the structure is that it allows us to deal with inter-constituency conflicts as they come up – 'cause they will come up. They have to meet together so they can't just sit there and fester.

Although this discussion focuses on the Ontario region of CUPE, which has taken the most extensive initiatives, coalition work and intersectionality across and among equity-seeking groups is also on the national agenda of CUPE. The Report of the Equality Branch (the national CUPE office responsible for coordinating equity work) to the 2007 national CUPE convention (CUPE Equality Branch 2007, 1) notes: "The Equality Branch has adopted an intersectional feminist analysis as our framework and we have been working hard at understanding this analysis and trying to operationalize it. An intersectional feminist framework tries to understand how multiple forces work together and interact to reinforce conditions of inequality and social exclusion."

The report of the National Women's Committee to the 2007 national CUPE convention highlights a concern about "the lack of diversity" on the committee and calls for greater representational intersectionality "through the inclusion of Aboriginal, racialized, lesbian, bi-sexual, transgendered women, women with a disability and young women" (CUPE National Women's Committee 2007, 5). The 2007 report of the National Aboriginal Council notes that "some of the issues identified by the Council are similar to what all equality-seeking groups have been working on. It is crucial that all these groups continue to work together on such important issues" (CUPE National Aboriginal Council 2007, 5). The 2007 National Pink Triangle Committee report calls for a meeting with "the National Women's Committee to discuss ways to continue to press for the decriminalization of sex work and to promote unionization and healthy and safe work for sex workers" (CUPE National Pink Triangle Committee 2007, 6).

British Columbia Teachers' Federation (BCTF)

The British Columbia Teachers' Federation represents 41,000 public school teachers, almost 70 percent of whom are women. It was incorporated as a benevolent society in 1919 and achieved full collective bargaining rights in 1987. As a teachers' union, the BCTF approaches equity issues from two perspectives: first, it tries to encourage teachers, through professional development workshops and curriculum development, to take up social justice issues in the classroom. Second, although to a lesser extent, it takes up equity issues inside the union and in the community. This dual equity agenda is often in tension. BCTF also differs considerably from CUPE and CUPW, both of which focus more extensively on organizing equity-seeking constituencies inside their unions and supporting their efforts to seek social justice in the workplace and community.

In 1973, the BCTF had a high-profile Task Force on the Status of Women; in 1977, the task force became an activist Provincial Status of Women Committee (PSWC).[14] Coincident with celebrating the twenty-fifth anniversary of this committee in March 1998, a controversial resolution to amalgamate the Status of Women Committee into a larger Social Justice Advisory Committee (SJAC) passed by a tiny margin: 334 votes for and 322 votes against.

Those who argued against the motion feared that integration would "dilute and make invisible the voices of women" (*Kinesis* 1998, 8). The mandate of this new SJAC was to advise the executive on social justice issues. Patrick Clarke, who is responsible for coordinating BCTF social justice programs, indicated that members of the SJAC were "named to the committee by the executive. They apply to a posting, which is sent out to all members. And then selection is done trying to be mindful of gender, proportionate to the membership of the federation, geographic considerations, visible minorities, sexual minorities. We try to be as inclusive as we can."[15] However, there are no rules governing selection, the BCTF has never had constituency groups select their own representatives, and according to Clarke, the "appointment process has been a bit controversial."

The meaning of the social justice frame in the BCTF is an important backdrop to understanding the motivation for the shift from constituency committees to an integrated social justice committee, and what happened once the new SJAC was in place. Louise de Bruijne (1999, 94), an activist on the PSWC, argues: "The BCTF's use of the term 'social justice' tried to acknowledge social oppression and validate teachers' responsibility to act to change society. However, at the same time, the Federation's discourse and SJ committee representatives were hesitant at separating any one group's issues around the type of oppression it might experience." She concludes that "the Federation's concept of social justice and its issues ... led to a marked decrease in its naming separate social oppressions as part of the social issue discourse" (ibid., 93). Jane Turner, also a member of the BCTF PSWC from 1977 to 1981, and currently on staff at the BCTF and responsible for social justice work, suggests that "the social justice focus has been more comfortable for the BCTF. It's more comfortable to be the middle class trying to deal with larger social issues [like poverty] than to say there's racism in our midst."[16]

By 2004, it had become clear that the new SJAC was not effective. As Turner describes it:

> The six years of the social justice advisory committee without the action groups were basically six years of frustration and futility. These were great people who were really trying to do good jobs. But they only met three times a year, they saw their mandate as only to advise the executive not to do anything, because the executive told them that was their mandate and they believed them. They didn't come out of that kind of history of activism, of doing, of taking it on. There was very little of substance that came out of that committee.

The lack of success with the SJAC structure encouraged the BCTF to move back to constituency-type structures.[17] In response to a 2004 convention resolution, the BCTF set up four social justice action groups, each with a three-year mandate, to address the issues of homophobia and heterosexism, the status of women, poverty, and anti-racism. Each group was composed of four classroom teachers and an SJAC member. The goal of these groups was to provide information, lesson ideas, and professional support for classroom teachers. These groups reinserted constituency reference points into the social justice program, and on occasion they met together to help build what might be called an intersectional practice. However, according to Turner, they had only a tenuous relationship with the SJAC.

Following another review of its social justice structure, the 2007 BCTF convention passed motions to set up a new form of dual structure that will maintain constituency groups within an umbrella structure. The BCTF plans to establish a twenty-member Committee for Action on Social Justice that will comprise five action groups with four members each. Furthermore, the mandate of the Social Justice Program has shifted from solely advisory to both action-oriented and advisory.

The BCTF history underscores the difficulty of dealing with issues of equity-seeking groups solely through an integrated or generic equity formation, especially given the lack of clear mandates about who should sit on the SJAC, and the absence of constituency committees as a foundation for cross-constituency organizing. Over the decade in question, the BCTF moved increasingly toward intersectional practices.

Equity Organizing under Attack

Despite innovative moves toward new forms of intersectional practice, equity organizing faces a continuing struggle to legitimize and relegitimize its work. The history of the demise of the BCTF PSWC is instructive. Although there are multiple reasons for the introduction and success of the motion that dissolved the effective PSWC, one key reason was the activist and outspoken nature of the committee, which, even in a female-dominated union, became a target of anti-feminist forces. Evidence suggests that the committee's radical position on social change, its overt feminism, and its support for women's reproductive rights all contributed to the considerable attack it sustained. Based on the account by de Bruijne (1999) and confirmed in interviews with both Clarke and Turner of the BCTF (2007), over a number of years the BCTF executive undermined the committee's mission, cut its funding dramatically, removed its role in training, and limited its communication vehicles and thus its connection to its grassroots constituency, all of which set the stage for the narrow vote that led to its demise in 1998. Turner concludes: "A lot of it was to control the uppity women."

Although the attack on women's organizing in the BCTF was quite overt, CUPE and CUPW equity structures also face a continuing struggle to legitimize and relegitimize their work. On the issue of financing equity organizing in CUPW, Pollack notes that a focus on costs is partly a cover for racism, homophobia, or sexism, but also points to several other interlocking issues: "I think there's a sense that people of equity-seeking groups have made it so we don't need to spend all this money on them; second, it's a concern that the committees haven't been as effective as people thought. And third, there's a continual tension between spending money on direct servicing and grievance arbitration, and dealing with equity-seeking issues." Similar to the way equity issues are dropped at the bargaining table (Briskin 2006b), equity organizing is seen as dispensable. However, this chapter argues that, given the contribution of equity work to union revitalization, unions need to reposition equity from the margins. From a union renewal perspective, then, the cost of equity work is legitimized and mainstreamed.[18]

Such attacks on equity structures are not new. Since their inception and perhaps because of their successes, union women's committees have faced challenges that highlight the constant renegotiation and struggle around constituency organizing. For example, the 1994 Report of the Women's Rights Committee to the Convention of the British Columbia Federation of Labour states: "The formation of the first federation Women's Rights Committee in Canada by the B.C. Federation of Labour was a progressive yet controversial step. There probably has not been a Federation Convention since that year that has not, at some point, debated the merits of a women-only committee ... After 24 years of due consideration, we still believe in the necessity of 'women only' committees and forums" (British Columbia Federation of Labour 1994, 4).

Just as cross-constituency organizing is emerging out of the success of constituency committees, new forms of organizing also surface out of the attacks on equity structures. For example, with the dissolution of the BCTF PSWC, an informal Feminist Caucus was established to continue activist work on women's issues. Turner commented: "The feminist caucus saw its role as ensuring women's presence, women's voice, and women's activism; that the issues are kept in front of the BCTF ... that there's a place for women to talk to each other and that it's coordinated. It has also maintained the link and liaison between women in teaching and women's organizations in the community." De Bruijne (1999, 112) notes that "there have been significant positive effects from the informal non-institutional organizations ... For example, the [Feminist Caucus] ... succeeded in raising important issues among women, the membership and the union's political caucuses. Their role and stature grew within the feminist community and the BCTF ... This group's strength to organize, which comes in part from being outside the institutional authority of the BCTF, has allowed them to act without depending on union resources and thus being limited by its sanctioned processes and bylaws.'"

The informality of the Feminist Caucus is both a strength and a weakness. Open to all BCTF members, it can reach out widely. As Turner remarked: "The strength is, you're not constrained. You get to do what you want. The weakness is that you don't have access to the communication networks and you don't have financial support."

Informal structures, then, play a very different role from formal structures, and may in some instances be more effective in outreach and mobilizing, given their democratic and participatory thrust. Since the inception of separate organizing in Canadian unions in the 1970s, the strategic trajectory has been to seek the legitimization of constitutionally mandated committees with elected and representative memberships. However, the tendency to assume a linear path from informal to formal, the latter replacing the former, may limit the potential of constituency organizing to contribute to union renewal. As a reference point for evaluating the viability of structures, BCTF's Turner suggests this question: "Does this structure prompt local action, local involvement, and widespread mobilization?" It may be that informal structures play this role more effectively. At the same time, the leverage from formal structures may enhance the power and efficacy of such informal organizing. As part of the renewal project, then, unions need to commit resources to both formal and informal equity structures.

Conclusion

This chapter analyzes the cross-constituency organizing efforts inside three unions – the Canadian Union of Postal Workers (CUPW), the British Columbia Teachers' Federation (BCTF), and the Canadian Union of Public Employees (CUPE) – that involve respectively parallel, integrated, and dual structures. The first and relatively common approach, that of CUPW, involves two parallel and coexisting committees: a human rights committee (representing four groups) and a women's committee. As is evident in CUPW, it is often the case that the relationship between the two is unclear, the women's committee having a long history and the equity committee newly established to address the "other" equity-seeking groups.[19] The second approach, that of BCTF, involves an amalgamation of all equity-seeking committees into one integrated social justice committee. In this model, the lack of constituency committees is significant. The third approach, that of CUPE, involves a dual structure that supports separate constituency committees but also formalizes mechanisms for cross-constituency work through an umbrella human rights committee. CUPE institutionalized this structure in 2003. It is noteworthy that in 2006 the Communications, Energy and Paperworkers Union of Canada set up a similar dual structure, that is, a national equity committee with representatives from national level constituency groups for women, workers of colour, Aboriginal workers, persons with disabilities, and gay, lesbian, bisexual, and transgendered workers.[20]

Although it is too early in the history of the dual structure of organizing to come to definitive conclusions, the research does highlight the significance and the potential of cross-constituency organizing. Perhaps counterintuitively, it suggests that a dual structure may facilitate intersectionality. Combining umbrella equity or human rights committees with constituency-based organizing for marginalized groups may help maintain the delicate balance between addressing the concerns of specific equity-seeking groups and working across these constituencies to develop an intersectional politic, and a culture and practice of alliances.

In principle, intersectionality and cross-constituency organizing may also address the interrelationship of equity issues, decrease the potential polarization among various equity-seeking groups, and demonstrate that solidarity can be built on a foundation of diversity. Situating claims for justice by particular groups within the complex web of equity issues may help reveal the power structures that maintain inequality for all equity-seeking groups. The extent to which cross-constituency organizing and a political commitment to and practice of intersectionality will reap these political benefits remains to be seen.

The capacity of union movements to reinvent themselves is critical to challenging restructuring and defeating the neo-liberal agenda. In the current context of increased competition among workers, coalition building inside unions and across unions, with social movements and across borders, is a vital aspect of that revisioning. Unions should vigorously support cross-constituency organizing – a form of coalition building *inside* unions. It is a vehicle for building solidarities across identities and advancing equity organizing in Canadian unions that supports, at one and the same time, union renewal and the union equity project.

Notes

1 There is extensive literature on the importance of coalition building for union renewal; see, for example, Kainer (2006) and Kumar and Schenk (2006) on Canada; Clawson (2003) on the United States; and Frege, Heery, and Turner (2004), who compare union coalition building in five countries.

2 Murray (2005, 108) notes: "Both social and social-movement unionism embrace a much wider definition of solidarity, e.g., that unions should defend all workers and not just their members. Moreover, both seek to promote the interests of the worker as citizen as well as wage earner and, in so doing, emphasize the importance of unions' political activity."

3 Chen and Wong (1998, 230) make this point explicitly in their discussion of the United States: "Constituency groups within the AFL-CIO [American Federation of Labor and Congress of Industrial Organizations], who have long served as a voice for people of color and women, are strategic bridges between labor unions and these neglected communities."

4 The idea of a caucus of caucuses, a singular thread picked up in a variety of sessions at the conference on Advancing the Union Equity Agenda sponsored by the Centre for Research on Work and Society at Toronto's York University in March 2005, encouraged me to pursue further research on cross-constituency organizing. See Briskin (2006c). This chapter is a shortened and somewhat revised version of "Cross-Constituency Organizing in Canadian

Unions," *British Journal of Industrial Relations* 46, 2: 221-387. That 2008 version distinguishes among constitutional, organizational, and representational intersectionality.

5   The CLC is the largest central labour body in Canada. It represents about 3 million workers and has 114 union affiliates, which include twelve provincial and territorial federations and 137 district labour councils that are regionally based cross-sector umbrella organizations of unions.

6   In her seminal study of violence against women of colour, Crenshaw (1991) coined the term "intersectionality," later taken up in much writing by anti-racist feminists (e.g., Zinn and Dill 1996).

7   From the CUPW website, at http://www.cupw.ca/index.cfm/ci_id/1288/la_id/1.htm.

8   Marion Pollack works for CUPW as a union representative. She describes herself "as a proud and active CUPW member." She has "worked for Canada Post for thirty-two years and has been an active participant in CUPW for most of that time. She is committed to advancing women's rights and the rights of all equity-seeking groups." Unless otherwise specified, this short bio and all comments in the chapter are from a telephone interview with Marion Pollack conducted on 21 December 2006. Permission to quote.

9   In some other unions, a women's committee and a human rights or equity committee coexist. It appears that the relationship between the two is often unclear, the women's committee having a long history and the equity committee newly established to address the "other" equity-seeking groups. For a comment on the problems with this model in the Canadian Association of University Teachers, see Briskin (2001).

10 HRC reports are available for 1999, 2002, and 2005; NWC reports for 1996, 1999, 2002, and 2005. Thanks to Geoff Bickerton from CUPW for sending me this material.

11 The CUPW constitution is available at http://www.cupw.ca/index.cfm/ci_id/7167/la_id/1. htm.

12 Since joining CUPE in 1990, Fred Hahn has served as a steward, a health and safety activist, a pay equity and contract negotiator, and recording secretary for Local 2191. In 1996, he became president of that local and within six months led the over 1,000 workers through a three-month strike against concessions. Fred has also been active since 1996 in the provincial and national union: sectorally, as an equality activist, and on the CUPE Ontario executive board since 1998. He was elected secretary treasurer of CUPE Ontario in 2006, making him the first openly gay man to be elected to a full-time officer position in CUPE Ontario. All comments are from the telephone interview with Fred Hahn conducted on 20 December 2006. Permission to quote.

13 In a 13 April 2007 email, Hahn clarifies: "The women's committee in its new formation will require other constituencies to be on it – like young women and women of colour. It is the only one that does so – although there are informal guidelines in the other committees regarding 'gender balance.'" The CUPE Ontario constitution is available at http://www.cupe.on.ca/www/constitution.

14 For a detailed history of the BCTF PSWC, see Foley (1995, 2000).

15 Patrick Clarke works for the BCTF, where he is responsible for coordinating BCTF social justice programs. He works on various social issues (poverty, homophobia, anti-racism, environmental, and global education) and has also written on curriculum issues related to social justice. He is a frequent sessional instructor on social studies methods and curriculum at the University of British Columbia and Simon Fraser University. All comments are from the telephone interview with Patrick Clarke conducted on 2 February 2007. Permission to quote.

16 Jane Turner has been on staff at the BCTF since 2004, responsible for social justice work and the training of school union representatives. She is a member of the Communications, Energy and Paperworkers Union of Canada. Before working for the BCTF, she was a secondary social studies teacher since 1975. She was an activist in her local and president of the Burnaby Teachers' Association. She was a member of the BCTF Status of Women Committee from 1977 to 1981, chairing the committee for two of those years. All comments are from the telephone interview with Jane Turner conducted on 21 February 2007. Permission to quote.

In her discussion of the early years of the BCTF's Social Justice Advisory Committee, 1977-81, Foley notes that her informants "indicated that the committee was aware that improving the lot of students was more acceptable to the membership than was improving the lot of the female membership of the federation" (2000, 517).

17 My own experience in 1998-99 as the first coordinator of the Equity Committee in the York University Faculty Association, a certified bargaining unit, highlighted problems with an organizational approach that starts with an integrated equity structure without previously existing and functioning constituency committees. For more details, see Briskin (2006c).

18 "Mainstreaming involves ensuring that gender perspectives and attention to the goal of gender equality are central to all activities – policy development, research, advocacy/dialogue, legislation, resource allocation, and planning, implementation and monitoring of programmes and projects." From the Office of the Special Adviser on Gender for the United Nations, http://www.un.org/womenwatch/osagi/gendermainstreaming.htm. For a discussion of mainstreaming equity in collective bargaining, see Briskin (2006b).

19 For an earlier comment on the problems with this model in the Canadian Association of University Teachers, see Briskin (2001).

20 See http://www.cep.ca/policies/policy_913_e.pdf.

References

Briskin, L. 1999a. Autonomy, diversity and integration: Union women's separate organizing in North America and western Europe in the context of restructuring and globalization. *Women's Studies International Forum* 22, 5: 543-54.

–. 1999b. Feminisms, feminization and democratization in Canadian unions. In *Feminist Success Stories/Célébrons nos réussites féministes*, ed. K. Blackford, M. Garceau, and S. Kirby, 73-92. Ottawa: University of Ottawa Press.

–. 2001. Crafting an effective equity strategy. CAUT Bulletin: A12. http://www.caut.ca/english/bulletin/2001_dec/commentary/equity.asp.

–. 2002. The equity project in Canadian unions: Confronting the challenge of restructuring and globalization. In *Gender, Diversity and Trade Unions: International Perspectives*, ed. F. Colgan and S. Ledwith, 28-47. London: Routledge.

–. 2006a. *Union Leadership and Equity Representation*. Gender and Work Database, Union Module. http://www.genderwork.ca.

–. 2006b. Equity bargaining/bargaining equity. Working Paper Series 2006-01, Centre for Research on Work and Society, York University.

–. 2006c. A caucus of caucuses: The next stage in union equity organizing. *Just Labour* 6, 1: 101-12. www.justlabour.yorku.ca.

–. 2008. Cross-constituency organizing in Canadian unions. *British Journal of Industrial Relations* 46, 2: 221-387.

British Columbia Federation of Labour. 1994. *Report of the Women's Rights Committee to the Convention of the British Columbia Federation of Labour*. Vancouver: British Columbia Federation of Labour.

Canadian Labour Congress. 1994. *Confronting the Mean Society, Policy Statement 20th Constitutional Convention*. Ottawa: Canadian Labour Congress.

Chen, M., and K. Wong. 1998. The challenge of diversity and inclusion in the AFL-CIO. In *A New Labor Movement for the New Century,* ed. G. Mantsios, 213-31. New York and London: Garland.

Clawson, D. 2003. *The Next Upsurge: Labor and the New Social Movements*. Ithaca, NY: ILR Press.

Cobble, D., and M. Michal. 2002. On the edge of equality? Working women and the US labour movement. In *Gender, Diversity and Trade Unions: International Perspectives*, ed. F. Colgan and S. Ledwith, 232-56. London: Routledge.

Crenshaw, K. 1991. Mapping the margins: Intersectionality, identity politics, and the violence against women of colour. *Stanford Law Review* 43, 6: 1241-99.

CUPE Equality Branch. 2007. Report of the Equality Branch to the 2007 national CUPE convention. Ottawa: Canadian Union of Public Employees.

CUPE National Aboriginal Council. 2007. Report of the National Aboriginal Council to the 2007 national CUPE convention. Ottawa: Canadian Union of Public Employees.

CUPE National Pink Triangle Committee. 2007. Report of the Pink Triangle Committee to the 2007 national CUPE convention. Ottawa: Canadian Union of Public Employees.

CUPE National Women's Committee. 2007. Report of the National Women's Committee to the 2007 national CUPE convention. Ottawa: Canadian Union of Public Employees.

de Bruijne, L. 1999. Feminist networks and institutional change: A case study of the British Columbia Teachers' Federation's provincial Status of Women Committee. Master's thesis, University of British Columbia.

Foley, J. 1995. Redistributing union power to women: The experiences of two women's committees. PhD diss., University of British Columbia.

–. 2000. Developing an explanatory framework for the demise of a women's committee. *Economic and Industrial Democracy* 21, 4: 505-31.

Frege, C.M., E. Heery, and L. Turner. 2004. The new solidarity? Trade union coalition-building in five countries. In *Varieties of Unionism: Strategies for Union Revitalization in a Globalizing Economy,* ed. C.M. Frege and J. Kelly, 137-58. Oxford and New York: Oxford University Press.

Hunt, G., and D. Rayside, eds. 2007. *Equity, Diversity and Canadian Labour.* Toronto: University of Toronto Press.

Kainer, J. 2006. *Gendering Union Renewal: Women's Contributions to Labour Movement Revitalization.* Gender and Work Database, Union Module. http:// www.genderwork.ca.

Kinesis. 1998. BCTF vote a step backward. *Kinesis* 8.

Kumar, P., and C. Schenk, eds. 2006. *Paths to Union Renewal: Canadian Experiences.* Peterborough, ON: Broadview Press.

Kurtz, S. 2002. *Workplace Justice: Organizing Multi-Identity Movements.* Minneapolis: Minnesota University Press.

Murray, G. 2005. Unions: Membership, structures, actions, and challenges. In *Union-Management Relations in Canada,* 5th ed., ed. M. Gunderson, A. Ponak, and D. Taras, 79-111. Toronto: Pearson Addison Wesley.

Ontario Human Rights Commission. 2001. An Intersectional Approach to Discrimination: Addressing Multiple Grounds in Human Rights Claims. http://www.ohrc.on.ca/english/consultations/intersectionality-discussion-paper.shtml.

Tatum, B. 1994. Teaching white students about racism: The search for white allies and the restoration of hope. *Teachers College Record* 95, 4: 462-76.

Thompson, B. 2001. *A Promise and a Way of Life: White Antiracist Activism.* Minneapolis: University of Minnesota Press.

White, J. 1990. *Mail and Female: Women and the Canadian Union of Postal Workers.* Toronto: Thompson Educational.

Zinn, M., and B. Dill. 1996. Theorizing difference from multiracial feminism. *Feminist Studies* 22, 2: 321-31.

Part 4
International Perspectives on Equity and Union Renewal

9
Gender Politics in Australian Unions: Gender Equity Meets the Struggle for Union Survival

Barbara Pocock and Karen Brown

The unique characteristics of Australian unions, through two phases of recent Australian political history – the Labor years (1982-96) and the Howard years (since 1996) – provide a telling perspective on gender politics and the strategies that may be employed to effectively advance equity. Although it is a rough generalization, these two periods represent contrasting phases of the equity trajectory in Australian unions: a feminist organizing phase that began in the early 1970s and persisted through to the mid-1990s, and the Howard government years of conservative offence against organized labour, which from 1996 saw feminist organizing efforts in retreat as Australian unions circled the wagons to fend off attack. The chapter concludes with a look to the future, and the prospects for social justice and equity through unions, and the challenges that remain.

Throughout the chapter we utilize quantitative data on rates of unionization, as well as qualitative data arising from interviews and a survey we conducted in late 2006 in a large Australian union where women make up a minority of members.

The history of gender issues in Australian unions is complex. Gender politics play out in different ways at different levels of unionism: in the workplace, the local union branch, the state branch level, the regional union council, and in the national peak body, the Australian Council of Trade Unions (ACTU). Gendered power structures throughout the horizontal sediments of unionism differ widely, and the prospects for more representative unionism vary between these sediments. They also play out differently in different vertical segments of the economy: by industry, occupation, and blue/pink or white collar and public/private employment.

After considerable progress leading up to it, the past decade has seen practical steps toward more representative structures overwhelmed in some locations as unions faced a conservative onslaught and dramatic falls in unionization. On the positive side, a vigorous campaigning response to this onslaught has seen new inclusive forms of campaigning that have in themselves transformed gender politics in unions in significant ways. However, the deep masculinist traditions and practices of Australian trade unionism are hardy creatures with deep roots. The history of gender politics in Australian unions shows how the effort to increase the voice of women, immigrants, and indigenous workers requires meticulous attention to detail and persistent, well-resourced efforts, with attention to patterns of male over-representation and their redress. Without them, old habits prevail: men resist women, old organizing habits screen women out of unions and representative structures, and key positions within the movement remain in men's hands.

Some Background Features of Australian Unionism

To make sense of equity in Australian unions requires some understanding of the structure and origins of unionism in the nation. After a series of union defeats in the "freedom of contract" strikes in the late 1890s, Australian unions regrouped, with unionization in Australia growing to comparatively high levels in the twentieth century. This period of union membership growth was fostered by strong unions in the maritime, pastoral, and building industries – all male strongholds. In the twentieth century, manufacturing expanded and was also strongly unionized and male dominated.

Much of this growth in unionization was fostered by Australia's industrial regime, which – like New Zealand's – was built upon a set of independent national and state statutory arbitration tribunals that recognized the key representative roles of employer and employee organizations. Unions were integral to the tribunal approach and the system of national industrial awards that it established. Unionization peaked at 61 percent in 1962 (Australian Bureau of Statistics 2007, 187). Awards set comprehensive labour standards on wages, hours, and other conditions for industry sectors, and unions were integral to their amendment and enforcement. This took unions into many workplaces, and they enjoyed a privileged status through the tribunal system. Relatively high rates of unionization reflected this status and created tribunal-dependent unionism in some locations, a form of unionization that was, in places, characterized by weak workplace strength and low levels of membership activism.

These forms of industrial organization began to unravel in the late 1980s as the pressures of globalization undermined unionization and national award standards, while fostering more local enterprise-based bargaining – first in a relatively benign collective way under federal Labor governments and then in a more anti-union, individualistic way from the late 1980s onward and especially after 1996 under the Howard government. The national rate of unionization fell from 41 percent in 1990 to 26 percent in

1999 as unions lost approximately 80,000 members per year through much of the 1990s (Peetz 2006, 162).

Australian unions have always enjoyed the strength that flows from having a single national peak council, the ACTU, with its set of unified state-based peak council equivalents. The movement undertook a radical program of union amalgamation in the 1980s and 1990s, moving from over three hundred national unions to forty-seven, with about three hundred branches and four thousand officials and staff (Hubbard 2007; Walton 2007). Although these amalgamations had significant negative fallout in some important cases (especially where the new unions lacked genuine political or industrial unity or were marked by long-lived personality cleavages), they allowed unions to consolidate resources and increase their efficiency. They were not, however, always kind to women, as officials sought to secure their place in a shrinking union structure. In some unions, the representation of women fell, especially at more senior levels, and particularly where no monitoring or quotas were in place. Furthermore, while these reforms generated organizational efficiencies in unions, they did little to stem membership declines as highly unionized jobs disappeared while poorly unionized jobs expanded.

The roots of Australian unions thus lay in male-dominated workplaces among full-time, permanent, male employees. Although the growth in public sector and service-based employment saw some shifts in this starting in the 1970s, women have always been under-represented in Australia's unions. This under-representation extends from the membership and workplace delegate levels through all levels of union representation. It is, however, especially pronounced among both elected and appointed officials at the most senior levels. (Note that, in Australia, union officials include both elected and appointed officers. Those at the most senior levels, such as union secretary – usually the most powerful officer – are generally elected by members, while many other union officials, such as organizers and legal staff, are appointed.)

Thus, Australian unions have a masculinist history, but this is far from a simple unitary tale. There were always unions and unionists with concern for women alongside men, indigenous Australians alongside non-indigenous, recent immigrants alongside long-standing settlers. Like movements in other countries, the Australian union movement has been historically characterized by wide differences in politics; many of these were around familiar left/ right agendas, but there were also significant cleavages around gender politics. For example, some unions vigorously resisted the organization, leadership, and representation of women or their issues, while others strongly endorsed women's voice and issues such as equal pay.

The Australian union movement has always had a close – if sometimes uncomfortable – association with the Australian Labor Party (ALP). It gave birth to the party, and unions continue to act as a significant conduit to parliamentary office. This has given unions an influential – though far from dominant – voice in the parliamentary sphere. In terms of gender politics, this has meant that in its first century, the ALP reflected the male domination of the union movement. However, in recent decades, both the parliamentary and union wings of the labour movement have turned their attention to mechanisms that increase women's voice, under pressure from women activists. This success has had its dividends both in parliament and beyond.

The Australian union movement's attachment for most of the twentieth century to maintaining basic standards such as minimum wages across the labour market, through industry-based awards, functioned as a transmission belt of industrial gains from the industrially strong (mostly men) to the weaker (mostly women). This explains the relatively narrow gender pay gap in Australia. However, the masculinist nature of Australian unions – with their deep roots in men's employment, Australian male identity, and the male breadwinner wage-earner model – created significant negative legacies for working women and their representation, as successive generations of Australian women unionists and academics have chronicled (Game and Pringle 1984; Ryan and Conlon 1975). These cultures partly explain Australia's laggardly work and family regime and the presence of advanced conditions such as long service leave (three months for those who spend a decade or more in one job, more available to men) and the absence of paid maternity leave (which benefits women). Male unions were resistant to women, and their powerful masculinist cultures worked against women as members, activists, and leaders (Pocock 1996).

The Labor Years 1983-96: "Women Need Unions, Unions Need Women"

The slogan "Women Need Unions, Unions Need Women" epitomizes the strategy of feminist union activists who made their mark in the labour movement in the thirty years from 1970 to the mid-1990s, including the thirteen years of Labor in federal government from 1983 to 1996. As second-wave feminism took hold, many Australian feminists took up their activism through the vehicle of trade unions, seeing possibilities for unions to lift the living conditions of women. As a consequence, this period saw important advances in action and understanding in relation to women in unions, and the justice of and pragmatic arguments for more inclusive and representative unionism.

These feminist union activists also saw that unions resisted women's interests (Franzway 2001; Pocock 1997a). Nonetheless, the movement and voice of feminists in the labour movement in Australia was stronger than in the United States and Canada, for example.

This period of feminist activism in Australian unions saw significant advances in equal pay in Australia and greater attention to issues such as child care, sexual harassment, the segmentation of the labour market, and discrimination. It also saw increases in women's voice and leadership in unions: by 1992, approximately one-quarter of union officials were women, up from about 3 percent in 1971 (Pocock 1997b, 18).

This period also saw women making arguments for greater attention to the recruitment of women, and for new forms of unionism in which the active voices of members were more openly represented in union structures and leadership (McManus 1997). The ACTU implemented affirmative action strategies for women in its structures, as did individual unions. Some encouraged separate organizing of women through annual women's conferences and women's councils.

In the early 1990s, as union membership figures continued to decline, Australian unions began to reflect on the passive habits of Australian unionism – that is, the effects of living inside the arbitration system, which delivered improvements in general wage and conditions but undermined the incentives for workplace activism, leaving some unions very vulnerable to changes in employment and to employer and state government anti-union attack. This debate was framed, from the early 1990s, in terms of traditional "servicing" versus "organizing" forms of union activism (McManus 1997). The latter had important potential for women: surely a more representative, active union movement, which truly reflected the interests of its actual and potential members, had to better reflect women? Organizing strategies that connected to community issues, used organizers who shared the values and characteristics of those they sought to recruit, and linked to social justice had obvious potential for women – both in Australia and elsewhere (Hallock 1997; McManus 1997).

Unfortunately, from the mid-1990s onward, advances in women's share of union leadership and understanding about the importance of new approaches to union organizing were overshadowed as a new and much more serious set of challenges emerged. The ongoing feminist struggle within unions has been overshadowed in the past decade by the more fundamental problem of union survival.

Unionization in Australia: The Thirty-Year Free Fall
In the first six years of the twenty-first century, growth in Australian women's participation in paid work – continuing the trend of the closing decades of the twentieth century – outnumbered men's. Between 2000 and 2008, growth in women's employment was equivalent to men's (Australian Bureau of Statistics 2008). Increasing numbers of women are joining men in their paid work, and Australian governments want more women to do so as economic growth remains high and the working population ages. Indeed, some

government policies are pitched to require it, with new participation requirements imposed on sole parents (mostly mothers) receiving social security
benefits, and some modifications of tax and benefit policy to reduce the
disincentive for second earners in the labour market.

However, while Australian women have been diligently increasing their
attachment to paid work, their union foothold has not strengthened, and
unionization generally has continued its three-decade-long downward trend.
In August 2007, only 18.2 percent of all Australian workers were members
of trade unions (Australian Bureau of Statistics 2007). This is less than half
the rate of thirty years before.

In 2007, only 13.7 percent of private sector workers were members of trade
unions, compared with 41.1 percent of public sector workers. In August
2007, a slightly higher proportion of male workers than female workers were
members of trade unions: 19.5 percent compared with 18.2 percent. This
contrasts with the United Kingdom, where since 2003 unionization among
women (29.7 percent in 2006) has been higher than among men (27 percent),
reflecting in part women's employment growth (Grainger and Crowther
2007, 3).

In recent years, unions have made persistent efforts to reach out in new
ways to members. There have been many contributors to this effort. Much
of it has focused on the Organising Works program, which has trained young
organizers in new methods of union organizing since 1994, and which has
been complemented by a raft of other organizing and educative initiatives
(including union management training for senior officials) (Crosby 2005).
Much of this effort has been encouraged by many officials of individual
organizing unions and union educators, as well as ACTU leaders Greg Combet
(secretary of the ACTU 2000-07) and Sharan Burrow (president of the ACTU
since 2000), among others.

Chris Walton (2007, 2) estimates that without these innovations union
density would be at around 11 percent, or less than half its current level.
Although these efforts are stemming the tide and have increased the absolute
number of union members, the overall picture is one of persistent union
decline in the presence of rapid growth in the size of the labour market.

What explains this free fall? Changes in the structure of the labour market
are of great significance (Peetz 1998, 2006). These changes include growth
in the proportion of Australian workers who are employed part-time and/
or precariously. Part-time work has grown strongly in Australia in the past
thirty years, as has insecure employment. Over one-quarter of all Australian
workers are employed part-time (and over 40 percent of all women, much
higher than in other comparable Organisation for Economic Co-operation
and Development countries). What is more, over one-quarter of all Australian workers are employed on casual terms, that is, on an hourly contract

without any guarantee of ongoing employment. Most of these are women, and many are part-timers. Unionization is very low among both part-time and casual workers.

There have also been significant changes in the industry composition of employment, which has seen very large falls in the share of employment in highly unionized industries. Employment growth has been strong, for example, in poorly unionized sectors such as property and business services; accommodation, cafés, and restaurants (both have approximately 7 percent union density); and wholesale trade (9 percent).

Union habits have also been highlighted as important contributors to the decline in union density, not least the habitual tendency to approach men more often than women to join, be involved, and take up union roles. This set of habits extends to ways of recruiting, involving, communicating with, and actively resisting women (Elton 1997; Forbes-Mewett and Snell 2006; Sudano 1997).

The Howard Government 1996-2007: A Movement under Attack

Since 1996, Australian unions have been haunted by a second major threat: alongside the continuing steady downward trend in unionization has been the assault of an aggressive anti-union federal government against collective organization of workers through unions. These threats are not wholly unrelated, of course. Although the downward spiral in unionization predated the Howard government's election in 1996, the Party's anti-union stance has played some role in the decline of union density. However, autonomous factors, such as the changing shape of the labour market, have also been and remain important.

Against this background, during the Howard years, the place, voice, and power of traditionally under-represented groups such as women have not been the central focus of union strategy. However, the gender challenge – which lies in some ways at the heart of the union renewal project, given the increasing feminization of work – remains a significant element in strategic union thinking and practice, but this varies widely among unions and among levels of union structure, whether at workplace, union state branch, or national union level.

After thirteen years of a federal Labor government (1983-96), the Australian union movement endured eleven years of federal conservatism (1996-2007). This has had important implications for the voice of women and other disadvantaged groups in the union movement. As so often occurs in social movements, an overwhelming threat has encouraged unity across the movement, and minority interests have often been set aside within the larger fight for survival. Fortunately, the union movement's renovations in the Labor years preceding the Howard government – including steps to increase the representation of women and to renovate its structure through amalgamation – have probably served it well in preventing a disintegration under extreme pressure.

The post-1996 assault on unionism has had several elements. Labor law was significantly modified soon after the Howard government won office, making recruitment and industrial action much more difficult. In 1996, a disastrous rally protesting the new industrial laws was held at Parliament House in Canberra. A group of male protesters engaged in violent action, generating powerful and bloody images and seriously undermining the rally's message and union standing (Muir 1997). The lesson was not lost: any movement that wants to link to its larger community cannot afford undisciplined violence, and this was a powerful lesson many union leaders – men and women – took to heart.

Two years later, the 1998 Maritime Dispute saw the full power of the federal government arraigned, in consort with key corporate interests, against one of Australia's oldest unions, the male-dominated Maritime Union of Australia. The movement engaged in a legal and community-based campaign that saw it wrest a successful defence from the jaws of disaster (Pocock 1999). Women were crucial to the campaign's success, comprising a large proportion of community pickets and rallies. Many women (and men) from beyond the union movement participated in peaceful assemblies that essentially picketed key sites and sent strong signals to the government, courts, and general public about community support for the principles of job security, collective bargaining, and the right to unionize. The dispute's leaders took great care to locate this dispute in its community and household context, arguing that its assault on job security was harsh and un-Australian. The dispute's images consistently included women, families, and children. Unionists from female-dominated unions, such as those of nurses, teachers, and public sector workers, were prominent in the dispute and critical to the eventual success of unions in negotiating a settlement on acceptable terms.

Since then, the Howard government has particularly focused on breaking effective unionism in another male bastion, the construction industry, by attacking the Construction, Forestry, Mining and Energy Union (CFMEU), traditionally a left-aligned, more industrially militant union.

While many of the central attacks on unions by the Howard government have concentrated on male-dominated unions such as the CFMEU, women have been prominent in defensive struggles against these attacks, and the union movement has managed to avoid falling into the trap of sectarian or gender-based division, and become increasingly unified under the banner of its national peak council, the ACTU. The authority of the peak council has probably never been greater than in the years of Greg Combet's and Sharan Burrow's leadership, since 2000.

WorkChoices and the Radical Rewrite of Australian Labour Law

A more general attack – with particular implications for low-paid, less powerful women workers – was unleashed in the aftermath of the 2004 election, when the Howard government unexpectedly achieved control of the federal Senate. This allowed it to fully implement its industrial vision through a historic rewrite of Australia's industrial law, titled WorkChoices, which was enacted in March 2006.

Specifically, the WorkChoices amendments allow employers unilateral scope to impose individual agreements (Australian Workplace Agreements, or AWAs), even in workplaces where collective agreements exist and the majority of employees wish to bargain collectively (Statement by 151 Academics 2005). These AWAs (to be repealed by the Rudd Labor government) could significantly reduce the overall wage of workers below the pre-existing award levels and impose much lower employment standards, including the loss of conditions such as extra pay for working on public holidays, rest breaks, extra pay for casual workers who miss out on paid vacation and sick leave, or for working at night or on weekends or on shifts, and a range of other special rates and allowances that are traditionally part of award pay and conditions.

Although the government amended some aspects of the law in May 2007 in response to public concern, the law resulted in lower pay and poorer conditions, weaker workplace voice, and decreased job security (Elton et al. 2007; Elton and Pocock 2007; Peetz and Preston 2007). The new law also curtailed the practical capacity of workers to join unions or take industrial action, and removed protection from unfair or arbitrary dismissal for the many Australians working in workplaces with less than a hundred employees (excluding discriminatory dismissal on the grounds of, for example, sex). It also reduced work and family supports, such as the recently introduced right for employees to request to work part-time when they return to work after having a child (Pocock 2006).

Evidence about the new law shows that non-managerial workers on individual contracts were worse off in terms of their pay, that the gender pay gap widened, and that vulnerable workers – including many women – felt less secure at work and more pressured, and had less predictable hours. The climate in their workplaces changed (Elton et al. 2007; Elton and Pocock 2007; Peetz and Preston 2007; Preston, Jefferson, and Seymour 2006).

Many workers on AWAs lost compensation for working outside normal hours or for working shifts. These losses had a serious negative effect on working families, lowering take-home pay, removing the disincentive to employers to employ staff for long hours or on weekends or at night, expanding the employment of workers at unusual times, and lengthening the number of hours they need to work to earn a living wage. The evidence on negative impacts on families from such outcomes is persuasive (Strazdins et al. 2004).

Qualitative studies of low-paid workers, mainly women, across several states suggest that many workers were worse off and became more time- and money-poor (Elton et al. 2007). Some found that their hours were manipulated to cut wages, making working hours unpredictable and increasing the difficulty of finding child care (Masterman-Smith, May, and Pocock 2006; Pocock and Masterman-Smith 2005). These studies also suggest that employers were exercising greater control over the amount and timing of leave entitlements, changing regulations on annualized average hours of work, meaning some employers were forcing workers to take annual leave at times that did not suit their families. This undermines family-friendly work practices and therefore the quality of family and household life, with important effects on women workers and their households.

There is evidence of growth in a 24/7 approach to working hours in Australia, which does not differentiate unsocial hours (by which we mean work performed outside "normal" hours of from 8 a.m. to 6 p.m. on weekdays) and is premised on the need of low-paid workers to work around the clock to supplement their incomes, leaving less scope for quality family time. Alongside this, unpredictable shifts and rosters, with sudden changes in working time or very short shifts, jeopardize the capacity of workers on low wages, especially mothers, to supplement their incomes through a second job, which is often necessary to ensure a decent standard of living for families.

The Shift to an Organizing Approach

The assault on unions, collective bargaining, and wages and conditions dominated union strategy in the period of the Howard government. At the same time, unions responded to the decline in union density arising from structural change in the labour market and failures in traditional methods of recruitment. A series of strategy documents since 1993 chronicle this response (see, e.g., ACTU 2006; Crosby 2005). They all speak of the urgency of the task to renew organizing efforts and build union power from the workplace up, especially through recruitment in non-union sites and new layers of workplace-based activism.

Many Australian unions – though not all – have been working hard to renovate their ways of organizing and recruiting, to focus efforts more intensively on organizing young and non-unionized workers, many of them women. Much of this activity has been framed around the servicing versus organizing dichotomy, though most commentators agree that unions need to do both: that is, service existing members (though perhaps in new, less resource-intensive ways, and making greater use of workplace delegates) while increasing organizing activity, especially through new levels of delegate activity and new recruitment methods (ACTU 2006).

These efforts have met with mixed success (Peetz, Pocock, and Houghton 2007), as the union density figures described above show. Although without these efforts the situation would no doubt have been even worse for unions, it is clear that working harder and in new ways has been barely up to the task of maintaining absolute membership numbers, and inadequate to the job of increasing union density (Peetz 2006). Nonetheless, unionism remains essential to the protection of wages and conditions for working Australians, especially women in low-paid work and, more generally, where they are affected by pay inequity, discrimination, and the need for improved work and family supports.

As Chris Walton (2007, 2) summarizes, the outcomes of new organizing strategies have been uneven: "Many branches have been building the capacity to do well in a difficult environment. These unions have been growing. Other unions have been slow to change, as if waiting for 'the good old days' to return, for the state systems of the ALP Government to save them." At his farewell appearance at the 2007 organizing conference, Greg Combet emphasized that unions cannot expect the election of a new federal Labor government in late 2007 to save them. Chris Walton (2007) similarly dismisses any reliance on a Labor government to turn around union fortunes: the union-ALP relationship has changed forever, as the ALP has moved to the right and is eager to demonstrate its independence from trade unions.

Instead, ACTU leaders Combet, Walton, and Burrow emphasize the need for greater union strength through active campaigning, internal renovation, and more attention to new organizing strategies, new industrial campaigns, and new union management approaches. In response to WorkChoices and in the lead up to the pivotal Australian election in late 2007, unions began this work in earnest.

Campaigning for Workers Rights: "Your Rights at Work: Worth Fighting For"

In 2006, the Australian movement decided to undertake the largest community-based campaign in its history in response to the WorkChoices legislation (ACTU 2007a). The movement made extensive use of television and radio advertising in an extended saturation prime-time media campaign, using images of women and men "negotiating" over their working time and job security, in ways that connected workers' rights such as pay and control over working time with family issues, community involvement, and fairness.

The union movement also made extensive use of web-based tools, focus-group research, polling, and targeted efforts to connect with workers at their desks and in their homes. The campaign occurred through a series of sustained waves, including mass rallies that made use of new technologies, music, and popular public figures, and met with extraordinary success. As WorkChoices took effect, the union campaign struck a chord, making industrial relations a prominent political issue in the pre-election climate.

The campaign also delivered support to the ALP in the lead up to the 2007 election and was expanded to include a very specific and detailed strategy in twenty-two marginal electorates in Australia, drawing local union members into the election campaign. This element of strategy included polling over 250,000 union members.

The union movement raised funds by increasing union fees and affiliation fees, and devoting very sizable sums to the campaign. The professional, well-targeted campaign outspent and outwitted the heavy-footed approach of the Howard government and employers. In an answering campaign of substance, the employers failed to unify, and the union movement was able to make significant progress, winning hearts and minds to its opposition to WorkChoices. Many images and experiences of women were mobilized in this process, as the union movement spoke directly and effectively to a new demographic: working women and youth – far from the traditional terrain of male unionists and the "union boss" of anti-union propaganda. This was a new scale of sophisticated strategic activity by a united movement, which, while in decline, decided to expend its resources in a struggle it saw as definitive in terms of the future of unionism in Australia.

This concerted campaign pushed many other regular activities aside, including those focused on women and their fair representation in union structures. This reflects the nature of the crisis in Australia and the widespread sense that another term of the Howard government in control of both houses of parliament for 2007-10 would change union fortunes forever. Male and female members and officials were unified in their support of an all-out effort focused on changing the government. As Chris Walton (2007, 7) puts it, "Internal barriers and divisions have been overcome with a clear-sighted determination and focus on the goals of the campaign. Whatever the outcomes of the [2007] election, unions will continue to meet the challenges ahead, and continue to drive change."

Women were prominent throughout this campaign, and old habits of unionism – such as violent protest, bad language, aggressive behaviour, and strident leadership – were for the most part set aside for new behaviours and strategies. "Ordinary" women were the targets, and they were the dominant images of the campaign. They were also prominent in the personnel advising unions on strategy, in the leadership at peak councils, and in many key unions.

The election of the Rudd Labor government in late 2007 was very significantly shaped by the Your Rights at Work campaign.

Whether women emerge from this period holding up half the union sky (i.e., holding half the powerful positions in unions) remains to be seen. However, the union movement will never go back to male business as usual – at least in terms of national campaigning – after the success of the Your Rights at Work campaign.

The Mixed Picture at the Local Level: Business as Usual for Gender Politics?

At the local level, the picture is more mixed than at the national level. Some unions now firmly embrace new union approaches that recognize that different practices of recruiting and organizing, and new types of industrial goals, are necessary to involve and link to women. These unions have in some cases renovated their pathways to leadership, setting aside the long-lived "time served" criterion for union leaders in favour of a focus on ability. The Liquor, Hospitality and Miscellaneous Workers Union, with its base among women and men in low-paid employment, is one clear example, but there are others. These unions see an increasing voice for women, more women leaders, and action on industrial issues affecting women, as critical to their efforts to build union power.

However, not all unions reflect this path. Some, especially those that remain dominated by men in their leadership and workplace delegate structures, are virtually unchanged. Their micro-level practice fails to recognize and stop resisting women as members, activists, and leaders.

We cite one example with which we are familiar, of a long-established, male-dominated union, whose predominantly male leaders are genuinely unsure about how to change their union to better represent women. In 2006-07 we interviewed eighty-seven officials in this union (31 percent of the total), including officials in each Australian state, in each part of the union, and in all types of union positions (from senior leaders to the union's administrative staff). The confidential interviews were on average each one hour long. They were conducted as part of a strategic review of the union and examined all aspects of the union's activities and organization, though in what follows we refer only to the gender equity issues that arose from the study.

Women now make up about one-third of the workforce in the industry sectors covered by this union (compared with 45.1 percent of the total workforce (Australian Bureau of Statistics 2008). However, in this union, women remain at approximately 10 percent of total union membership. Interviews reveal that organizers readily recognize that past efforts to involve women have not been effective. As one organizer put it, "Every affirmative action effort has failed." Most women members in the union are in a particular industry subgroup, while in other areas women's membership has not tracked upward with its increasing share of employment.

In fact, the number of women members has declined at an accelerated rate over the past few years, outstripping the decline in male membership in the union. Women made up only a small number of officials – 12 percent of the total number nationally, with very few of them in senior positions. Specific structures for women's voice in the union have not been well supported and, by and large, have relied on the over-extension of dedicated women officials and activists, many of whom face burnout, not least from the continued expectation that they outperform their male peers and because they are immersed in a culture that is frequently hostile to their sex. This is not to deny the many male leaders who support women leaders and their presence in the union, but this support is rarely backed up with specific resources in an environment of union decline. Such declines are often marked by internal factional struggle, and this union is no exception, with specific efforts to assist minority groups, such as women, caught up in or simply crowded out by the factional crossfire.

In this union, the fortunes of young members and potential members have not been better; attention to these groups has generally received more lip service than material support. The low level of material support was made clear in interviews we conducted across the union; interviewees were far from positive about what women officials have experienced. Many observed that turnover among women organizers, for example, was high and that their union was not good at retaining women organizers. Research in the union a decade earlier (conducted by one of the authors) showed that women members in the union had half the level of contact with delegates and officials as did male members. More recent surveys of members show that that situation has barely changed.

Research tells us that strategies to involve women in unions are not mysterious. Studies consistently demonstrate that women are not more anti-union in their attitudes than men (Cobble 1993) and that they respond to the same strategies as men: union attention to the workplace issues that matter to them, using "like" to recruit "like" (e.g., using a woman organizer to organize women), allocating them the same per capita attention and conversation as men and scheduling union activities (including education, conversation, and meetings) at times that suit women's work and family schedules, and so on. This union's failure to adopt these strategies with vigour and persistence is reflected in its membership numbers among women.

There is also evidence of outright male resistance to women members; even male organizers volunteered that women members and organizers faced internal hazards. As one organizer put it, "I believe we need strong women members, but we don't look after them or give them a positive experience in the union office."

Many discussions about this problem in this union have taken place but have not met with success. Specific strategies and policies to increase women's participation in the union have been discussed at the most senior policy-making forums of the union for almost a decade, but resource allocation and senior leadership follow-through was slow to occur or failed on the ground.

To successfully employ and engage women organizers, a union like this needs to review its employment practices and the attitudes of some of its staff and leaders, and introduce flexible working arrangements that suit the needs of both the union and different types of employees. The introduction of part-time working arrangements for organizers, for example, would assist. Greater flexibility in hours of work arrangements and after-hours child care support would also be of benefit to both women organizers and women activists in the union. In addition, the union could adopt measures that other unions have used with success, including mentoring programs for both officials and activists and review of union communication strategies, to ensure they are appropriate and appealing to all aspects of the union's membership and potential membership, and reflect and value women's role in the union and in the workplace. Senior leadership support for such steps, their review and evaluation, and the allocation of resources to underpin them are all critical to success.

Unfortunately, as this case illustrates, the decline in union density, and the urgent priority of managing union decline with careful attention to finances, human resources, and internal politics, have crowded out effective strategies for women's voice and power in the union. The difficulties of recruiting new, more representative organizers, and employing them in a renovated and more supportive culture, are a big task, even for a large union.

If unions such as this are to pay more than lip service to their commitments to increasing women's membership and involvement, they have some distance to travel in setting clear goals, allocating responsibility for them, and ensuring that appropriate resources underpin action. This union is not alone in struggling with the practical realities of changing union practice and culture at a moment of serious attack and decline. However, its experience reveals how better representation for women and youth is a casualty of decline, rather than being viewed as a potential pathway to a more effective and powerful union, with increasing union membership through the recruitment of women workers.

Women in Union Leadership

Turning to the larger issue of women's leadership across the movement, the ACTU has been committed for more than a decade to affirmative action for women, creating new places for them on its key bodies (rather than displacing men and thus fuelling their active resistance to women). It has encouraged unions – with variable success – to increase women's voice in unions, as delegates and leaders. It has also encouraged coalitions with women's and community organizations, and this strategy has provided an important bulwark at moments of attack from the Howard government. This strategy has met with some success on peak council bodies at the ACTU and in state labour councils. However, affirmative action approaches have met with more mixed success at the local union level.

Most of the key union power brokers continue to be men: in 2007, only six of the forty-seven national unions (or 12.8 percent) were led by a female national secretary (ACTU 2007b). Even unions with a high proportion of women members, such as the Shop Distributive and Allied Employees Association and the Australian Nurses Federation, are led by men, while more male-dominated areas, such as manufacturing, have never seen a female national secretary. Old habits and old attachments to power die hard. Against this, numerous state labour councils have recently been led by women; in 2007, two of the six (South Australia and Queensland) were led by women.

The ACTU introduced affirmative action strategies in 1995 when it elected its first female president, Jennie George. By 2000, the ACTU executive aimed at achieving 50 percent female representation. However, its current listing in the 2007 directory includes only seven women out of thirty-eight members, although the directory notes that additional executive positions were not known at the time of publication (ACTU 2007b, 1).

Senior women officials, backed by formal and informal coalitions of women unionists, have seen to it that the ACTU agenda has regularly included attention to issues of importance to women, including work and family issues, pay equity, and decent minimum wages. However, in a conservative environment where unionism is under attack, advances have been thin on the ground; indeed, significant rights have been lost and inequality has widened on several fronts, not least between women and men as well as between the top and the bottom of the labour market. Australia remains one of two developed countries (the other being the United States) without a universal system of paid maternity leave, and less than half of Australian women have access to some period of paid leave (usually just a few weeks) when they have a baby. Paid paternity leave is even rarer.

Sharan Burrow, the president of the ACTU, has been involved in international campaigns to support workers and especially women, taking a leadership role at the International Labour Organization and at the International Confederation of Free Trade Unions. The ACTU endorsed the World March of Women 2000 and has continued to campaign for child care, paid maternity leave, improved public health and education services, and services for indigenous Australians. In the area of wages and conditions, the ACTU and unions have attempted to protect and increase minimum wages in particular, given their importance to low-paid workers, a disproportionate number of them women.

The ACTU has also focused on improving work and family supports, campaigning for two years of unpaid parental leave, increased access to leave for carers, and the right to request to work part-time on return from parental leave. These measures were won in a test case in 2005 but did not survive as general rights with the passage of WorkChoices. Unfortunately, the union movement has not pursued with quite the same energy the issue of paid maternity leave. In part this is because of the Howard government's cash bonus for families upon the birth of a child (which some see as a substitute for paid maternity leave, despite its failure to guarantee a paid maternal rest upon childbirth). But it also reflects the power of significant social conservatives within the union movement who remain resistant to maternal employment and paid maternity leave.

The ACTU's Women's Congress is committed to "monitoring and regularly reporting on progress in achieving gender balance within union decision making processes and structures" (ACTU 2003, 5). However, this commitment is somewhat rhetorical, with most levels of leadership understandably more preoccupied with union membership declines and, in recent years, the assault of the Howard government than with women's place in unions.

Working Life and Time in Australia: A Pressing Future Agenda for Women – and Men

Women's place in the Australian movement is also reflected in the movement's industrial agenda on working conditions. Women's growing share of all employment has created new industrial issues begging for union attention, and many unions have risen to the challenge, pursuing improved, paid maternity leave, more flexible employee-driven employment conditions, and other family-friendly measures in collective agreements, awards, and labour law.

There are plenty of issues of significance. Recent nationally representative surveys of Australian workers have found – in a situation of so-called full employment – that more than half of all workers have a significant gap (of at least half a day) between the hours they would prefer to work and the hours they actually work, and these workers have poorer work-family spillover and health outcomes (Pocock, Skinner, and Williams 2007; Skinner and Pocock 2008). Two-thirds of these would like to work fewer hours. Further, approximately 55 percent of the workers in these surveys agreed somewhat or strongly that they are overloaded at work, half have little freedom to decide when to do their work, and just under a third are worried about the future of their jobs. Thirty-seven percent of Australian workers work overtime, many for long hours, and almost half of these are not paid for their extra hours (Australian Bureau of Statistics 2006). One in five Australian workers regularly works more than fifty hours a week, most of them men, with important implications for the women and children with whom they live.

Issues of job security, control of working time, fair recompense for working outside normal hours (again, usually defined as from 8 a.m. to 6 p.m., Monday to Friday), and control of unreasonably long working hours have been the subject of union campaigns that connect to women and men, especially around their family lives. This is fertile ground for union activity. The ACTU has picked up on these concerns and undertaken a range of union campaigns to help redress the poor work and family arrangements many Australians face, especially those in lower paid jobs where autonomy is low. Campaigns to increase rights around unreasonable hours and to give working carers access to two years of unpaid parental leave, a right to request to return to work part-time after having a baby, and more access to paid carer's leave are examples of this commitment at peak council level. This industrial agenda, alongside the efforts to increase minimum wages, illustrate the ways in which peak council union leaders have worked hard to win industrial gains with real salience for women workers, with plenty of scope to continue this work into the future.

Organizing Women: Future Strategies
Regardless of who is in federal government, there will be no return to some of the protections – such as closed shops or awards – that cushioned Australian unions against anti-union employers and the chill winds of conservatism and global pressures. It is clear to Australia's union leaders that they need to revitalize union organization and increase unionization; this involves new approaches and success among the growing proportion of workers who are women.

This is unlikely to be achieved through the Rudd Labor government alone (or perhaps at all, given its caution in reforming Howard's industrial law and its distancing from unions). Although more organizing-friendly labour law would help, new strategies to reach hard-to-organize workers who have no union tradition, work in small workplaces, or are casual or part-time or have hostile employers will remain an organizing challenge for Australian unions. Many of these workers are women. Significant numbers of unions understand how to organize women, but they will need to increase their resource allocation to increase unionization, and they will need to continue to listen to, understand, and connect with women workers. Moreover, they will need to better understand the resistance that many long-standing Australian unionists and unionized workplaces display toward women.

Nevertheless, some Australian unions do not understand this task or how to do it. Others simply struggle to find the resources to achieve it, in an environment where the employment relationship is being transformed or becoming more temporary. There is no substitute in this environment for a sustained union-based strategy, which makes union leaders accountable for the representative character of their union structures and agendas. The Howard years caused some to set aside (or defer) gender-specific strategies and efforts, and meant that some unions stalled their long and necessary gender revolutions.

Against this, the vigorous union fight back represented by the Your Rights at Work campaign demonstrates the power of effective, unified campaigns involving both women and men that mobilize a deliberately gendered discourse of fairness. If unions are to build on their campaigning success achieved in the 2006-07 Your Rights at Work campaign, and to authentically speak to and for Australian workers, they need to continue and deepen the gender renovation at the local union level. It will take ongoing organizing among women activists to ensure this happens.

References

ACTU (Australian Council of Trade Unions). 2003. *ACTU Women's Congress Document.* Melbourne: ACTU.

–. 2006. *Unions@Work.* Melbourne: ACTU.

–. 2007a. *Your Rights at Work Campaign.* Melbourne: ACTU. http://www.rightsatwork. com.au.

–. 2007b. *ACTU National Union Directory.* Melbourne: ACTU.

Australian Bureau of Statistics. 2006. *Working Time Arrangements, Australia.* Catalogue no. 6342.0. Canberra: Australian Bureau of Statistics.

–. 2007. *Year Book.* Canberra: Australian Bureau of Statistics.

–. 2008. *Labour Force, Australia.* Catalogue no. 6202.0. Canberra: Australian Bureau of Statistics.

Cobble, D.S. 1993. *Women and Unions: Forging a Partnership.* Ithaca, NY: ILR Press.

Crosby, M. 2005. *Power at Work: Rebuilding the Australian Union Movement.* Sydney: Federation Press.

Elton, J. 1997. Organizing unions in Australia. In *Strife: Sex and Politics in Labour Unions,* ed. B. Pocock, 133-55. Sydney: Allen and Unwin.

Elton, J., J. Bailey, M. Baird, S. Charlesworth, R. Cooper, B. Ellem, T. Jefferson, F. Macdonald, D. Oliver, B. Pocock, A. Preston, and G. Whitehouse. 2007. *Women and WorkChoices: Impacts on the Low Pay Sector.* Adelaide: Centre for Work and Life University of South Australia.

Elton, J., and B. Pocock. 2007. *Not Fair, No Choice: The Impact of Work Choices on 20 South Australian Workers.* Adelaide: Centre for Work and Life University of South Australia.

Forbes-Mewett, H., and D. Snell. 2006. Women's participation in "a boys' club": A case study of a regional trades and labour council. *Labour and Industry* 17, 2: 81-98.

Franzway, S. 2001. *Sexual Politics and Greedy Institutions.* Sydney: Pluto Press Australia.

Game, A., and R. Pringle. 1984. *Gender at Work.* Sydney: Allen and Unwin.

Grainger, H., and M. Crowther. 2007. *Trade Union Membership 2006.* London: Department of Trade and Industry.

Hallock, M. 1987. Organising and representing women. In *Strife: Sex and Politics in Labour Unions,* ed. B. Pocock, 45-66. Sydney: Allen and Unwin.

Hubbard, L. 2007. Hard questions facing Australian labour. In *Trade Unions in the Community: Values, Issues, Shared Interests and Alliances,* ed. D. Buttigieg, S. Cockfield, R. Cooney, M. Jerrard, and A. Rainnie, 11-22. Heidelberg, Australia: Heidelberg Press.

Masterman-Smith, H., R. May, and B. Pocock. 2006. "Low paid services employment in Australia: Dimensions, causes, effects and responses." In *21st Century Work: High Road or Low Road?* ed. B. Pocock, C. Provis, and E. Willis, 369-79. 20th Conference of AIRAANZ, vol. 1, Referred Papers, Association of Industrial Relations Academics of Australia and New Zealand, Adelaide, 1-3 February.

McManus, S. 1997. Gender and union organizing in Australia. In *Strife: Sex and Politics in Labour Unions,* ed. B. Pocock, 26-44. Sydney: Allen and Unwin.

Muir, K. 1997. Difference of deficiency: gender, representation and meaning in unions. In *Strife: Sex and Politics in Labour Unions,* ed. B. Pocock, 172-93. Sydney: Allen and Unwin.

Peetz, D. 1998. *Unions in a Contrary World.* Cambridge, UK: Cambridge University Press.

–. 2006. *Brave New Workplace: How Individual Contracts Are Changing Our Jobs.* Sydney: Allen and Unwin.

Peetz, D., B. Pocock, and C. Houghton. 2007. Organizers' roles transformed? Australian union organizers and changing union strategy. *Journal of Industrial Relations* 49, 2: 151-66.

Peetz, D., and A. Preston. 2007. *AWAs, Collective Agreements and Earnings: Beneath Aggregate Data.* Melbourne: Industrial Relations Victoria.

Pocock, B. 1996. Challenging male advantage in Australian unions. PhD diss., University of Adelaide.

–. 1997a. *Strife: Sex and Politics in Labour Unions.* Sydney: Allen and Unwin.

–. 1997b. Gender, strife and unions. In *Strife: Sex and Politics in Labour Unions,* ed. B. Pocock, 9-26. Sydney: Allen and Unwin.

–. 1999. Success in defence: Union strategy and the 1998 Maritime Dispute. *International Employment Relations Review* 5: 17-38.

–. 2006. *The Impact of WorkChoices on Australian Working Families.* Melbourne: Industrial Relations Victoria.

Pocock, B., and H. Masterman-Smith. 2005. WorkChoices and women workers. *Journal of Australian Political Economy* 56: 126-44.

Pocock, B., N. Skinner, and P. Williams. 2007. *Work, Life and Time: The Australian Work and Life Index 2007.* Adelaide: Centre for Work and Life University of South Australia. http://www.unisa.edu.au/hawkeinstitute/cwl/documents/AWALI2007.pdf.

Preston, A., T. Jefferson, and R. Seymour. 2006. *Women's Pay and Conditions in an Era of Changing Workplace Regulations: Towards a "Women's Employment Status Key Indicators" (WESKI) Database.* Sydney: Human Rights and Equal Opportunity Commission, National Foundation for Australian Women, and the Women's Electoral Lobby.

Ryan, E., and A. Conlon. 1975. *Gentle Invaders: Australian Women at Work 1788-1974.* Sydney: Thomas Nelson.

Skinner, N., and B. Pocock. 2008. *Work, Life and Workplace Culture: The Australian Work and Life Index 2008.* Centre for Work + Life, University of South Australia. http://www.unisa.edu.au/hawkeinstitute/cwl/documents/awali08.pdf.

Statement by 151 Academics. 2005. *Research Evidence about the Effects of the Work Choices Bill.* Submission into the inquiry of the Workplace Relations Amendment (Work Choices) Bill 2005. Submission 175. Canberra: Australian Parliament. http://www.aph.gov.au/Senate/committee/EET_CTTE/wr_workchoices05/submissions/sub175.pdf.

Strazdins, L., R.J. Korda, L.L. Lim, D. Broom, and R.M. D'Souza. 2004. Around-the-clock: Parent work schedules and children's well-being in a 24-hour economy. *Social Science and Medicine* 59, 7: 1517-27.

Sudano, L. 1997. Union leadership. In *Strife: Sex and Politics in Labour Unions,* ed. B. Pocock, 112-32. Sydney: Allen and Unwin.

Walton, C. 2007. The Future of the ACTU. Unpublished paper. Melbourne: Australian Council of Trade Unions.

10

Sites for Renewal: Women's Activism in Male-Dominated Unions in Australia, Canada, and the United States

Mary Margaret Fonow and Suzanne Franzway

Women union activists are in a unique position to develop strategies that can revitalize the labour movement so that unions are able to rebuild their organizational and industrial strength. Women workers generally are critical to the renewal of the labour movement, but unions must find ways to encourage their union membership and activism. Unions need to learn to "resonate more deeply with current and prospective members" (Cornfield and McCammon 2003, 16) in order to overcome the gendered impediments to women's participation. We argue that if unions are to achieve equity for their current and future women members on the path to renewal, women need political spaces where they can identify and articulate their needs and create feminist politics.[1]

However, making feminist politics within and through the trade union movement involves contesting explicit and complex structures of power. In all labour movements, women's participation rates are quite disproportionate to their low leadership rates and, on any measure, inequalities continue. As one woman official we spoke to in our research observed, "When I go to the national office I look around their walls and their photographs over years and years, and there is not one woman in sight, not one." It takes considerable effort for women to gain recognition as union members whose issues are central to programs for renewal and growth, as well as influence over union agendas and the allocation of political resources. Women in male-dominated unions are likely to face unique challenges in overcoming barriers to participation and recognition.

Nevertheless, contemporary union feminists are bringing their concerns into the traditional trade union movement and developing new and productive spaces for union renewal. As Healy, Hansen, and Ledwith (2006) observed, the move toward self-organizing groups has been a major structural change in trade unions. By creating women's committees, forums, conferences, and women's centres or units, women activists within the labour movement have developed effective mobilizing structures that can be used to harness the resources of their organizations to build solidarity among women. Union feminists who participate in the networks, discourses, and campaigns of the labour movement and the women's movement are creating overlapping spaces between movements for making feminist politics.

This chapter is part of a larger project on transnational feminist alliances between women and labour, which offers an analysis of the efforts of union feminists to secure workplace rights and economic and social justice for women in the global economy (Fonow and Franzway 2007; Franzway and Fonow 2008).[2] Here, we focus on three sites that exemplify differences and complexities in these strategies. Women in the United Steelworkers of America in Canada and the United States developed and utilized a union leadership course as a mobilizing structure. The Australian-based biannual conference of Women in Male Dominated Occupations and Industries campaigns for national and international industrial rights. And feminists and unionists succeeded in gaining state support for Working Women's Centres in Australia, which advocate gender equity policies and practices for women workers.

Sexual Politics

We adopt the concept of sexual politics to identify the complex gender relationships of power as domination, resistance, alliances, and pleasures that are central to all social institutions, including the trade union movement (Franzway 2001). Sexual politics typically works through practices of invisibility. When women are absent from or insignificant to discussion and analysis of the central concerns of work, politics, and labour movements, it is not just a matter of ignorance or carelessness. Rather, it is a strong signal that an inegalitarian or patriarchal sexual politics that advantages men is in play. The concept of sexual politics not only recognizes that men's concerns and practices are the norm but also draws attention to the invisibility of men's power. In unions, for example, questions rarely arise about how men achieve and maintain their leadership and political dominance.

In spite of the obstacles of sexual politics, women's workplace and political commitment, activism, and militancy are not insignificant (see Briskin; Kainer; this volume). The minority positions of union women activists in trade unions together with their feminist politics give them strong incentives to work across state and union borders to make alliances that are creative and productive. For example, the World March of Women 2000, born out of the experience of a Women's March against Poverty held in Canada in 1996, brought women together from peace organizations, community groups, and trade unions in an explicitly global campaign for peace and equality (Fonow 2003). Union feminists in Australia held a national conference explicitly linked to the march's themes, while the United Steelworkers in Canada mobilized over 1,000 of their members to participate in the march. Carolyn Egan, president of United Steelworkers Toronto Area Council and assigned to lead the mobilization, reported, "The World March brought together the incredible strength of the women's movement and the labour movement. It showed real potential for the change that's possible" (Fonow 2003, 194).

Unions have the resources to bring together women from different countries and different sectors of the economy to exchange information about their experience of globalization and to build new forms of labour solidarity. Feminists are constructing a solidarity that does not ask women to repress the differences among themselves but, rather, encourages the productive use of these differences to expand ideas about democracy and human rights. Without the material resources, networks, and rhetorical tools of their unions, fewer working-class women from any part of the world would have the opportunity to participate in the debates and struggles concerning the politics of trade and globalization.

Mobilizing Structures for Gender Equity

Social movement theorists have debated at some length the relationship between structural inequality and collective action. Although they differ from each other in significant ways, new social movement (NSM) theory and resource mobilization (RM) theory challenge the idea that there is a direct, unmediated relationship among structural conditions of exploitation, dissatisfaction, and collective action. Both perspectives view the transition from condition of inequality to action as a contingent and open process mediated by several factors. NSM theory places an emphasis on cultural factors (particularly expressive aspects) to explain social movements as struggles for control over the production of meaning and the constitution of new collective identities. RM theory, in contrast, stresses the political nature of the new movements and interprets them as conflicts over the allocation of goods in the political market. Hence, it focuses on the strategic-instrumental aspects of action (Canel 2007).

We integrate insights from both approaches as we examine the discourses, resources, and networks mobilized by feminists for collective action within male-dominated unions. From RM theory we employ McCarthy's (1996, 149) notion of mobilizing structures as "those collective vehicles, informal as well as formal through which people mobilize and engage in collective action," to evaluate union gender equity structures as both tools for and the outcome of mobilization. We see gender equity mobilizing structures within unions as (potential) organizational mechanisms to collect and use the resources of both the labour and women's movements. If mobilizing structures are to be useful as tools for movement activity, however, they must be culturally framed as such, and here the emphasis in NSM theory on culture and discourse is helpful.[3] Although we understand that the political opportunity structure is also important for successful movement outcomes, we intentionally focus on how activists challenge the sexual politics of male-dominated unions and in the process create mobilizing structures for collective action on behalf of women's interests.

Union feminists have created gender equity structures and separate self-organizing sites within unions that have been framed as legitimate sites for feminist politics. These "protected" spaces are "where activists meet, share experiences, receive affirmation, and strategize for change" (Katzenstein 1998, 33). Brown (1995) argues that the development of feminist politics actually requires the cultivation of such spaces for constructing feminist political norms, strategies, and agendas. Women's self-organizing in unions provides the political space to construct union feminism, and it is within these spaces that women's economic interests get defined. According to Curtin (1999, 33), "Separate spaces provide the opportunity for women to alter the discursive frameworks through which women's claims are constituted." They serve as mobilizing structures, not ends in themselves, and they are useful not only for internal mobilization but also for building alliances with feminist supporters in other unions and with women's organizations in the community.

Marie Clarke Walker, executive vice-president of the Canadian Labour Congress, makes clear in her chapter (this volume) that equity structures *alone* do not result in equity for racialized workers. She argues that workers of colour have had to organize both inside as well as outside the labour movement, and we have found this to be true for women in male-dominated unions, many of whom are women of colour. In the United States, for example, women's self-organizing within the United Steelworkers was modelled after the Ad Hoc Committee of Concerned Black Steelworkers, which gained a good measure of its influence within the union from its alliance with the civil rights movement. Black women steelworkers who were active in both the Ad Hoc Committee and in the civil rights movement brought with them this deep understanding of how to link internal struggles with external movements and were instrumental in creating a multiracial women's caucus within the United Steelworkers that was connected to the broader women's movement and civil rights movement.[4]

Women of Steel Leadership Course

The United Steelworkers, one of the few unions representing workers on both sides of the US-Canadian border, provides an interesting case study of how women, who were historically excluded or marginalized, gained a foothold in a union during a time of crisis and renewal. During the 1970s, women successfully used the equity legislations and mechanisms created by the women's movement and the civil rights movements in the United States and Canada to gain access to employment in basic steel (Fonow 2003). Thus they became members of the United Steelworkers at a time when the union was compelled to grapple with the long-term effects of deindustrialization, globalization, and economic restructuring (ibid., 136). Plant closings, downsizing, and outsourcing greatly reduced the membership base of the organization. Paradoxically, this crisis produced changes in the union that resulted in greater opportunities for women's participation and activism.

The union responded to the challenges of globalization by restructuring its own administration, merging with other unions, increasing its international activities, and allocating more funds for organizing sectors of the economy that traditionally employ women. As their proportion of the membership increased, women mobilized from within the union to campaign for women's rights and for women's participation in the leadership of the union. In the process of mobilizing, women developed a collective identity of themselves as political actors and challenged the organization to respond to their concerns and to the concerns of women outside the organization. Women's increased activism is both a consequence of and an impetus for union renewal.

We focus our attention on the Women of Steel leadership course, which was designed and implemented in Canada in 1992 with the support and assistance of the now defunct Ontario Women's Directorate and eventually exported to the United States. The purpose of the course is to provide leadership training to women, with the goal of increasing their participation in union activities and in leadership positions. But in reality, the course is much more than an educational tool. It brings together women who often work in isolation from each other to help them understand the systemic nature of sexism and other systems of inequality in the workplace, in the union, and in society. It builds solidarity across the social lines of division that often divide workers, such as race, ethnicity, language, and occupational categories. Finally, it provides opportunities for consciousness raising and mentoring. The course serves as a mechanism for rank-and-file social-movement mobilization and is part of a broader process of the participants acquiring and solidifying a sense of political efficacy, a sense of themselves as political actors – as citizens, as union members, and as women.

The course employs a very broad understanding of successful activism that is not measured solely in terms of how many women are elected to formal leadership positions. It embraces a feminist approach to politics by expanding activism to include a wide range of activities, from speaking up at meetings to talking about an issue at work, volunteering for routine tasks around the union hall, and participating in organizing drives. Cuneo's definition (1993, 111) of activism as "the capacity and willingness to act, and the practice of taking the initiative, of beginning new actions, of going on the offensive, of making things happen rather than waiting for them to happen" comes close to what the course organizers had in mind. One of the facilitators of the course said, "It's not necessarily about developing the next president of the Steelworkers – but hopefully someday that'll happen. It's activating the women and showing them that they have the skills already to become active. Every one of them will come out being more knowledgeable about their union, feeling less isolated. We've got a woman where she's the only woman in the plant, but when she went back she also took some skills with her to help build some support among her brothers out there" (Fonow 2003, 155).

In 1999, Fonow conducted a telephone survey of Canadian women who had participated in the course, in an effort to measure the impact of the course on women's activism and participation in the union.[5] Respondents were asked to indicate whether they thought their level of activism had changed after they took the Women of Steel course. Fifty-one percent said their involvement had increased after taking the course, 39 percent said it had remained the same, and 10 percent said it had decreased. The survey measured a number of specific dimensions of participation, including attending meetings, speaking at meetings, serving on committees, volunteering, running for office, and attending union programs. The most significant positive changes in participation were for speaking at meetings, attending meetings, and committee service. Before and after differences for voting in union elections, running for office, and being elected to office were not statistically significant (Fonow 2003, 157). But a closer look at the data revealed that women were running for and being elected to more influential positions on executive boards after taking the course than they had before taking the course.

Respondents were asked to identify what they thought were important outcomes of taking the course. More than half (53 percent) strongly agreed that the course helped them to better understand the importance of networking with other women, and 51.8 percent strongly agreed that the course helped them to understand the importance of building solidarity among women (Fonow 2003, 159). In an open-ended query about what they thought they had gained from taking the course, the respondents' most common answer was confidence, followed by consciousness about women's issues, new information about the union, solidarity and networking, voice and empowerment. Half of the respondents felt the course made them more confident about their abilities, and nearly 40 percent thought the course helped them to become more effective communicators (ibid., 161). Finally, when asked what factors contributed to increasing the participation of women in their local, 83.1 percent said that union-sponsored courses and training programs were very important, in fact the most important factor. Next was the presence of a mentor (79.5 percent), followed by encouragement from the local president or other officers (75.9 percent).

In general, unions have turned to women's leadership training as part of a renewal strategy because they believe that women's increased activism will make unions more attentive to equity issues and therefore more attractive to women (Greene and Kirton 2002). To be effective as a renewal strategy, leadership training must be attached to real opportunities for women to participate in the decision-making bodies of their union. It is doubtful that education alone will bring about changes in the opportunity structure within unions; this will require more sustained forms of activism. What the course does do, however, is connect participants to other networks within the union and help to build solidarity and collective identity among those who have taken the course.

The course laid the foundation for building or revitalizing women's committees in the union and was the impetus for appointing regional coordinators for Women of Steel activities, including regional and national women's conferences. The concerns of the women's committees included pay equity, promotion, sexual and racial harassment, domestic violence, and respect on the job and from their union brothers, double-day work loads, dependent family members, job training, and the culture of male-dominated union locals. Typically, these committees rotate the decision-making roles within the division of labour of the committees so that women gain as much organizational experience as possible. The reason for establishing separate women's committees is based on women's minority status in a male-dominated union and their experiences of sexual harassment and sex discrimination on the job (Fonow 2003, 153). According to union documents about the women's committees, "In many workplaces: mines, factories, and offices, women are in a minority. The work environment – from the physical layout of the office or plant, to the behaviour of management and the traditional shoptalk – creates barriers to women's employment and training. In the retail and service sectors, where work is traditionally undervalued and underpaid and hours of work vary tremendously, women struggle to organize and fight for job security and decent wages. In every sector across Canada, women continue to face workplace harassment and discrimination."[6]

Women's committees provide separate autonomous space where women can strategically mobilize on behalf of their emerging interests as women workers in a male-dominated union (Fonow 2003, 154). Separatism is not the goal of the committees but rather, as Briskin (1993) suggests, a strategic move, a reflection of gender significance and specificity already built into the power arrangements within the workplace, the union, and society.

The union builds on the momentum of the course by connecting participants with local women's committees, thus creating a more permanent structure for activism (Fonow 2003, 162). Women who take the course report that they maintain contact with other women in their local who have taken the course and with the women with whom they took the course. The course creates an incipient network that can serve the purpose of mobilizing women on specific issues and campaigns. Almost half (45.1 percent) of the women who live or work in regions where there is an existing women's committee belong to it. The majority (65.2 percent) say they were motivated to join because of their interest in pursuing the issues covered in the course, and 43.5 percent said the encouragement of a union official was very important in their decision to join the women's committee. Those who join (91.3 percent) do so because they value the work done by women's committees and because they believe there is the need for women to have separate spaces to discuss issues such as sexual harassment. Slightly less than half (49.4 percent) think their local is very supportive of women becoming more active in the local (Fonow 2003).

However, as Foley (this volume) discovered, the success of women's committees as advocates for equity depends on whether committee leaders can frame injustices in a way that reinforces the efficacy of collective action and whether the political opportunity structure within the union is favourable to the ideas and demands of the activists. When they work well, women's committees can be a route by which women become more active in the life of their local. It is really through attending local union meetings, union schools, and conventions that women gain the information and skills they need to be effective change agents within their union when it comes to achieving equity outcomes. Whether they are listened to by union leadership depends in part on how central to union survival equity advancement is seen to be, and if they can make that message resonate with a broad base of the membership (Briskin; Foley, Chapter 7; this volume).

Gender equity norms have been institutionalized in the United Steelworkers. The leadership course is offered in all twelve districts in the United States and Canada, and women's committees that are organized into regional councils are now required by the union's constitution. International, national, and district women's conferences are held regularly, and a website facilitates organizing and the exchange of information. Ann Flener serves as director of the Women of Steel office and special assistant to the president for women's issues and programs, and Carol Landry, one of the first women to attend the Women of Steel course and who rose up through the ranks to become the president of a large copper-mining local in British Columbia, was named as the first women to serve on the International Executive Board. The position is a newly created one – vice-president at large – and as Clarke Walker (this volume) points out, these set-aside seats can be problematic if there is not also an all-out effort to integrate and make visible the concerns and issues of workers of colour and of women in the entire union and in society.

Women in Male-Dominated Occupations and Industries (WIMDOI)

Political spaces that are less resource intensive than union courses, such as focused conferences, have also proved to enhance the mobilization of women unionists and the promotion of women's issues and concerns. Union feminists need to organize within the labour movement in order to obtain the resources necessary to create such a space. The case of the Australian biannual conference for women in male-dominated occupations and industries (WIMDOI) is typical.[7]

The idea for this conference came from a union shop floor delegate, Tania Courtney, who had attended a national women's forum conducted by the peak union body, the Australian Council of Trade Unions (ACTU), and thought a similar event would be useful for the women in male-dominated unions who often felt marginalized by the men in their own unions and by women unionists from more feminized areas of work. She talked with other women from male-dominated unions whom she met at the forum, who also felt like outsiders at the one place where they expected to feel supported. She approached Max Adlum, a union women's officer, to see if the women's committee of the Australian Manufacturing Workers Union could sponsor a conference. Adlum took the idea to her executive but met with resistance. Officials told her it was too costly, that the women should be focusing on organizing and recruiting more women into the union, and that focusing especially on women was "not core union business." She was told to come back when she "had the numbers." Rather than be limited by the attitude of one union, Max and Tania developed alliances with other interested women unionists to lobby ACTU to sponsor a conference across the spectrum of male-dominated occupations.

Interest in establishing a national WIMDOI conference developed at a time when the unions in Australia were going through a major restructuring, with many union mergers and amalgamations. Women found themselves in reconfigured union bodies with other women from different unions and political factions. According to Max Adlum, they did not always trust or like each other, but they found they could leave those feelings outside the door so they could work together on women's issues. WIMDOI was an intentional space for building solidarity among women across Australia that could focus some of their political energy on national and international campaigns.

The point of the conferences, the first of which was held in 1993, is to bring women together to share experiences and ideas about how to survive in occupations that place them outside the social norms for their sex and isolate them in environments dominated by male culture. Much like the Women of Steel leadership course, the WIMDOI conference seeks to inspire participants to return to their local branches and organize and recruit more women. In addition to skill- and confidence-building activities and workshops and presentations by labour experts and activists, each conference typically includes a solidarity action with a local strike or labour campaign and group-building activities designed to build a collective identity or spirit among the women at the conference. WIMDOI conferences have built an international focus by developing connections with union women from New Zealand and Canada. The 2003 conference facilitator, Kathleen Galvin, a metalworker and an ACTU labour educator, also consults for the International Labour Organization in the Asia-Pacific region and leads workshops with labour educators from India, Pakistan, Korea, Mongolia, and the Philippines. In her training workshops with other unionists she uses the WIMDOI conference as a case study of a unique strategy of women's activism.

We attended the 2003 WIMDOI conference in Adelaide, Australia, where we collected documents, conducted interviews, and made observations. We talked with women who worked in steel, auto, furniture making, lumber and paper mills, construction, prisons and policing, shipping, trucking, and small-scale manufacturing. Delegates at the conference represented a wide range of unions, including the West Australian Prison Officers Union; Maritime Union of Australia; National Distributors Union of New Zealand; Australian Manufacturing Workers Union; Construction, Forestry, Mining and Energy Union; National Union of Workers; and New South Wales Police Association. Many of the 2003 conference sessions centred on recruitment, organizing, and strategies to increase women's participation in trade unions. Speakers were very aware of the impact of globalization on their unions and talked of the necessity of linking the organization of women to the survival of their unions. Union renewal was seen as a key and necessary objective toward achieving both the women's goals and the union movement's programs. Reports by delegates indicated that organizers are being trained to recruit new types of workers – immigrants and women – and to focus more on the ways unions provide a better life for workers, rather than only on the more traditional union issues of wages and conditions.

WIMDOI conferences provide space to debate union strategies. For example, the session on women's ways of organizing drew a mixed response. The facilitator presented an organizing model that emphasized women's embeddedness in relational networks. Since building unions is essentially about building relationships, she believed women with their relational advantages were natural organizers. Women share and value each other's stories and develop creative and safe places to learn. Since being active in the union is another responsibility added onto those of work and family, it often takes women longer to become active, but Kathleen Galvin saw that they usually demonstrate high levels of commitment when they do get involved. In the small discussion groups on this topic, in which we participated, the younger women disagreed. They thought the model old-fashioned and preferred a more analytic, task-oriented model that focused on ways women can be more effective in the union and on the job. They did not see women as natural allies and thought that some women played power games just as well as men. They rejected essentialist ideas about womanhood and the idea that women were more altruistic than men, interested in what they could do for others and not in what they might get in return.

Conference participants also discussed the workplace issues that feminists have succeeded in bringing onto union agendas, such as work-family balance policies, paid maternity leave, and sexual harassment. Sandra Dann, the director of the Working Women's Centre in Adelaide, drew an enthusiastic response when she presented a workshop on workplace bullying, which has become a visible workplace issue in the last decade. This is a result of successful feminist campaigns, achieved in part by framing it as an occupational health and safety issue. As Sandra Dann said, "A bully in the workplace is just as dangerous as a broken piece of machinery." In the short term, the individual worker who is the target of bullying needs support and help, so workmates and the union should make it clear that bullying creates an unproductive and stressful workplace and will not be tolerated. Sandra encouraged workers who experience workplace bullying to file complaints with the occupational health and safety office of their state governments, explaining the technical aspects of remedies available in law. However, implementation of appropriate policies in workplaces remains inadequate according to Sandra, who advocated a long-term strategy of political campaigning, which would need to draw on union resources and mobilizing structures developing, for example, through WIMDOI.

Finally, the participants utilized their WIMDOI experience to become involved in their own unions' international networks and campaigns. Sue Virago of the Maritime Union of Australia in Sydney described how involvement in earlier conferences motivated her to persuade her union to establish an office that would develop programs to encourage women's union participation. As the only woman "wharfie" on her shift for nine years, Sue was the ideal person to head the new office. The union extended its support of women's participation by sending her as a delegate to an Asian-Pacific women's conference held by the International Transport Federation, which was exerting pressure on its affiliated unions, such as the Maritime Union of Australia, to strengthen women's union membership. In turn, Sue was able to leverage the international networks she developed through these efforts to support her work in Sydney.

Although WIMDOI conferences are relatively small events, they are the result of successful union feminist campaigns to gain resources from their unions that they can then turn toward identifying and engaging women's workplace issues in male-dominated occupations and industries. Women are minorities in their specific unions, but by developing alliances across the unions, as well as with other political spaces, they are able to challenge sexual politics in both their own unions and their workplaces. One such political space that has been created in Australia is the group of Working Women's Centres.

Working Women's Centres

Australian Working Women's Centres (WWCs) sit between the state and the union movement. Not unlike American worker centres, with their goals to support low-wage workers through advocacy, services, and organizing (Fine 2006), the WWCs share characteristics with women's services or centres that have been, and still are, central to the women's movement in Europe, the United States, Canada, New Zealand, and Australia (Hercus 2005; Weeks 1994). This reflects their origins in alliances of union and non-union feminists working with unions, community groups, and state agencies. WWCs generally employ several people with industrial relations expertise and are managed by boards drawing their membership from community, state, and union organizations.

The WWCs also typify the Australian feminist strategy of seeking and relying on funding by the state (Franzway, Court, and Connell 1989; Sawer 1999). The South Australian centre, which is also the longest standing, was established by feminists working within and around the state and the peak union body, the South Australian United Trades and Labour Council. It is mainly funded by an annual grant from the South Australian state government, supplemented in recent years by smaller, more conditional grants from the federal government. Such a strategy has often caused difficult and knotty problems for feminists around roles, alliances, and political autonomy, and the WWCs have been no exception. All centres have experienced conflicts over the politics of funding that have been exacerbated by increased controls imposed by funding bodies, particularly at the federal level. Two centres (out of five) were forced to close in 2007 (in Tasmania and in New South Wales) as a result of insufficient funding.

As the Australian industrial landscape has become increasingly harsh, the main focus of activity and case work has become vulnerable working women, including those who work in precarious and/or low-status employment, Aboriginal and Torres Strait Islander women, women from non-English-speaking backgrounds, women in regional or remote areas, women with disabilities, and women with family responsibilities (Working Women's Centres 2006). The WWCs frame their goals from feminist perspectives on women's work, and economic and social justice. As the South Australian WWC states, it campaigns for the achievement of access to work, and fair pay and conditions for all working women, so that they may enjoy a balanced and quality life. Issues of equity, education, and opportunities are translated into tangible goals and campaigns to gain access to political agendas of unions, the state, and even some areas of the women's movement.

The WWCs are sites of advocacy and empowerment for women in relation to employers, the state, and the union movement. They build knowledge gained from their educational, advocacy, and case work, from action research projects, and from alliances with union and feminist activists at local and international levels. The centres have created spaces in which major issues such as outwork (Tassie 1989), sexual harassment, homophobia, workplace bullying, and the impact of domestic violence on women's work (Franzway and Chung 2005) are identified and debated. Sexual harassment, for example, proved to be a critical issue for union feminists as they struggled to develop appropriate union policy, especially where both perpetrator and victim were union members. How could the union represent the interests of both?

Unions are often confronted by members' conflicting interests, yet when sexual harassment was recognized as a critical issue for working women (through the efforts of feminist activists), the sexual politics of both workplaces and unions were thrown into sharp relief. Sexual harassment for (mainly) women workers, and (less visibly) for gay and lesbian workers, raised questions about gendered and unequal relationships of power, the discursive dominance of masculine heterosexuality, and practices of invisibility, none of which is easily resolved by the application of feminist or union principles. These issues have a particular bite in male-dominated occupations and industries, where women are in the minority and so struggle to have them recognized in workplaces and in the relevant unions. WWCs were able to provide relevant research and industrial experience, based on their case and advocacy work, as well as political space for the necessary debates among union and other feminists (Franzway 2001; Working Women's Centre 1994).

The service focus of the WWCs has a double edge to it. Responding to individual women's work problems and taking up individual cases of workplace discrimination provides centres with obvious and tangible evidence of continuing need, and therefore grounds for continued funding for campaigns for change in policies and practices by unions and the state. However, case work is voracious and almost infinite so that WWCs always struggle to balance the needs of clients with their advocacy and policy work. The challenge is how to measure and maintain an appropriate level of case work, and how to set and meet its other priorities, particularly in an increasingly difficult industrial climate. Nevertheless, centres continue to participate in advocacy and campaigns with union feminists. Such work contributes to the union movement's moving to confront difficult political and strategic issues that are relevant to working women.

Conclusion

Each of the examples discussed above is a form of feminist organizing constituted by the ongoing and shifting forms of interactions among various groups of participants within the labour movement's organizational environment. This kind of activism is crucial if women are to play their part in the revitalization of trade unions. In spite of the considerable obstacles they face from the sexual politics in workplaces and labour movements, women's political commitment and activism are not insignificant. Union feminists in alliances with the women's movement are creating and using political spaces, national and international networks, and community organizations for mobilizing women's participation to address workers' issues and concerns that arise out of the rapidly changing impact of globalization. Union feminists' activism is a site of the contestation of sexual politics, as well as a vehicle for its transformation. We argue for a better recognition and understanding of the mobilizing structures and strategies that encourage women's union participation and help to shed light on the role unions can and do play in improving the lives of working women. As union feminists develop strategies to achieve gender equity, they also contribute to the necessary revitalization of the labour movement itself.

Notes

1 For a comprehensive discussion of the ways women are transforming labour in the United States see Dorothy Sue Cobble, ed., *The Sex of Class: Women Transforming American Labor* (Ithaca, NY: ILR Press, 2007).
2 Franzway and Fonow, *Making Feminist Politics: Transnational Alliances between Women and Labor*, forthcoming from the University of Illinois Press, argues that union feminists are bringing qualities of the women's movement into the traditional trade union movement, not only to make their claims about union gender politics but also to develop strategies that revitalize the labour movement itself. We employ a multi-sited ethnography of labour institutions, networks, and campaigns. The sites include the World Social Forum (actual and virtual), the International Confederation of Free Trade Unions, global union federations, national peak union bodies, non-governmental labour organizations such as Working Women's Centres, intergovernmental agencies such as the International Labor Organization, free trade activism, and labour rights campaigns. Our data draw on research conducted by the authors that is extended and deepened by interviews with union women activists about their everyday lives, observations of relevant events and campaigns, and textual analysis of documents.
3 See Fonow (2005) for a discussion of the role of discourse in framing mobilization structures.
4 The details about this strategy can be found in Fonow (2003, chapter 5).
5 A more extensive analysis of the survey results was published by Fonow in *Union Women: Forging Feminism in the United Steelworkers of America* (Minneapolis: University of Minnesota Press, 2003), 157-64. The telephone survey was conducted with the help of the Survey Research Center at the Ohio State University. Data were collected between 29 June 1999 and 31 July 1999 from a random survey of 191 participants of the Canadian Women of Steel course. Eighty-three completed interviews were obtained using CATI process.
6 Women of Steel development course, *Building Solidarity*, section 1, p. 1. Toronto: United Steelworkers.
7 In the Australian system, workers may be members of unions without the whole workplace being organized or unionized. Recruitment may be a much more accumulative process. However, recent legislation, the Workplace Relations Amendment (Work Choices) Bill 2005, has seriously restricted union access to workers and workplaces.

References

Briskin, L. 1993. Union women and separate organizing. In *Women Challenging Unions: Feminism, Democracy, and Militancy*, ed. L. Briskin and P. McDermott, 89-108. Toronto: University of Toronto Press.
Brown, W. 1995. *States of Injury: Power and Freedom in Late Modernity*. Princeton, NJ: Princeton University Press.

Canel, E. 2007. *New Social Movement Theory and Discourse Mobilization Theory: The Need for Integration.* International Development Research Centre. http://www.idrc.ca/en/ev-54446-201-1-DO_TOPIC.html.

Cornfield, D., and H. McCammon. 2003. *Labor Revitalization: Global Perspectives and New Initiatives.* Amsterdam: JAI Press.

Cuneo, C. 1993. Trade union leadership: Sexism and affirmative action. In *Women Challenging Unions: Feminism, Democracy, and Militancy,* ed. L. Briskin and P. McDermott, 109-36. Toronto: University of Toronto Press.

Curtin, J. 1999. *Women and Trade Unions: A Comparative Perspective.* Brookfield, VT: Ashgate.

Fine, J. 2006. *Worker Centers: Organizing Communities at the Edge of the Dream.* Ithaca, NY: Cornell University Press.

Fonow, M. 2003. *Union Women: Forging Feminism in the United Steelworkers of America.* Minneapolis: University of Minnesota Press.

–. 2005. Human rights, feminism, and transnational labour solidarity. In *Just Advocacy? Women's Human Rights, Transnational Feminism and the Politics of Representation,* ed. W. Kozol and W. Hesford, 221-42. New Brunswick, NJ: Rutgers University Press.

Fonow, M., and S. Franzway. 2007. Transnational union networks, feminism and labour advocacy. In *Trade Union Response to Globalization,* ed. V. Schmidt, 165-77. Geneva: ILO Press.

Franzway, S. 2001. *Sexual Politics and Greedy Institutions: Union Women, Commitments and Conflicts in Public and in Private.* Sydney: Pluto Press Australia.

Franzway, S., and D. Chung. 2005. Domestic violence and work. Paper presented at the Australian Sociological Association annual conference, Hobart, Australia.

Franzway, S., D. Court, and R.W. Connell. 1989. *Staking a Claim: Feminism, Bureaucracy and the State.* Sydney: Allen and Unwin.

Franzway, S., and M. Fonow. 2008. An Australian feminist twist on transnational activism. *Signs: Journal of Women in Culture and Society* 33, 1: 537-44.

Greene, A., and G. Kirton. 2002. Advancing gender equality: The role of women-only trade union education. *Gender, Work and Organization* 9, 1: 39-59.

Healy, G., L. Hansen, and S. Ledwith. 2006. Still uncovering gender in industrial relations. *Industrial Relations Journal* 37, 4: 290-98.

Hercus, C. 2005. *Stepping Out of Line: Becoming and Being Feminist.* London: Routledge.

Katzenstein, M. 1998. *Faithful and Fearless: Moving Feminist Protest Inside the Church and the Military.* Princeton, NJ: Princeton University Press.

McCarthy, J. 1996. Constraints and opportunities in adopting, adapting, and inventing. In *Comparative Perspectives on Social Movements,* ed. D. McAdam, J. McCarthy, and M. Zald, 141-51. Cambridge, UK: Cambridge University Press.

Sawer, M. 1999. The watchers within: Women and the Australian state. In *Women, Public Policy and the State,* ed. L. Hancock, 36-53. Melbourne: Macmillan.

Tassie, J. 1989. *Out of Sight – Out of Mind: Outwork in South Australia.* Adelaide: Working Women's Centre.

Weeks, W. 1994. *Women Working Together: Lessons from Feminist Women's Services.* Melbourne: Longman Cheshire.

Working Women's Centre. 1994. *Stop Violence Against Women at Work: An Information Guide for Women Dealing with Sexual Violence and Sexual Harassment in the Workplace.* Adelaide: Working Women's Centre.

Working Women's Centres. 2006. *About Us.* http://www.wwc. org.au/about.html.

11
The Representation of Women and the Trade Union Merger Process
Anne McBride and Jeremy Waddington

Throughout many industrialized countries the loss of political influence, membership decline, and substantial changes in the composition of the labour market have led many trade unionists to seek to renew their organizations to adjust to new circumstances. Attempts to renew unions have embraced a wide variety of policy options. Integral to most of these attempts to renew, however, are institutional and procedural reforms intended to encourage greater numbers of women to join unions and to stimulate higher rates of participation and involvement in union activities by women members. In addition, within several unions, attempts have been made to mainstream gender-related issues.

Concurrent with attempts to renew union organization and to ensure greater gender equity has been the extensive restructuring of union representation through the merger process. Proponents of the merger process argue that mergers are a means through which renewal can be achieved, as they are a means to restructure union movements in a manner consistent with changes in labour markets. In addition, merger proponents claim that mergers generate economies of scale, thus releasing resources for renewal activities. They also eliminate costly disputes over union jurisdictions and present opportunities to introduce institutional and procedural reforms intended to move toward or result in gender equity. Although there is a wide-ranging literature on the process whereby mergers are completed, there is limited research on merger outcomes (Chaison 2001; Waddington, Kahmann, and Hoffmann 2005). Assessments of the claims of the proponents of merger activity are thus in short supply. Furthermore, where such assessments are available, they review the impact of mergers by reference to specific questions: are mergers integral to union renewal (Behrens, Hurd, and Waddington 2004b); do mergers allow unions to extend membership coverage within private sector services (Waddington, Kahmann, and Hoffmann 2005); are post-merger unions responsive to members in the workplace (Sverke and

Sjöberg 1997); are post-merger unions more effective than pre-merger con-
stitutents in financial management and related activities (Willman 2004)?

One outstanding question is whether mergers lead to improvements in
the representation of women. This stands aside from the question of whether
mergers actually lead to renewal but is inextricably linked, since an increase
in women's involvement could lead to a renewal of union goals or an extension of union recruitment bases. A considerable literature now exists on the
effectiveness of union attempts to adapt to increasing diversity in the labour
market and, in particular, to increase women's participation and representation (Colgan and Ledwith 1996; Healy and Kirton 2000; Parker 2002). Given
the amount of merger activity throughout European and North American
union movements, much existing material on mergers and women is derived
from newly formed unions. Within this material, however, the role of women
necessarily takes centre stage, and conclusions usually relate to the effectiveness of new structures for women's organization, rather than the commenting
on the impact of mergers per se.

This chapter is an attempt to do some ground clearing of existing European
research against a series of questions. First, what is the current state of
women's representation within trade union confederations and national
trade unions?[1] Second, to what extent do these organizations implement
measures to increase women's representation? Third, have merger reforms
contributed to women's representation within trade unions and, if so, how?
Fourth, how widespread is merger activity that impacts upon the participation and representation of women? Finally, how does the material that links
the representation of women and merger activity affect our understanding
of mergers and renewal?

The material in this chapter is derived from European research primarily
published in the English language. The statistical material on women's
representation and equality measures results from surveys conducted by the
European Trades Union Confederation (ETUC); the Landsorganisationen i
Danmark (LO), the Danish Confederation of Trade Unions; the Deutscher
Gewerkschaftsbund (DGB), the German Trade Union Confederation; the
Trades Union Congress (TUC); and Southern and Eastern Regional Trades
Union Congress (SERTUC) in the United Kingdom. A review of published
case study material that examines gender equity in mergers led to the iden-
tification of three categories of interest: a merger involving a union that
organized and represented only women, mergers involving male-dominated
unions, and "big bang" mergers, which involve unions that consist either
of a majority of women or at least equal membership. This material relates
primarily to mergers brought about by amalgamations, rather than by acquisition. Amalgamations are probably the best cases to illustrate change,
since they tend to involve greater disturbance of vested interests within

unions and more fundamental changes to structures and practices. The
material that underpins our analysis is therefore not representative of all
merger activity but is representative of material that examines gender equity
in union amalgamations throughout Europe.

The chapter comprises two substantive sections and a brief conclusion.
The first section identifies the female representation gap in unions and
examines measures to increase women's representation. This section also
introduces the conceptual links between restructuring and renewal as a
backdrop to examining evidence on mergers and women's representation.
The second section presents survey and case study material on mergers in
Denmark, Germany, and the United Kingdom. The distinctiveness of these
mergers and their implications for women's representation and union renewal is then discussed in the context of merger activity in the concluding
section. The overall argument of the chapter is that the merger process
represents a key opportunity to reform union structures to increase women's
representation, but it is acknowledged that this opportunity is rarely taken.
Furthermore, we argue that where reforms are introduced during the merger
process that are appropriate to encourage the participation and improve the
representation of women, there is no certainty that these reforms will lead
to increases in the number of women members or the extension of union
recruitment bases into areas of the labour market heavily populated by
women. A wide range of other factors may preclude these developments and
effectively overpower the impact of the internal union reforms.

The Context: Gender Equity and the Merger Process
In order to situate the merger process in the context of gender equity within
unions, this section reviews the current situation of the representation of
women within trade unions and identifies recent trends toward gender equity
in trade union confederations and affiliated unions in Denmark, Germany,
and the United Kingdom. The character and the intensity of the merger
process are also examined.

Women's Representation within Unions
Women make up about 39 percent of global trade union membership but
constitute only 1 percent of the decision-making bodies of unions worldwide
(ILO 2001) and in 1999 held less than a third of senior decision-making
posts in over 60 percent of trade unions in a European study (Garcia 2002).
The 2002 ETUC survey (ibid.) indicated that within Europe, women remain
under-represented in leadership and in most confederal congresses and
executive committees. Only five of twenty-five confederal congresses could
claim attendance proportional to female membership, and only three of
twenty-four confederal executives could claim proportional representation

of women. When compared with the previous survey (Hacourt and Garcia 1999), however, these data reflect an increase in the overall number of women in decision-making bodies. Confederation-wide surveys in Denmark (LO 2005), Germany (Jenter, Tondorf, and Jochmann-Döll 2004), and the United Kingdom (SERTUC 1997, 2004; TUC 2005) indicate that women are under-represented within affiliated unions, too. The Danish survey concluded that there had been no major changes during the past ten years. The UK surveys show an improving pattern of representation but no dramatic changes either. For example, although the proportion of women delegates to the Trades Union Congress (TUC) has risen over the past five years, if progress were maintained at the current rate it would take thirty years for the congress to proportionately represent women (SERTUC 2004).

Improving Women's Representation: Theory and Practice

The word "representative" implies at least two duties of the representative: to represent the interests and views of the represented, and to share at least some of the characteristics of the represented. Theories of representative and participatory democracy, however, assume that men and women have equal opportunity to engage in the democratic process of being a representative or participating in meetings. Numerous trade union studies have shown that this is not the case, the key obstacles being women's unequal share of domestic responsibilities, women's oppressed status within society (McBride 2001a), and "simultaneously interlocking oppressions" (Brah and Phoenix 2004, 78), which exclude black women (Munro 1999) and lesbians (Humphrey 2002). Much attention has been paid to ensuring gender equality within unions, but the primary means of improving women's representation is through providing family-friendly practices, such as job sharing and the provision of daycare facilities or child care allowances for activists attending meetings; reserving seats for individual women to specific quotas or proportionality; developing structures that enable oppressed social groups such as those consisting of women, black members, members with disabilities, and lesbian/gay/bisexual/transgender members, to determine their own priorities. Sometimes members of these structures are representatives on mainstream committees, enabling group representation (McBride 2001a, 19-26).

Family-Friendly Practices

Garcia (2002) indicates that despite recognition within European confederations that women's lack of time and the timing of meetings represent major obstacles to women's representation, only a minority of confederations have a policy for making women's attendance easier. Only four of the thirty-one confederations provided child care facilities, and only six reimbursed child care during congress and other meetings. This is in contrast to national unions in the United Kingdom where only four unions in the SERTUC (2004) survey did not provide support for members with children at their annual conferences, and twelve of the thirty-three provided support for members with other caring responsibilities. There is no comparable data for Denmark or Germany.

Reserving Seats for Women

Nearly 40 percent of European confederations indicate that they use reserved seats or quotas to promote representation of women (Garcia 2002). Four confederations had started using either reserved seats or quotas since the 1999 survey, though two other unions had stopped using reserved seats.

The LO survey does not identify the extent to which its affiliated unions use reserved seats, but quotas have been rejected by the Danish union movement in the past (Silvera 2004, 29). There is no national picture of German usage either, but an example is provided below. In the United Kingdom, ten out of thirty-three TUC affiliates have some guaranteed representation for women, which correlates with proportionality of representation in seven of them. Of the ten largest UK trade unions, five have reserved seats for women on their national executive committee (NEC), and each of these has female representation on the NEC within eight percentage points of the size of the female constituency (sometimes even higher).

Equality Structures

The majority of European confederations have a women's committee, with 60 percent of these having their own budget. Forty-four percent of these committees have a joint advisory and decision-making role, and this represents an increase in power given to these committees. Seventy-two percent have links to other bodies, though only 11 percent have voting rights on these other committees.

At the national level, there is little specific information on women's committees in the LO affiliates, but the newly merged Fagligt Fælles Forbund (3F, the United Federation of Danish Workers) has established a women's network that meets after work hours every two months. The German confederal survey does not contain any data on this aspect. The SERTUC (2004) survey indicates that only five of thirty-three TUC affiliates do not have an equality group of some description. Eighteen of the thirty-three affiliates have a women-only environment, and six have equality committees. Twenty-eight percent of unions in the TUC Equality Audit 2003 had women's or equality committees at regional or sub-national level. Heavily male- or female-dominated unions tend to develop fewer and a smaller range of women-only groups (Parker 2002). The SERTUC survey notes that only four of the thirteen unions with a predominantly female membership have women-only fora. The survey also notes that eleven of these unions do not reach proportionality on their executives, and questions the connection between the two features.

In summary, there has been an increase in practices intended to improve women's representation, but these increases have not been dramatic. There has thus been a slow growth in the participation and representation of women within trade unions. The literature suggests that organizational restructuring might provide a much-needed boost to women's participation and representation. It is to this issue that we now turn.

Restructuring for Renewal

Behrens, Hamann, and Hurd (2004a, 20) conceptualize union renewal as "(re)gaining power along the various dimensions that capture the main orientation or spheres of union activity." Three dimensions (membership, economic, and political) are derived inductively by observing patterns of union decline and revitalization, while a fourth (institutional) dimension is designed to encompass a union's internal structure, dynamics, and identity. The membership dimension relates to membership numbers, membership density, and changes in membership composition. The economic dimension includes bargaining power and labour's impact on the distribution of wealth, and thus Behrens, Hamann, and Hurd (2004a, 21) indicate that union renewal along this dimension could include the use of innovative ways of increasing economic leverage. Renewal along the political dimension involves unions being more effective in influencing the policy-making process. Of particular interest to our discussion is the fourth dimension, which addresses the organizational structures and governance of unions, and encompasses internal enthusiasm to embrace new strategies and structures (ibid., 22). It is anticipated that renewal along this dimension relates to changes in the other three dimensions. The example given is that organizing previously marginalized groups, for example women or immigrants, could lead to the creation of new structures to encourage participation and representation, which may then influence union goals and eventually lead to a redefinition of strategies.

Since there has been considerable union restructuring across Europe (Waddington 2005a) and slow changes in women's representation, it is important to revisit the propositions of Behrens, Hamann, and Hurd (2004a). This chapter focuses on one aspect of restructuring, trade union mergers, and their impact on improving women's representation.

Union Mergers

A merger is the combining of two or more unions to form a single union. Mergers take the form of amalgamations or acquisitions. An amalgamation consists of the formation of a new union from at least two pre-merger unions, whereas in an acquisition a large union absorbs a smaller union (Chaison 2001; Waddington 2005b).

Merger activity has been relatively intense since the mid-1970s in Australia, Canada, New Zealand, the United States, and throughout much of Europe (Chaison 1996; Waddington 2005a). The same sources indicate that while there are national variations, a significant proportion of successful mergers are acquisitions. A consequence of this activity is that the number of trade unions is decreasing and membership is becoming increasingly concentrated in a few large unions within each country or confederation (Waddington 2006). Another consequence is that membership of the larger unions is becoming more heterogeneous. This raises questions about how different groups of members are to be represented within trade unions. All mergers are characterized by some degree of negotiation between the parties, both before and after the ratification of the formal merger agreement. These negotiations overcome barriers to mergers, reconcile differences in union government and administration, and seek new means of member representation (Chaison 2001; Waddington, Kahmann, and Hoffmann 2005).

The dynamics of merger negotiations have been conceptualized in terms of the politics of bargaining, which comprises three sets of relationships that link the range of influences on trade union structure and the merger process (Waddington 1995; Waddington, Kahmann, and Hoffmann 2005). These relationships are the bargaining position of unions relative to employers and the state; the bargaining position of unions relative to that of competitor unions; and factional bargaining within unions. This approach demonstrates that variations in union policy toward union structure and a range of external pressures may change the circumstances under which unions operate and thus stimulate merger activity, but internal union politics are shown to be influential on the form of post-merger union constitutions. For example, tensions between and within shop stewards and full-time officers in pre-merger unions, and between and within different political factions, are likely to influence the form of post-merger representation.

There is less material on the politics of bargaining between groups identified by sex, but two citations related to the United Kingdom are worth mentioning, since they illustrate the influence of gender on union structure and the merger process. The first is the withdrawal of the Federation of Women Civil Servants from the Civil Service Alliance, as the efforts of the latter to secure equal pay were seen by women as inadequate. The second relates to the breakaways (of men and women) from the National Union of Teachers over equal pay policies (Waddington 1995, 127, 153). There is even less material on the politics of bargaining in merger negotiations between groups identified by race (see McBride 2001a, 84-94); Marie Clarke Walker's comments (Edelson, this volume) are a valuable contribution to our knowledge of the impact of mergers on representation from communities of colour.

Mergers and Gender Equity

Most of the material on mergers does not examine gender relations. Indeed, most material on mergers addresses only issues associated with gender when women are the focus of attention or when mergers explicitly identify gender equality objectives (Colgan and Ledwith 2002; Behrens, Hurd, and Waddington 2004b). Extant studies thus present only a partial picture of the relationship between mergers and gender equity, since unions are selected precisely *because* they are doing things. The material in this chapter has been organized into the three categories noted above, namely, a merger involving a union that represented and organized only women; mergers of male-dominated unions; and big bang mergers. Analysis of survey data has focused on reserved seats, equality structures, and numerical impact. Case study material has been analyzed for factional bargaining on these principles and qualitative outcomes. Where possible, reference is made to the four dimensions of renewal identified by Behrens, Hamann, and Hurd (2004a): membership, economic, political, and institutional.

Mergers Involving Women-Only Unions

Women-only unions are rare in Europe, but a recent merger in Denmark provides insights into the consequences for structures initially set up to campaign for the interests of women. Kvindeligt Arbejderforbund i Danmark (KAD, Danish Union of Women Workers) exclusively organized women from its formation in 1901. In 2005, KAD merged with Specialarbejderforbundet i Danmark (SiD, General Workers Union of Denmark) to form 3F. It was joined in 2006 by the RestaurationsBranchens Forbund (RBF, National Restaurant Trade Union). 3F is the largest trade union in Denmark, representing approximately 360,000 members, almost 25 percent of the membership of unions affiliated to the LO, who work in industry, building and construction, transport, or the public sector.

In the merger, 20 percent of 3F members came from KAD, and 80 percent from the male-dominated SiD, leading to 32 percent of 3F members being women. Since the later acquisition of RBF, women comprise 34 percent of 3F membership. Merger negotiations between KAD and SiD resulted in an Agreement on Fair Representation. This agreement sets out the principle of proportional representation and details several features to support gender equity but also references the internal politics of bargaining. The demand for gender quotas from KAD representatives is noted alongside the comment that some can perceive these negatively, and recent research indicates that SiD negotiators thought quotas was a "dirty word" (Hansen 2006). The process for ensuring proportional representation, as outlined in the agreement, is limited to eight years, after which "elections take place according to ordinary rules and regulations."[2] The agreement also establishes a Committee of Equal Treatment; a Committee for Family Policy, with options to establish subcommittees for women and ethnic minorities; and a Secretariat of Equality and Family Policy.

3F thus has four aspects of equal opportunities practice that its former partner union SiD did not have in 2004 (equal opportunities and/or family policies, committees, a budget for equal opportunities work, and target figures for equal opportunities work) (LO 2005). Early indications are that the quota system is enabling women to attain proportional representation. 3F is the only affiliated union that responded to the LO survey to have an over-representation of women in its executive committee, and one of only two unions that has an under-representation of men among congress delegates (ibid.). Branch chairs, however, are less likely to be women, and branches have been slow to work with the concepts of gender equality and gender mainstreaming.[3] In addition, proportional representation in the agreement related to the former partners' unions, rather than gender, with the impact that SiD women appear to have less influence than in their former union (Hansen 2006).

In terms of renewal, it is too soon to assess the impact of this merger on membership, but one consequence could be the increase in the economic power of KAD members. A consequence of being a women-only union was that KAD represented members across a wide range of industries but was not the majority union in any of the key bargaining fora where it was present. In the absence of majority bargaining positions, KAD representatives found it difficult to advance the interests of women, though by definition these interests were mainstreamed within KAD (Due and Madsen 2005). In practice, the central issue was not gender mainstreaming within KAD but the bargaining position of KAD relative to employers and other trade unions. The merger with SiD, which also represented members across a wide range of industries, arguably presents the opportunity to strengthen the bargaining position of KAD, albeit as part of 3F, with employers and other unions. The paradox that bargaining strength could be gained through a merger at the expense of representational equity is also raised by Edelson (this volume). There, Marie Clarke Walker refers to mergers that strengthened bargaining sectors but also led to a decrease of racialized local leaders.

Mergers of Majority-Male Unions

This section provides a gendered analysis of a series of UK mergers involving twelve unions over a period of nineteen years. Most of the unions are male dominated. Parallel and consecutive merger action led to them becoming part of Unite in 2007. Unite is now the largest British union, with approximately 2 million members, of which 21.7 percent are women, although the proportion varies markedly between the different sections of the union. Tables 11.1 to 11.4 focus on four episodes of merger activity involving these unions and contain data on the membership of women, equality measures, and the representation of women in these unions.

Table 11.1 relates to the merger in 1988 of two unions that organized technical and managerial staff in manufacturing and services: Technical, Administrative and Supervisory Staff (TASS) and Association of Scientific, Technical and Managerial Staffs (ASTMS). They merged to become Manufacturing, Science and Finance (MSF), which organized skilled and professional staff in the public and private sector. In 1990, MSF acquired the Health Visitors' Association (HVA), increasing the proportion of female membership within MSF.

Table 11.2 indicates how MSF merged with the engineering union Amalgamated Engineering and Electrical Union (AEEU) in 2002 to become Amicus. In 2005, Amicus acquired Unifi (the union that organized workers in the finance industry) and the Graphical, Paper and Media Union (GPMU. The name Amicus was retained. GPMU organized workers in the print, publishing, paper, IT, and media industries and was itself the result of a 1992 merger.

Table 11.3 contains data on the constituent unions of GPMU: the National Graphical Association (NGA) and Society of Graphical and Allied Trades (SOGAT '82), both of which organized in the print industry. Table 11.4 focuses on the 2007 merger between Amicus and the Transport and General Workers' Union (TGWU) to form Unite. As its name suggests, TGWU organized workers in a range of industries and sectors. Unite represents workers employed in each of the principal sectors of the economy, with particular membership concentrations in road transport, finance, manufacturing, print, aviation, food and farming, and public services. Although it could be classed as a big bang merger, it is included here, as Unite remains a male-dominated union.

Four observations can be drawn from this material. First, as indicated in the case of 3F, the merger of female- and male-dominated unions can bring positive and negative gender impacts to the former partner unions. As noted earlier, the impact of any merger on the bargaining position with employers or competitor unions will be a main priority when seeking merger partners, rather than the gender balance among members. Some mergers can increase the critical mass of women in more male-dominated former partner unions, for example, TASS (Table 11.1) and AEEU (Table 11.2). Conversely, the impact of mergers on reducing the critical mass of women can be seen in the case of the Amicus merger (Table 11.2) and the GPMU merger (Table 11.3). In 2000, women comprised 31 percent of the MSF membership but

Table 11.1

Equality structures and women's representation in pre-merger unions TASS and ASTMS, and merged union MSF

Union/membership/year	% women members/ year	Reserved seats (women)	Equality structures	% women on NEC	% women at national conference
TASS: 253,000 (1987)	11% (1987-88)	Yes		n/a	
ATSMS: 400,000 (1987)	19% (1987-88)	None		n/a	
TASS and ATSMS merge to form MSF in 1988; 653,000 members at amalgamation.	20% (1988)	4 on NEC (from national women's committee)	NWC; NW conf; race, L&G, disabled workers committees and conferences; NWC reps on NEC	8%	
MSF: 653,000 (1988)	19% (1989)			10% (1989)	
HVA: 16,019 (1989); acquired by MSF in 1990	99% (1989)				
MSF: 552,000 (1994)	27% (1993)	1995: quota system to ensure women's proportional representation at all levels		24% (1993)	
MSF: 446,000 (1997)	31% (1997)			38% (1997)	22% (1997)
MSF: 400,000 (2000)	32% (2000)				
MSF merge with AEEU to form Amicus (see Table 11.2)					

L&G = lesbian and gay; NEC = national executive council/committee; NWC = national women's committee; NW conf = national women's conference
Sources: Annual report of certification officer various; Healy and Kirton 2000; Kirton and Healy 1999; SERTUC 1997, 2004.

Table 11.2

Equality structures and women's representation in pre-merger unions MSF and AEEU, and merged union Amicus

Union/membership/year	% women members/ year	Reserved seats (women)	Equality structures	% women on NEC	% women at national conference
MSF: 400,000 (2000)	31% (1997)	1995: quotas/ proportionality introduced		38% (1997)	22% (1997)
AEEU: 546,000 (1994)	9% (1994)	Not known	Not known		
AEEU: 727,369 (1999-2000)	10% (2000)			10% (2000)	10% (2000)
MSF and AEEU merge to form Amicus in 2002; 1,080,046 members at amalgamation	16% (2002)	4 out of 48 on NEC	NWC; biennial NW conf; race, disability, youth, LGBT committees and conferences		
Amicus post-merger: 935,321 (2003-04)	16% (2003-04)			19% (2004)	
Amicus acquires GPMU (see Table 11.3) and Unifi in 2005	22% (2005)				
Amicus merge with TGWU to form Unite (see Table 11.4)	22% (2007)				

LGBT = lesbian, gay, bisexual, and transgender; NEC = national executive council/committee; NWC = national women's committee; NW conf = national women's conference

Sources: Certification officer various; Healy and Kirton 2000; Kirton and Healy 1999; SERTUC 1997, 2004.

Table 11.3

Equality structures and women's representation in pre-merger unions NGA and SOGAT '82, and merged union GPMU

Union/membership/year	% women members	Reserved seats (women)	Equality structures	% women on NEC	% women at national conference
NGA: 131,538 (1988)	5% (1987-88)	None (1988 proposal rejected)	NWC	n/a (1987-88)	
SOGAT '82: 185,150 (1988)	33% (1987-88)	None	NWC from 1990	n/a (1987-88)	
NGA and SOGAT '82 merge to form GPMU in 1991; 269,881 members at amalgamation.	17% (1992)	None	NWC; biennial NW conf; equality committee		
GPMU: 250,230 (1994)	17% (1993)	993 conference accepted principle of proportional representation for national executive 1995 rule change for guaranteed proportional representation at all levels, on all delegations, requires addition of women if not proportionate	NWC; biennial NW conf; disabled members committee; young members' committee	5% (1994)	11% (1993)
GPMU: 250,230 (1997) GPMU: 170,279 (2003)	17% (1997)			23% (1997)	11% (1997)
GPMU: 102,088 (2004)	17% (2004)			22% (2004)	13% (2004)
2005 GPMU merges with Amicus (see Table 11.2)					

L&G = lesbian and gay; LGBT = lesbian, gay, bisexual, and transgender; NEC = national executive council/committee; NWC = national women's committee; NW conf = national women's conference

Sources: Certification officer various; Colgan and Ledwith 1996; Colgan and Ledwith 2002; Healy and Kirton 2000; SERTUC 1997, 2004.

Table 11.4

Equality structures and women's representation in pre-merger unions Amicus and TGWU, and merged union Unite

Union/membership/year	% women members	Reserved seats (women)	Equality structures	% women on NEC	% women at national conference
Amicus (see Table 11.2): 1,080,046 (2004)	16% (2004)	4 out of 48 on nec	NWC; biennial NW conf; race, disability, youth, LGBT committees and conferences	19% (2004)	
TGWU: 1,348,712 (1987)	17% (1987-88)		NWC; biennial NW conf; biennial equality conference; race, disability committees and conferences; LGBT working party; young members' forum	5% (1987-88)	
TGWU: 958,834 (1994)	19% (1994)				
TGWU: 884,669 (1997)	19% (1997)	reservation of 6 seats for women on executive (1998)		6% (1997)	10% (1997)
TGWU: 823,312 (2004)	21% (2004)			33% (2004)	19% (2004)
Amicus and TGWU merge to form Unite in 2007	22% (2007)	Draft rules allow for proportionality in all conferences and committees; inclusion of designated seats to achieve proportionality of women and of black, Asian, and ethnic minority members.	Draft rules allow for NWC; NW conf; committees and conferences for black, Asian, and ethnic minority, and for disabled and LGBT members. Representation of women and of black, Asian, and ethnic minority members on NEC.		
Approximately 2 million members					

LGBT = lesbian, gay, bisexual, and transgender; NEC = national executive council/committee; NWC = national women's committee; NW conf = national women's conference

Sources: Certification officer various; SERTUC 1997, 2004; Unite 2007.

the post-Amicus merger comprised only 16 percent of the new union. Likewise, Table 11.3 shows the dilution of women's membership from 33 percent of SOGAT '82 to 17 percent in GPMU (Colgan and Ledwith 1996). The most dramatic dilution is seen in the acquisition of the almost exclusively female HVA by MSF in 1990 (Table 11.1), though it has a positive impact on the proportion of women in MSF overall.

Second, a union becoming more male dominated does not mean that pre-merger equality measures are axed or equality measures cannot be established. On the contrary, the cases of TASS, ASTMS, MSF, Amicus, NGA, SOGAT '82, and GPMU (Tables 11.1 to 11.3) illustrate that existing structures remain throughout merger activity. One example of continuity is the passing of the women's committee and conference from MSF into Amicus, despite the fall in women's membership from 31 percent in the pre-merger union to 16 percent in the post-merger union. Likewise, a quota system was introduced within MSF seven years after the merger, and guaranteed proportional representation was introduced in GPMU four years post-merger.

As noted above, internal union politics are influential on the form of post-merger constitutions (Waddington 1995). Case-study research indicates how women activists make alliances with male trade union activists sympathetic to an equal opportunities agenda once mergers reduce the proportion of women members and women activists. Such alliances were noted in the survey and interview responses in Colgan and Ledwith's longitudinal case study (1996, 2000, 2002) of GPMU. This case shows how support for the 1995 rule change for guaranteed proportional representation cut across political views and was linked to the need to recruit and organize a diverse workforce. The GPMU case also indicates how key women in the former partner unions determined that the women's committee of NGA and the women's conference of SOGAT '82 should be embedded in the constitution of the new union (Colgan and Ledwith 1996). Indeed, the period before, during, and after the merger is seen as an opportunity for women to push for change, either because they bring "freshness" or because "we can catch everybody napping while they're all worrying about their lost territory" (Colgan and Ledwith 2002, 171). Case-study research in MSF, which included interviews with ten women from the NEC, however, warns that although consensus alliances may facilitate evolutionary change, they may "inhibit the more contested transformational change" (Healy and Kirton 2000, 358). Indeed, the fierce factional competition noted within MSF was in danger of inhibiting women's influence within the union (Healy and Kirton 2000; Parker 2003). A further potential inhibitor with implications specifically for the influence of black women within the union is indicated by the norm for the MSF national women's committee to be dominated by white women and the national race equality committee to be male dominated (Kirton and

Greene 2002, 166). Hence the paradox that while women and black members are given organizational space to determine their priorities, black women may be organizationally silenced, a concept vividly illustrated by Beverley Johnson and Marie Clarke Walker (Edelson, this volume).

The third observation from Tables 11.1 to 11.4 is the impact of reserved seats. This impact can be seen in the increase in the number of women on the NEC of MSF after a decision in 1995 to use quotas (Table 11.1). It can also be seen in GPMU after a rule change in 1995 to guarantee proportional representation (Table 11.3). A dramatic illustration of the relationship between reserved seats and representation is also apparent in the TGWU, which increased the number of women on its executive by 27 percentage points between 1997 and 2004 through the introduction of reserved seats (Table 11.4). However, this latter rule change was introduced without a merger.

The last observation relates to the declining membership, including post-merger declines, of these unions. Table 11.1 indicates that MSF membership fell from more than 600,000 at amalgamation to 400,000 in 2000, despite the influx of members from the merger with HVA. GPMU also lost membership, from 269,881 at amalgamation in 1991 to 102,088 in 2004 (Table 11.3). This illustrates three points. First, mergers involving unions in contracting sectors of the economy are often defensive reactions to adverse environmental change and do not necessarily have any effect on the pattern of membership decline. Second, although post-merger efficiencies may be generated, the effects of these may be overpowered by environmental effects. Third, although post-merger reform may improve the representation of women, such reforms are no guarantee of increases in the number of women members.

Big Bang Mergers

Considerable study has been conducted on the implications for women's representation of the formation of UNISON in 1993 and of Vereinte Dienstleistungsgewerkschaft (ver.di, the United Services Union) in 2001. Interest in these cases developed for four reasons. First, representatives of UNISON and ver.di used the mergers to attempt to establish new unions that differed fundamentally from their constituent pre-merger parts (Waddington 2005c, 389). Second, a key of being "new" was the attention given to ensuring women's proportional representation. Third, at the time of merger, both amalgamations resulted in the largest unions in their respective countries. Fourth, and related to the above, these two amalgamations have been categorized as "transformative" in that they were not pursued to protect the vested interests of leaders and current members but to address new strategic priorities. Transformative mergers, however, are rare (Behrens, Hurd, and Waddington 2004b).

UNISON

Formed from three public sector unions in 1993 – the Confederation of Health Service Employees (COHSE), the National and Local Government Officers Association (NALGO), and the National Union of Public Employees (NUPE) (see Table 11.5) – UNISON has approximately 1.3 million members, 72 percent of whom are women. At amalgamation it represented about 16.5 percent of trade unionists in the United Kingdom. The following commitments were adopted in the founding Rule Book to support women's representation: proportional representation of women; reservation of seats for low-paid women;[4] fair representation of all members of the electorate; and provision for self-organized groups at national, regional, and branch levels for women, black members, members with disabilities, and lesbian and gay members.

When put together, these commitments represented new opportunities for women's participation and representation. Although NUPE and COHSE used reserved seats to facilitate the access of women to representative structures, proportionality (as a target outcome) was a new feature to all the former partner unions, as was the combination of fair representation and proportionality through seats for women with low pay. Likewise, self-organized groups provided new sources of authority and influence to women members in at least two of the former partner unions. Even in NALGO, the former partner union that had previously supported self-organization, it was not on the same scale as pursued within UNISON.

Despite its radical nature, the issue of guaranteeing effective representation was not central to merger negotiations that concentrated on the distribution of power between lay activists and paid officers, among former partner unions, and between service groups and regions (Fryer 2000; Terry 1996). The end result was a matrix structure with seven vertical service groups and thirteen geographical regions. The self-organized groups are vertical structures where group representation is possible at a regional level. In the run-up to amalgamation, women worked in strategic alliances to achieve constitutional legitimacy for self-organized groups (Colgan and Ledwith 1996) but arguably missed the opportunity to ensure group representation within the service groups or the NEC (McBride 2001b). Post-merger, self-organized groups have negotiated rights of representation at national and regional service group conferences, and self-organized groups now have the opportunity for group representation on the NEC, but only through open election. The study of fifteen representative bodies in UNISON, involving non-participant observation and interviews, indicates how post-merger bargaining surrounded the interpretation and practice of fair representation, and highlights differential impacts and divisions along the lines of class, occupation, former partner union, gender, and race (McBride 2001a). For example, given that low-pay seats were initially attached to annual salary

Table 11.5

Equality structures and women's representation in pre-merger unions COHSE, NALGO, and NUPE, and merged union UNISON

Union/membership/year	% women members	Reserved seats (women)	Equality structures	% women on NEC	% women at national conference
COHSE: 207,841 (1987)	78% (1987-88)	On regional councils	NWC (1991) Equal opportunities committee	15%(1987-88)	
COHSE: 200,000 (1993)	80% (1993)				
NALGO: 758,780 (1987)	51% (1987-88)	NW conf (1989); self-organized groups for black, disabled, and L&G members	36% (1987-88)		
NALGO: 750,000 (1993)	55% (1993)				
NUPE: 650,930 (1987)	67% (1987-88)	1975 introduction	NW Advisory Committee (1984)	50% (1987-88)	
NUPE: 550,000 (1993)	74% (1993)				
COHSE, NALGO, AND NUPE merge to form UNISON in 1993; 1,368,796 members at amalgamation	67% (1993)	Yes with proportionality, includes low-pay seats	NWC; NW conf; self-organization at regional and branch level for women, black, LGBT, and disabled members. Group representation at regional level. Possible at NEC but through open election.	42% interim committee	
UNISON: 1,301,900 (1997)	70% (1997)			65% (1997)	48% (1997)
UNISON: 1,289,000 (2004)	72% (2004)			65% (2004)	56% (2004)

L&G = lesbian and gay; LGBT = lesbian, gay, bisexual, and transgender; NEC = national executive council/committee; NWC = national women's committee; NW conf = national women's conference

Sources: Certification officer various; Colgan and Ledwith 1996; SERTUC 1997, 2004.

rather than an hourly rate, and as black women tend to work full time, low-pay seats as initially prescribed were unlikely to provide black women with specific representational opportunities, despite their overall lower pay. The rules related to the low-pay seats were amended at the 1997 conference, thus enabling more diversity for the seats reserved for low-paid women.

The combination of direct elections, multi-representative constituencies, and seats reserved for women, including low-paid women, pushed and pulled women into representative positions, and limited men's participation (McBride 2001a). At first sight, however, the absence of proportional representation on the NEC in 2004 appears to contradict this (see Table 11.5). The number of reserved seats to enable proportionality was calculated on pre-merger figures, thus women's NEC representation in 2004 (65 percent) is very close to women's representation in the union at the merger (in 1993) of 67 percent. It is only post-merger that the share of women members has risen to 72 percent. Self-organization has also encouraged the participation of new women activists in all four of the aforementioned self-organized groups (Colgan and Ledwith 2002; Humphrey 2002) and a national Black Women's Caucus (Healy, Bradley, and Mukherjee 2004) – choices that were not available in the former partner unions.

Although the proportion of women members is increasing, it is unclear whether these institutional changes attracted more women into the union. Detailed analyses of the total and disaggregated pre- and post-merger membership figures, employment trends in the segments of the economy where UNISON organizes, and the age profile of the membership of the union would be necessary in order to assess the direct impact of these institutional changes. What is clear, however, is that a greater proportion of women union leavers cite some form of dissatisfaction with UNISON as a reason for leaving than do their male counterparts (Waddington and Kerr 1999). In other words, these institutional changes have not been translated into the levels of support, contact, and information that women require at a local level. Notwithstanding the detail of the membership effect within UNISON, Tables 11.1 to 11.4 raise the possibility that other unions have followed UNISON's lead in developing comprehensive structures for encouraging full representation of formerly marginalized groups. More specifically, rule changes to introduce proportionality in MSF and GPMU were passed two years after their introduction in UNISON.

Turning to the impact of UNISON on regaining power on the economic dimension, an Equal Pay Campaign has been conducted since the formation of UNISON that is focused on collective action on low pay and the pursuit of equal pay claims, the latter resulting in numerous legal victories, including a historic award for 1,500 women workers (Thornley 2006). Although not the only union involved, the membership size of UNISON is arguably a factor in regaining some influence over government policy. This can be seen in three ways. First, the pay structures in the National Health Service (NHS) have been radically changed, and changes have been jointly introduced and implemented with the health services unions. Second, unions have played a key role in the continuation of learning accounts in the NHS. These entitle individuals to £150 of training or education per year. Individual learning accounts were introduced across all sectors in the United Kingdom to provide learning opportunities for traditional non-learners but were discontinued (with the exception of the NHS) because of instances of fraudulent administration of the accounts (McBride and Mustchin 2007). Third, earlier government policy, which allowed the subcontracting of work in the public sector, had led to a two-tier workforce where workers working alongside each other were likely to be on different terms and conditions. This possibility has been reduced after continued pressure from public sector unions (Thornley 2006).

Ver.di

Ver.di was formed from five service sector unions in 2001 and represents workers in both public and private sector services in Germany. When ver.di was formed it had a membership of approximately 2.5 million members, which represented 31 percent of trade unionists affiliated with Deutscher Gewerkschaftsbund (DGB, German Trade Union Confederation). Forty-nine percent of ver.di members are women, a higher percentage than in most German unions. Women make up only 32 percent of the membership of the DGB and only Gewerkschaft Erziehung und Wissenschaft (Education and Science Union) has a larger female membership at 67 percent.

Given the concentration of ver.di members in the service sector, the female membership of the five partner unions was relatively high. In 1999, the female membership of the unions was Gewerkschaft Handel, Banken und Versicherungen (Retail, Banking and Insurance Union), 66 percent; Gewerkschaft Öffentliche Dienste, Transport und Verkehr (Public Services, Transport and Traffic Sectors Union), 46 percent; Deutsche Postgewerkschaft (Postal Workers' Union), 44 percent; and Industriegewerkschaft Medien (Media Union), 32 percent. No figures are available for Deutsche Angestellten-Gewerkschaft (Union of Salaried Employees) (Jenter, Tondorf, and Jochmann-Döll 2004). These membership demographics, and a desire to become more attractive to currently unorganized female employees, led ver.di to make proportional representation of men and women binding from its creation, and to be the first German union to implement gender mainstreaming (Keller 2005, 214). During the years that preceded the union's foundation congress, women activists of the merging unions were working out basic structures, and the following statutory regulations were agreed upon (Jenter, Tondorf, and Jochmann-Döll 2004): (1) minimum quotas for women's representation, proportionate to membership, for all bodies and panels (including collective bargaining commissions and delegations); (2) establishment of women's councils at national, regional, and district levels with representation to executive committees, and national collective bargaining committees; (3) representation of women's council interests in executive committees; (4) provision of budget resources for work on women's issues and gender equality; and (5) equal treatment of men and women, a core task at all levels and departments.

Commentators note that this post-merger structure is the most wide-ranging reform of German union government since 1950 (Waddington, Kahmann, and Hoffmann 2005), but there is limited discussion about the provisions for women's representation within the former partner unions and the detail of their negotiation. Instead, authors focus on the matrix structure adopted within ver.di and rules for proportional representation among the former partner unions, which are the outcome of "continuing micro-political bargaining processes and enduring power struggles between rational, self-interested actors" and concerns that the largest partner union would gain too much power in the new union (Keller 2005, 215-16). The union has a matrix structure, with thirteen trade sections running vertically through the union, and three geographical levels running across the union (national, regional, and district) where the women's councils reside. Although the matrix model was intended to address heterogeneity, this has been impeded by the lack of experience in handling such a complex model, the unequal size of the trade sections, and their financial autonomy, which allows some of them to almost act as independent unions (Waddington, Kahmann, and Hoffmann 2005).

Annesley's interviews (2006, 175) with eight ver.di trade union officials (one national and seven regional) prompted the conclusion that ver.di has "fallen short of its goals" for female equality and gender mainstreaming. Only two regional officers claimed that women's issues were being taken seriously and had established posts for women. An east German regional officer indicated that there was resistance to quotas among female members "because they had been socialized with a different understanding of equality" (ibid., 176). Other obstacles included the lack of support given to women "parachuted" into local areas they did not know and women meeting with hostility from established male trade unionists. Given the small size of the study and the complexity of the union, this presents a very partial view, and more material is required from the trade sections and activists on the women's councils.

In contrast to this negative picture, ver.di's "gender card" (Jenter, Tondorf, and Jochmann-Döll 2004, 34) indicates that women have achieved proportionality in several fora, including congress; finance, health, and collective bargaining commissions; and the Trade Negotiation Commission. Figures indicate that women's overall share in collective bargaining commissions is

57 percent, and that the share in negotiation commissions is 52 percent. Among the eight unions affiliated to the DGB, no union had proportional representation on the four fora of congress, executive committee, collective bargaining commission, and negotiation commission, and of those providing data on all four, only ver.di and Industriegewerkschaft Metall (the engineering union), which has about 19 percent female membership, had proportional representation on at least three of these fora.

Mergers, Women's Representation, and Renewal

Although Frege and Kelly (2003, 9) identify mergers as a potential strategy for renewal, the majority of mergers are defensive, rather than the result of a positive strategic choice, and constitute a response to an adverse environmental change or a failure to reform union practices (Waddington 2005a). While trying to survive, such unions have little energy to renew. Myriad factors have been identified as promoting mergers, prominent among which in recent years are membership decline and financial difficulties. It is generally accepted that membership decline results from the influence of external factors such as macro-economic context, the changing composition of the labour force, management resistance, and workplace practices (Mason and Bain 1993; Metcalf 1991) and internal factors including inadequate recruitment campaigns (Kelly 1990; Voos 1984).

The impact of the changing composition of the labour force is particularly marked in countries where unions are organized by industry. In practice, industrial unions cannot extend their recruitment bases to areas of employment growth without generating disputes over jurisdictions. Apart from continuous membership decline and internal cost cutting, an industrial union that represents workers in a contracting industry may thus have no alternative to a merger. In many countries, employment in mining, clothing, textiles, and woodworking industries, for example, has contracted to the extent that, even if density is high, there are insufficient employees to sustain an independent trade union. In this context, union practices might include strategies to reverse membership decline, to introduce forms of representation appropriate to changed circumstances, and to reduce costs. Indeed, in some instances it would appear that a merger was pursued as a means to avoid making difficult decisions on internal union reform (Waddington 2005a).

Taking each of the four dimensions of renewal in turn, Behrens, Hurd, and Waddington (2004b, 131, 132) analyzed the impact of restructuring in four European countries and the United States. Regarding the membership dimension, they concluded that merger activity rarely resulted in union organizing in new areas or indeed intensifying activity in established areas. They did not find any significant evidence of renewal along the economic dimension, and they found little evidence of an associated increase in political influence. Lastly, despite finding examples of restructuring that contributed to institutional vitality, they had to conclude that "structural change in itself does not hold great potential to drive revitalization. Without more substantial progress in the membership, economic, and political dimensions, this institutional progress will have little substantive impact" (ibid., 133).

That said, 3F, ver.di, UNISON, and Unite do represent a significant proportion of union members in Denmark, Germany, and the United Kingdom, and it is worth returning to examine these issues over a longer period post-merger.

Discussion: Where Now?

This chapter has presented a review of material on the relationship between mergers and women's representation. However, the material does not relate to a broad sweep of mergers but only to those mergers where women's participation and representation has been studied. These mergers are by definition exemplar cases that have attracted research interest. Other exemplar cases may still require study, or may not be accessible in English-language texts. Also, these mergers are primarily amalgamations. Material is still required on women's representation in union acquisitions. Nonetheless, this review provides a useful base from which to work.

This research indicates that women have been able to use the circumstances of amalgamation to secure institutional and procedural development toward gender equity. Such development is certainly not universal but in certain circumstances can be marked, as illustrated by the UNISON and ver.di cases. The data presented here suggest that amalgamations that are defined in terms of creating "new" unions, that do not merely adopt the institutions and practices of the pre-merger constituent unions and involve parity or majority women membership, constitute circumstances favourable to developments toward gender equity. This is not to say that women's representation suffers in mergers of male-dominated unions. On the contrary, the material indicates developments in these mergers, too. Moreover, it shows that once equity measures have been established in these unions, there is no reversal of policy; successive mergers retain these aspects. This can be seen in the comprehensive nature of the draft rules for Unite (2007), which is the culmination of many mergers. The politics of merger bargaining in male-dominated unions, however, requires considerable energy. Indeed, all of these cases have shown how women have been agents of change in pre- and post-merger negotiations, making alliances where necessary with other identified factions. In terms of outcomes for women, these can be seen most clearly in the impact of reserved seats, though we appreciate that these can be instituted without mergers, a point to which we return later.

The detail of these mergers underlines the linkages between the institutional, membership, political, and economic dimensions (Behrens, Hamann, and Hurd 2004a) but also confirms that institutional vitality is not sufficient on its own (Behrens, Hurd, and Waddington 2004b). The data on male and female members' decision to leave UNISON provide us with a pertinent reminder that institutional changes need to be translated into the needs of members, particularly women, in the workplace (Waddington and Kerr 1999). In the context of falling membership, is there a danger that these changes, however seemingly radical, are not radical enough for the needs of workers today? As those unions involved in a series of mergers demonstrated, the introduction of institutions and procedures directed toward gender equity may not be sufficient to ensure the independent survival of unions. To the contrary, mergers may be a means to postpone a range of difficult internal union decisions directed toward union survival, such as reducing the number of staff, cutting running costs, shifting resources toward recruitment and organizing, or conceptualizing different organizational forms of unionism. It remains to be seen whether the recent emphasis that unions throughout much of Europe have placed on recruitment and organizing is sufficient to reverse the membership declines of the past twenty-five years.

In conclusion, this preliminary analysis raises a series of questions that require further examination. First, to what extent, if at all, can developments toward gender equity be implemented without amalgamations? All mergers, but particularly amalgamations, disturb vested interests within trade unions. In practice, the key question in this context is, does the disturbance of vested interests create the opportunity for women to progress toward gender equity at a higher rate than otherwise? Examination of gender equity practices in unions that have not engaged in amalgamations and a comparison with those formed through merger is necessary to address this issue. Second, the focus of this chapter has been on the representation of women members within trade unions. Analysis of the impact of mergers on the composition by sex and race of the union leaders and the full-time officer corps, on the character and quality of internal union gender mainstreaming, and on the extent of participation by women in unions is necessary if the relationship between mergers and gender equity is to be examined more fully. Third, do institutional and procedural changes directed toward gender equity attract more women into membership and, if so, what are the most effective features of these changes in attracting new women members? In combination, of course, these questions and the issues raised in this chapter raise a more wide-ranging question, namely, what structures, procedures, and practices are appropriate for all women in trade unions?

Acknowledgment
We would like to thank Kluwer Law International for permission to make use of some material previously presented in Anne McBride and Jeremy Waddington, "Union mergers and gender democracy," *Bulletin of Comparative Labour Relations* 67 (2008): 133-54.

Notes

1   North American practice is to refer to the AFL-CIO (American Federation of Labor and Congress of Industrial Organizations) and the Canadian Labour Congress as union federations, whereas in Europe peak union organizations are referred to as confederations. For the purpose of this chapter the term "confederation" is used throughout.
2   Fagligt Fælles Forbund, Agreement on Fair Representation, 17 October 2006, p. 4. A feature of many mergers is that constitutional or governance arrangements remain in place for a stipulated period after the merger. In practice, such arrangements are interim and subject to post-merger review. The particular circumstances of the 3F merger, namely, the involvement of the women-only KAD, result in these interim arrangements referring specifically to an issue concerned with the representation of women.
3   In most European countries, the local unit of union organization is the union branch, rather than the union local, as in North America. The branch chair is thus the person elected to chair meetings of the branch during his or her tenure.
4   Within UNISON, the seats for women with low pay are reserved for women who earn below a defined basic hourly rate. This rate is uprated annually by the increase in median earnings, as defined by the Annual Survey of Hours and Earnings in the October immediately preceding the election. As at October 2007, the rate is £7.25 per hour. The rate excludes all supplements, such as overtime.

References

Annesley, C. 2006. Ver.di and trade union revitalisation in Germany. *Industrial Relations Journal* 37, 2: 164-79.
Behrens, M., K. Hamann, and R. Hurd. 2004a. Conceptualizing labour union revitalization. In *Varieties of Unionism: Strategies for Union Revitalization in a Globalizing Economy,* ed. C.M. Frege and J. Kelly, 11-30. Oxford: Oxford University Press.
Behrens, M., R. Hurd, and J. Waddington. 2004b. How does restructuring contribute to union revitalization? In *Varieties of Unionism: Strategies for Union Revitalization in a Globalizing Economy,* ed. C.M. Frege and J. Kelly, 117-36. Oxford: Oxford University Press.
Brah, A., and A. Phoenix. 2004. Ain't I a woman? Revising intersectionality. *Journal of International Women's Studies* 5, 3: 75-86.
Chaison, G. 1996. *Union Mergers in Hard Times.* Ithaca, NY: Cornell University Press.
–. 2001. Union mergers and union revival. In *Rekindling the Movement: Labor's Quest for Relevance in the 21st Century,* ed. L. Turner, H. Katz, and R. Hurd, 238-55. Ithaca, NY: Cornell University Press.
Colgan, F., and S. Ledwith. 1996. Sisters organising: Women and their trade unions. In *Women in Organizations: Challenging Gender Politics,* ed. S. Ledwith and F. Colgan, 152-85. Basingstoke, UK: Macmillan.
–. 2000. Diversity, identities and strategies of women trade union activists. *Gender, Work and Organization* 7, 4: 242-57.
–. 2002. Gender, diversity and mobilisation in UK trade unions. In *Gender, Diversity and Trade Unions: International Perspectives,* ed. F. Colgan and S. Ledwith, 154-85. Abingdon, UK: Routledge.
Due, J., and J-S. Madsen. 2005. The survival of small trade unions in the context of centralised bargaining. In *Restructuring Representation: The Merger Process and Trade Union Structural Development in Ten Countries,* ed. J. Waddington, 87-112. Brussels: P.I.E.-Peter Lang.
Frege, C.M., and J. Kelly. 2003. Introduction: Union revitalization strategies in comparative perspective. *European Journal of Industrial Relations* 9, 1: 7-24.

Fryer, B. 2000. The making of UNISON: A framework to review key events, processes and issues. In *Redefining Public Sector Unionism,* ed. M. Terry, 23-48. London: Routledge.

Garcia, A. 2002. *Women in Trade Unions: Making the Difference.* Brussels: European Trade Union. http://ww.etuc.org/IMG/pdf/genre_an_080403.pdf.

Hacourt, B., and A. Garcia. 1999. *The Second Sex of European Trade Unionism.* Brussels: European Trade Union Confederation.

Hansen, L-L. 2006. Fair representation and gender equality in 3F: A new trade union in the making. Paper presented at the Women and Trade Unions Round Table seminar, Ruskin College, Oxford.

Healy, G., H. Bradley, and N. Mukherjee. 2004. Inspiring activists: The experience of minority ethnic women in trade unions. In *The Future of Worker Representation,* ed. G. Healy, E. Heery, P. Taylor, and W. Brown, 103-26. Basingstoke, UK: Palgrave Macmillan.

Healy, G., and G. Kirton. 2000. Women, power and trade union government in the UK. *British Journal of Industrial Relations* 38, 3: 343-60.

Humphrey, J. 2002. *Towards a Politics of the Rainbow: Self-organization in the Trade Union Movement.* Aldershot, UK: Ashgate.

ILO (International Labour Organization). 2001. *Promoting Gender Equality: A Resource Kit for Trade Unions.* Geneva: International Labour Organization. http://www.ilo.org/public/english/employment/gems/eeo/tu/cha_2.htm.

Jenter, A., K. Tondorf, and A. Jochmann-Döll. 2004. *Equal Participation of Women and Men in Trade Unions.* Final report to the DGB (Germany). http://www.ugt.es/Mujer/proyectoeuropeo/informedgbeng.pdf.

Keller, B. 2005. Union formation through merger: The case of Ver.di in Germany. *British Journal of Industrial Relations* 43, 2: 209-32.

Kelly, J. 1990. British trade unionism 1979-89: Change, continuity and contradictions. *Work, Employment and Society* 4 (special issue): 29-65.

Kirton, G., and A-M. Greene. 2002. The dynamics of positive action in UK trade unions. *Industrial Relations Journal* 33, 2: 157-72.

Kirton, G., and G. Healy. 1999. Transforming union women: The role of women trade union officials in union renewal. *Industrial Relations Journal* 30, 1: 31-45.

LO (Landsorganisationen i Danmark). 2005. *LO's Equal Opportunities' Accounts for 2005.* Copenhagen: Landsorganisationen i Danmark.

Mason, B., and P. Bain. 1993. The determinants of trade union membership in Britain: A survey of the literature. *Industrial and Labor Relations Review* 46, 2: 332-51.

McBride, A. 2001a. *Gender Democracy in Trade Unions.* Aldershot, UK: Ashgate.

–. 2001b. Making it work: Supporting group representation in a liberal democratic organization. *Gender, Work and Organization* 8, 4: 412-29.

McBride, A., and S. Mustchin. 2007. A beneficial combination? Learning opportunities from union involvement in career and pay progression. In *Learning with Trade Unions: A Contemporary Agenda in Employment Relations,* ed. S. Shelley and M. Calveley, 81-100. Aldershot, UK: Ashgate.

Metcalf, D. 1991. British unions: Dissolution or resurgence? *Oxford Review of Economic Policy* 7, 1: 18-32.

Munro, A. 1999. *Women, Work and Trade Unions.* London: Mansell.

Parker, J. 2002. Women's groups in British unions. *British Journal of Industrial Relations* 40, 1: 23-48.

–. 2003. We're on a road to somewhere: Women's groups in unions. *Industrial Relations Journal* 34, 2: 164-84.

SERTUC. 1997. *Inching (Extremely Slowly) Towards Equality.* London: Southern and Eastern Regional Trades Union Congress.

–. 2004. *Waving Not Drowning.* London: Southern and Eastern Regional Trades Union Congress.

Silvera, R. 2004. *The Challenge of Mainstreaming for Trade Unions in Europe.* Brussels: European Commission. http://ec.europa.eu/research/social-sciences/knowledge/projects/article_3517_en.htm.

Sverke, M., and A. Sjöberg. 1997. Short-term union merger effects on member attitudes and behaviour. In *The Future of Unionism,* ed. M. Sverke, 247-60. Aldershot, UK: Ashgate.

Terry, M. 1996. Negotiating the government of unison: Union democracy in theory and practice. *British Journal of Industrial Relations* 34, 1: 87-110.

Thornley, C. 2006. Unequal and low pay in the public sector. *Industrial Relations Journal* 37, 4: 344-58.

TUC (Trades Union Congress). 2005. *TUC Equality Audit 2005.* London: Trades Union Congress.

Unite. 2007. *Schedule General Rules.* http://www.amicustheunion.org/PDF/newunion_generalrules14dec06.pdf.

Voos, P. 1984. Trends in union organizing expenditures, 1953-1977. *Industrial and Labor Relations Review* 36, 2: 576-91.

Waddington, J. 1995. *The Politics of Bargaining.* London: Mansell.

–. 2005a. *Restructuring Representation: The Merger Process and Trade Union Structural Development in Ten Countries.* Brussels: P.I.E. – Peter Lang.

–. 2005b. Charting the dimensions of the merger process. In *Restructuring Representation: The Merger Process and Trade Union Structural Development in Ten Countries,* ed. J. Waddington, 11-44. Brussels: P.I.E. – Peter Lang.

–. 2005c. Conclusions: What difference has the merger process made? In *Restructuring Representation: The Merger Process and Trade Union Structural Development in Ten Countries,* ed. J. Waddington, 375-92. Brussels: P.I.E. – Peter Lang.

–. 2006. The trade union merger process in Europe: Defensive adjustment or strategic reform? *Industrial Relations Journal* 37, 6: 630-51.

Waddington, J., M. Kahmann, and J. Hoffmann. 2005. *A Comparison of the Trade Union Merger Process in Britain and Germany.* London: Routledge.

Waddington, J., and A. Kerr. 1999. Trying to stem the flow: Membership turnover in the public sector. *Industrial Relations Journal* 30, 3: 184-96.

Willman, P. 2004. Structuring unions: The administrative rationality of collective action. In *Union Organization and Activity,* ed. J. Kelly and P. Willman, 73-88. London: Routledge.

12
Old Tracks, New Maps?
The Meaning of Women's Groups
for Trade Union Revival in Britain
Jane Parker

The decline of UK trade unions is a familiar story. Mass unemployment, privatization, and deindustrialization in the 1980s were followed by the pressures introduced by globalization and a reluctance on the part of the Labour government (in power since 1997) to reverse the anti-trade union legislation introduced by its Conservative predecessors. The hemorrhage of members from unions, particularly in male-dominated, private manufacturing workplaces, has proved extremely difficult to remedy by organizing in new sectors and workplaces (Machin 2000). From a peak of 12.2 million in 1980, Trades Union Congress (TUC) affiliate membership almost halved by the mid-1990s and continued to drop until reaching a plateau at around 6.5 million in recent years, despite robust employment growth over the last decade. Women are now more likely to belong to a union than men, reflecting both a feminization of the workforce and the retreat of trade unionism into the public sector. Female membership density was 29.7 percent in 2006, according to the official Labour Force Survey, slightly higher than the 27.2 percent for men. However, fewer than one in six (16.6 percent) of private sector employees was a union member, compared with almost three in five (58.8 percent) in the public sector (for equivalent Canadian statistics, see Wall, this volume).

This highlights the importance of union revitalization strategies and the need to address the concerns of the female workforce and membership. The growth of women's groups (WGs) since the 1970s, which was originally associated with the influence of feminist/social movement organizing and equality ideas, advances in equality law, and recognition through formal union equality policies of women's growing labour market and union presence, is increasingly associated with trade union revitalization.[1] The most common forms of WG include women's committees, conferences, courses and workshops, discussion circles and, more recently, virtual networks (see also the WG examples examined by Fonow and Franzway, this volume). The objective of this chapter is to examine the nature of WGs in British unions and to assess their meaning for key union revival strategies, drawing on evidence from two national union surveys, qualitative interviews, and union/ WG documentation.

Union Revival Strategies

As Jan Kainer discusses in Chapter 1, unions have employed a range of revival strategies. In the UK setting, five approaches are commonly identified in the literature.

Organizing and Recruitment

Organizing and recruitment have always been natural trade union priorities, but more recent is the strategic adoption of a US-style organizing model (Heery and Adler 2004). In 1996, the TUC launched its New Unionism project to promote a return to grassroots union involvement, followed by the establishment of the Organizing Academy in 1998. However, it remains difficult to identify a significant "organizing union" (e.g., Wills 2001). Research suggests that most organizing and recruiting activity is aimed at consolidation rather than revitalization as such (Baccaro, Hamann, and Turner 2003; Heery, Kelly, and Waddington 2003), which is perhaps not too surprising given its resource intensity and limited legal support for trade union recognition campaigns.

Labour-Management Cooperation

Since 1997, the Labour government has sought to promote labour-management partnerships that emphasize cooperation over adversarialism (Martinez Lucio and Stuart 2002). The government has provided financial support through its Partnership at Work Fund, and the TUC has responded by setting up the Partnership Institute to provide advice and consultancy to employers and unions alike. Estimates of partnership arrangements in Britain vary greatly. However, assessments of their impacts on union membership and bargaining power are generally negative (Fichter and Greer 2004; Kelly 2004), and the introduction of limited consultation rights via the Information and Consultation of Employees Regulations 2004 is not thought to have made much difference (e.g., Hall et al. 2007; Terry 2003).

Restructuring

Union mergers and amalgamations have been a significant development in Britain over the past decade (Arrowsmith 2004). Much of this is defensive, driven by membership decline and associated financial weakness, with larger unions tending to extend their membership bases via mergers *and* recruitment efforts (e.g., Waddington, Kahmann, and Hoffman 2003). At the same time, internal restructuring has been partly designed to help renewal efforts, in political terms, by enhancing union representation of member diversity and thus organizing capacity (e.g., via WGs, reserved seats, identity groups, proportionality goals, alliances with identity and equality groups; see Clarke Walker, this volume, on organizing by workers of colour within and beyond the Canadian union movement). Administrative changes have emphasized efficiency, new management techniques and budgetary control (e.g., market research and the targeting of potential member groups, use of e-technology to improve services, replacement of formal standing committees with campaign- and duration-specific task groups). However, there is little evidence that any of this has had a real impact on reducing union bureaucracy, improving efficiency, or increasing membership overall (e.g., Behrens, Hurd, and Waddington 2004; Fichter and Greer 2004; McBride and Waddington, this volume).

Political Engagement

Unions have had a stronger political voice in the twelve years since the Labour Party was first elected. This has delivered gains such as the country's first national minimum wage and the transposition of European Union (EU) law such as that which governs working time. However, much of this has been cautious and weak in order for the governing party to maintain its pro-business face, and the laws governing industrial action and statutory trade union recognition are particularly limited and constraining (Dickens and Hall 2006). Notwithstanding limited gains (Hamann and Kelly 2003), the British labour movement has been unable to position itself as a major political actor with whom the government must interact, despite lobbying becoming an increasingly vital part of the policy-making process, and even though it provides a large part of Labour Party funding.

Alliance Building

British union coalition activity has traditionally been confined to political activity or enterprise-level partnerships. Increasingly relevant are alliances with non-labour or non-government institutions represented by feminist, community, human rights, welfare, peace, environmental, and anti-globalization groups. However, this activity remains limited in the British context. Although the union renewal literature emphasises the significance of coalition building for union revitalization (see Briskin's analysis, this volume), British unions' internationalism is underdeveloped in practice (e.g., Cumbers 2004; Parker 2008), and community unionism is often an "add-on" activity focused on ad hoc events such as factory closures (Wills 2001). However, Baccaro, Hamann, and Turner (2003) note that external social group bodies were important allies in the fight against privatization and the contracting out of public services during the last Conservative administration, and may again become so given current battles around further privatization and the quality of public services.

Research done thus far indicates that British union revival strategies are varied but without significant impact. Union decline has prompted energetic reinvigoration efforts, within and without the labour movement, but weakness begets weakness. Reduced membership numbers, financial resources, and political influence make it difficult for unions to reach out. However, revival is not merely about quantitative outcomes. One implication of the literature is that the qualitative processes that deliver the very confidence, energy, and self-belief that also help build membership and influence are frequently neglected. In other words, unions need to look inward as well as outward, emphasizing the value of members' involvement beyond traditional activism, and reaching out to build alliances where their presence may be weak.

WGs and Union Revitalization

Identity-based organizing has been used as one such approach to help increase membership and its mobilizing capacity (e.g., Flynn et al. 2004), with WGs forming the most widespread form of identity-based organizing within British unions (Parker 2003). Case evidence indicates that certain WGs act as agents for change in their promotion of equality and democracy approaches that inform union organization, such that unions not only come to numerically represent diverse constituencies but also empower those groups to better pursue their interests via the union (e.g., Colgan and Ledwith 2002).

Unsurprisingly, WGs have encountered opposition from those who, in privileging so-called common working-class interests over the interests of particular member groups, view WGs as a threat to union cohesion and strength. As a result, WGs – like their unions – expend considerable energy guarding against the active reversal or withering away of their achievements (Parker 2006). Indeed, in the face of such constraints, some commentators convey the broad impression that WGs have made little inroad on union thinking or the movement's public image (e.g., Aldred 1981; Cockburn 1995), while recent case work specifically emphasizes WG impacts on women's development and union representation (e.g., Colgan and Ledwith 2000; Healy and Kirton 2000).

Drawing on survey and qualitative sources, this study thus shifts the analytical lens to consider the meaning of WGs for the nature and furtherance of each of the five union revival strategies identified above.

Research Method

Data from two national union postal surveys, semi-structured interviews, and documentary evidence enabled in-depth exploration of the relationships between WGs and different union strategies. The first survey, distributed in November 2004, sought an official response from senior union and equality officials across all of the then seventy-one TUC affiliates about the nature of any WGs in their union. Combined with supplementary material from a Southern and Eastern Region Trades Union Congress Women's Rights Committee survey (SERTUC WRC 2004), it yielded data on at least 142 WGs in twenty-seven of fifty-six respondent unions (e.g., a 79 percent union response rate, covering 98.7 percent of members) (see Table 12.1).[2] The TUC Women's Equality Department helped circulate a second survey in April 2005 to equality officers in all unions with WGs, who then forwarded it to officials, paid and lay representatives, and activists. This questionnaire canvassed views about WG impacts in relation to union revitalization. Forty-six respondents from eight affiliates completed this survey, conjointly commenting on at least eighteen WGs.[3] The highest level of responses to the second survey (fourteen) came from the Public and Commercial Services (PCS) union. Further qualitative research was conducted using as a case study PCS, which comprises a national women's forum (NWF), group-level women's advisory committees (WACs), and, after recent efforts to reinvigorate local WG arrangements, a growing number of branch (local) women's advisory committees (BWACs). Between April and August 2005, semi-structured interviews were conducted with ten PCS survey respondents and a further fifteen union contacts suggested by them. Interviewees included officials, activists, and lay representatives from all levels of the union, who also facilitated access to various documentary sources. Thematic analysis of WG data from the above sources was structured according to the five key forms of union revival strategy highlighted above, each of which was underpinned by constructs drawn from the literature and empirical material to enable an examination of whether WGs contribute to existing strategies and/or develop or enlarge their range.

Key Findings

Organizing and Recruitment

Respondents from twenty-four affiliates supplied reasons for the establishment of their union's "most significant" WGs. Based on data for at least sixty-two WGs located in these unions, it emerged that most were conceived almost equally as a result of recognized union organizing strategy and as a response to related growing rank-and-file consciousness of the need to better serve (women's) members' interests via special representation. In a number of unions, for instance, WGs were seen as "providing a key opportunity for mainstreaming equality issues via wage and collective bargaining structures," according to a National Union for Journalists senior official.[4] By WG type, organizing and representation and internal reform strategy were cited almost equally as the key rationale for establishing many women's committees, conferences, and task groups, while women's courses and networks were

Table 12.1

Women's group types in TUC affiliates

Union level:
☐ National
▨ Other

Union	Committee	Conference	Course	Network	Email network	Seminar/meeting	Branch (local)	Informal self-organized group[1]	Section	Working/task/support group/caucus
Amicus	• •	• •	•							
ASLEF	•		•			•				
AUT	•					•			•	•
CATU	•					•				
Community	• •	•	○			•				
Connect				•	•					
CWU	• •	•	•• •						•	
EIS	•								•	
Equity	•					•				
FBU	• •••	• •	• ••	•	••	•	• ••	•	•	• •
GMB	•		•							
GPMU	•	•	• •			•				
NAPO	••					•				
NASUWT	••		•• •							
NATFHE	•	•	•• •	•		•	•	•	•	•
NUJ	•		•							
NUT	•		• •	•		•	•		•	
PCS	••[2] •••		• ••			••			•	•
POA	•									
Prospect				••						
RMT	•	••	○							
TGWU	•	••[3]	•							
TSSA			•						•	•
Unifi	•			•						
UNISON	•	•	• •	• •			•	•	• ••	•
USDAW	•	•[3]	•							
Total	21 26≥	15≥ 3≥	17≥ 10≥	7 3≥	4≥	10	5≥	1≥	1≥ 2≥ 2	8 6≥

Note: Union n = 26, WG n ≥ 142, where D = divisional and R = regional.

1 This type of WG recorded by the union and WG survey respondents constitutes the only informal WG form in the sense of not being sanctioned by the host union and conducting its activity independently of formal union operations.

2 Double or triple dots in a cell indicate more than one WG at national level, or WGs at more than one sub-national level. A hollow dot indicates a planned WG at the time of the survey.

3 Eight regional and seven divisional women's committees in TGWU and USDAW, respectively.

List of Unions

Amicus	Largest private sector union (second largest UK union, now part of Unite)
ASLEF	Associated Society of Locomotive Engineers and Firemen
AUT	Association of University Teachers (now part of the University and College Union)
CATU	Ceramic and Allied Trades Union (now Unity)
Community	Steel, clothing, and betting industries union
Connect	Union for professionals in communications
CWU	Communication Workers Union
EIS	Educational Institute of Scotland
Equity	Actors' trade union (formerly British Actors' Equity Association)
FBU	Fire Brigades Union
GMB	Britain's general trade union (formerly General Municipal Boilermakers)
GPMU	Graphical, Paper and Media Union (now part of Amicus)
NAPO	National Association of Probation Officers
NASUWT	National Association of Schoolmasters, Union of Women Teachers
NATFHE	National Association of Teachers in Further and Higher Education (now part of University and College Union)
NUJ	National Union of Journalists
NUT	National Union of Teachers
PCS	Public and Commercial Services Union
POA	Prison Officers' Association UK
Prospect	Engineers, managers, specialists, and scientists' union
RMT	National Union of Rail, Maritime and Transport Workers
TGWU	Transport and General Workers' Union (now part of Unite)
TSSA	Transport and Salaried Staff Association
Unifi	Banking and insurance union (now part of Amicus)
UNISON	Britain's public service union
USDAW	Union for Shop, Distributive and Allied Workers

more likely to be regarded as supporting general union organizing efforts. PCS's NWF and group WACs were said to put their weight behind "mainstream" issue-based union campaigns on pay, pensions, job losses in the civil service, and relocation, while asking, "What's our perspective?" And women's networks of Prospect (the engineers, managers, specialists, and scientists' union), whose principal role is advisory, similarly support union campaigns, including those that impact differentially on women and men (e.g., equal pay, women's position in the science and engineering sector). More generally, related activities include information dissemination to (women) members about union policy; consciousness raising activities about the implications of issues for different constituencies; training provision on certain concerns (e.g., domestic violence) through branches to all representatives; and seeking to develop debate to inform union executive decisions.

WGs, particularly committees and support and working groups, also lend support to national union conventions that are, to some extent, concerned with organizing and recruitment. This includes holding fringe meetings at their union's annual conference with the aim of supporting women delegates and helping them to organize in the workplace. For example, the PCS WAC's "meeting at Inland Revenue Group conference helps networking, and supports new women delegates, particularly from smaller branches which are only due one conference delegate," as one PCS Inland Revenue Group WAC member explained. Many individual WG members were reported to recognize the importance of recruitment, organizing, and income generation to ensure union vibrancy, and more experienced union women often mentor female newcomers to "learn the [existing union] ropes."

The decentralization of collective bargaining in Britain, including in the public services, also appears to have raised the profile of some WGs. PCS now hosts a growing number of BWACs that have close links to local union campaigns and organizing drives. Similarly in USDAW, the shopworkers' union, one senior full-time officer felt that this involvement encourages a greater sense of union ownership among female members, which was vital given the union's focus on the retail sector, where labour and member turnover is high. In the TSSA, the transport sector union, the regional Women in Focus (WiF) committee network has "gendered" local organizing initiatives by, for example, encouraging women members to attend union meetings in the form of small groupings at their homes. These initiatives have helped a number of women overcome child care and other obstacles to their participation in regular union meetings. The initiatives are thus regarded as "vital for helping women's union participation," a TSSA WiF member said, both in the mainstream and via their own fora such as women's conferences and courses. Typical of informants in other unions with WGs, for instance, a member from the former print union, GPMU (now part of Amicus), singled out its national women's conference as an important environment for enabling "the breadth of women members ... to meet and be encouraged to begin or continue organizing." At this and women's conferences elsewhere, the activities (e.g., small group role play, workshops), the direct relevance of the topics under discussion, and the highly supportive space at the fora where women feel able to ask questions and receive insights about organizing in the union, were all seen to provide momentum for women's politicization, mobilization, and organization.

As well as directly augmenting mainstream union organizing and recruitment, WGs were generally seen by informants to contribute to such via the substantive issues they raise to mainstream union platforms. Although several senior officials pointed out that WGs have experienced varying levels of success in terms of whether their mainstream union prioritizes or even takes up their specific approaches and interests, respondents to the first survey indicated that for at least ninety-one WGs across fourteen affiliates, the number and range of interests and concerns that had been raised to national union agendas and negotiations had increased in recent years. Further, just over half (representing eight unions) perceived that several issues, including equal and low pay, had become union priorities and likely to be presented as general rather than women-only matters. Other increasingly high-profile issues were said to include domestic violence, sexual harassment, bullying, flexible working, parental leave, and child care.

It emerged from the second survey and interviews that WGs were often perceived to contribute to member recruitment, both directly and by supporting wider union efforts. Local, decentralized WGs were considered to be particularly well placed for encouraging women to join and become active. TSSA's WiF network asserted that WiF groups have "made real progress in ensuring that [the union] continues to grow" but also noted "the need for us to continue to invest adequate resources to build sustainable activity of women throughout the movement" (TSSA WiF 2007, 1). Furthermore, as with organizing more generally, WGs have helped to "gender" or feminize elements of union recruiting processes, and sometimes their outcomes. For example, USDAW's Divisional Women's Committee members combine their meetings with workplace "walkabouts" in order to speak with employees on the job. While this helps them to engage both male and female potential members, the predominance of women in many of these workplaces (e.g., large supermarkets) means that activity akin to "like by like" recruitment and organizing takes place. Perhaps significantly, however, informants did not discuss WGs' contributions to union organizing and recruitment strategies in relation to the pursuit of recognition with employers, a key goal of such strategies. This might suggest that they are best able to contribute where the union is already established.

Restructuring

Analysis revealed that union mergers, a familiar activity in the contemporary British union movement, have often led to the introduction of or reforms to WG arrangements. For example, a national secretary in Community (the steel, clothing, and betting industries union) wrote that the formation of his union from a merger in 2004 of the male-dominated Iron and Steel Trades Confederation and the female-dominated National Union of Knitted, Footwear and Apparel Trades (KFAT) supported the arrival of WGs. The formation of PCS via mergers in 1998 was reported to have necessitated a review of its organization, with new structures, including WGs, put in place at all levels. By contrast, respondents from the former GPMU were concerned that the then imminent merger with Amicus, the largest private sector union, would mean that its existing WGs would not be transferred to new organizational arrangements, thereby "squeezing" women from mainstream posts.[5] The situation was resolved in PCS by a softening of the WG's formal status to reduce potential opposition to their continuation. As the union's head of equalities noted, "It's called NWF due to the merger and some resistance to the word 'committee' for having a formal status. Forum was a looser, more acceptable term ... The leadership, from various constituent parts, was more comfortable with this."

As well as merger activity, survey and interview evidence revealed that WGs have played a role in furthering union restructuring, for example, by injecting "new" or different principles for democratic organization (e.g., via identity-based structures and politics). Underscoring connections between restructuring and organizing revival strategies, this development was often seen to link to decentralization of union decision making and procedures, in turn supporting the introduction of local-level WGs (e.g., in PCS and TSSA). It also emerged that a number of WGs have become increasingly institutionalized within their union setting. The first survey found that all of the nineteen well-established WGs (mostly national-level committees, conferences, and support groups) were eventually formally incorporated via constitutional clauses, and respondents said that this helped to sanction WG access to union resources.

Only four WGs reported by survey respondents were able to make policy, and most of at least twenty-seven WGs (including committees, networks, conferences, and a task group) in sixteen unions were elevated to advisory status only. Nevertheless, the formal inclusion of WGs at a union's national organizational level also led in numerous cases to the introduction of more structures locally. For instance, as part of the former Association of University Teachers' (now part of the University and College Union) campaigning strategy, the union's National Women's Committee (NWC) helped to support WG establishment in local associations. The enthusiasm of regional women's officers (RWOs) and active regional women's committees in UNISON (the largest public sector union) was emphasized as stimuli for and coordinators of the development of existing and additional WGs. The TSSA's national WiF provided part of the catalyst for regional WiFs because, noted a TSSA National WiF member, "regional women-only spaces ... enable more women to become active within the union." This was, of course, more difficult in male-dominated unions, but some reluctance was also reported on the part of women themselves in these settings. For instance, another national WiF member from the TSSA commented that some younger women members in the union hold the view that "they will get on by merit and don't need a specialist WG," while the director of organization and development in Connect, the communications professionals union, commented on a "lack of motivation from women members [in her union] – they don't like to acknowledge discrimination in the workplace until they become victims of it ... They press the union towards a servicing model rather than an organizing model on equality matters."

Nonetheless, it also emerged that WGs have been bound up with initiatives to enhance the representation of particular constituent groups on mainstream union structures. Indeed, data from the first survey showed that for at least seventy-four WGs from twenty-five unions, the most common union-centred pursuits have been women's union representation and presence, union organizing and participation by women, and changes to structures and procedures to help women access their union. Their more informal and participative mode of operation, relative to traditional union structures, was commonly considered a role model and facilitating factor in this regard. For instance, one TSSA WiF member felt that "hierarchy and power struggles don't seem to exist within WiF, though it's early days ... There're no strict roles – everyone does what they can or feel comfortable with – you can volunteer to be chair or whatever." Similarly, a PCS BWAC member commented, "Committees put off women who don't engage with points of order, etc. We've found members are much more likely to engage [with a lunchtime meeting] on a single issue than sit through a tedious, twenty-item agenda when they've time pressures." One UNISON regional women's committee member cited "union objectives and priorities" as a key influence on the type of issues pursued by women's groups in her union.

Further, in the broadcasting and entertainment union, BECTU (the Broadcasting Entertainment Cinematograph and Theatre Union), a women's conference attendee said that WG operations broadly differ from national, mixed-sex union structures, since they are "less procedural," operate on the basis of "consensus not competition," and "are concerned with issues affecting all women – not just there for individual reasons." Similarly, in UNISON, a UNISON regional women's officer noted, it was felt that WGs are "better at reaching consensus." By raising women's interests and helping women to better engage with union channels to pursue their interests, WGs were thus seen by their supporters as vehicles for advancing union revitalization in terms of membership inclusivity and participation. This was thought to have various spillover effects, as WGs network to share experiences, as WG members advance into the mainstream, and as some mainstream bodies have sought to apply the approaches of WGs (e.g., rotating positions, non-hierarchical networking, less formal practices) to their work in order to raise levels of member engagement, mobilization, and procedural efficiency.

Alliance Building, Political Engagement, and Labour-Management Cooperation

Analysis of the survey, interview, and documentary evidence indicates that many of the WGs under examination have become increasingly involved in networking and coalition-building activity. Informants indicated that this broad development has occurred both as a matter of policy and in order to offer practical on-the-ground help for issues such as domestic violence and refuges within local communities. PCS interviewees in particular often related how WGs conceive of themselves as constituent parts of a larger women's network within and beyond their union setting, so it seems natural for them to have relationships with identity-based bodies such as the UK Women's Aid and Refuge, a national domestic violence charity and network of safe houses for women and children. Similarly, the TSSA's WGs campaign jointly with the National Childminding Association, as well as with women's health and safety organizations (e.g., the Suzy Lamplugh Trust for personal safety). Drug- and youth-crime-related issues were also common community concerns that saw WGs link up with local activist and government rehabilitation schemes. This emphasizes how WGs can be engaged in certain operations and causes relatively independently from their unions. For example, an ex-member of the Writers' Guild of Great Britain recalled how the small union had been unable to formally support the miners during the 1984 strike because of its non-political status and "the opposition of Thatcherite members," but its NWC contacted miners' wives directly and collected money to help their families survive.

Many WGs were also shown to be involved in alliances within institutions and parties in the wider labour movement, including identity-based TUC bodies such as the Black TUC Conference and Women's Conference, as well as various political structures and trades councils. These linkages and jointly organized initiatives straddle various workplace-, union-, and "other"-centred interests. Further, one PCS NWF member pointed out that these links and joint activities often have practical benefits for WGs and union vitality; for instance, "the theme of the TUC Women's Conference in 2005 was women's organizing. We learned from women in other unions and the TUC about attracting and mobilizing women in group activities designed to respond to their specific needs."

According to the evidence, many WGs coalesce with a range of local through international organizations and movements whose interests and campaigns encompass or intersect only in part with workplace concerns. Common examples of areas of WG alliances and alliance partners include internationalism and globalization, the environment (e.g., with Greenpeace), politics and peace (e.g., with Cuba Solidarity), and human and women's rights (e.g., with Amnesty International). Specific WG alliances with these bodies are sometimes reinforced by their union's wider links with the same organizations and related networks. For instance, WGs in the former National Association of Teachers in Further and Higher Education (now part of the University and College Union) and the union itself have supported Amnesty International's campaigns to counter violence against women and raise issues to do with women and poverty, asylum seeking, child labour, and international human rights. WG external activity was reported to have increased in about half of the unions with WGs, a finding that appears to fit with other research reporting that a "new generation" of union representatives (particularly women, black, and ethnic minority groups) were seen by senior TUC officials to be helping to develop understanding of the need for practices involving the TUC and its affiliates in civil and government alliances (Parker 2008).

However, most informants in this study perceived that the direct impact of such WG activity in terms of union revival was difficult to establish and, indeed, that this was not necessarily the purpose of all alliance-building initiatives. However, the process was certainly considered to be educational and empowering for those involved, with implications for future union vitality. For instance, a TSSA National WiF member commented, "The WiF hasn't made an enormous impact externally yet because it's a new union group. But we've given members more confidence in their own ideas, and introduced people who'd normally never have got involved in the wider women's movement ... Our links with sister organizations, other interest groups, and national movements are strengthening. Those ties are helping the WiF to grow."

On the other hand, a number of informants stressed that their WGs actively opted to contain their coalition activity. This was partly because of resource constraints, but it also reflected an attitude of wanting to "focus on and do what they do well," as one USDAW Divisional Women's Committee member put it, in order to better service, organize, and retain their existing support base. For instance, in the context of the then imminent merger with Amicus, a GPMU NWC respondent stressed how her union's WGs were simply trying to "consolidate and build on previous work, trying to ensure, through the women's conference and branch activities, that new people are involved ... [and] to build and strengthen the equality networks."

Finally, none of the data sources specified WG objectives or membership in relation to union revitalization via labour-management cooperation or partnership. This omission might stress difficulties with assessing the character or impacts of partnership arrangements; a perception that they do not equally empower all the parties that they involve and lack teeth in union renewal terms; or that union involvement in partnerships has thus far concerned national-level and mainstream union officers and structures. Indeed, recent case research on the information and consultation arrangements for employees in UK workplaces shows little to suggest that gender-based identities and union organizing forms inform the selection or election of information and consultation representatives in unionized settings (e.g., Hall et al. 2007).

Discussion and Conclusions

This research reveals that WGs are widely seen by their "insiders" to contribute to union revival efforts via organizing, recruiting, and internal reform, though it is difficult to measure or quantify their impact in these terms. Further, they are also regarded as valuable conduits for the dissemination of a wider gender or diversity consciousness within their union hosts, and for directly providing more effective voice mechanisms for neglected constituencies in traditional union structures. Indeed, unions can learn from WG ways of organizing and representing members, which are commonly marked by a level of informality, adaptability, and grassroots responsiveness that is less alienating than sometimes overly rule-bound procedures. The study also draws attention to a tendency for many WGs, as identity-based, activist networks, to develop alliances and links with labour and non-labour external parties, political and otherwise. This presents another opportunity for unions to benefit from closer links to the wider community, and the inward flow of fresh ideas, issues, and experiences. The apparent absence of a connection between WGs and labour-management cooperation or partnership arrangements contrasts with evidence of links between WGs and other union revival strategies. This could reflect limited exploration of such by WGs or a perception that there is little to be gained from partnerships in, among others, union revitalization and WG effectiveness terms. The need for further research examining WGs' meaning for union revival strategies, and labour-management cooperation in particular, is clearly signalled.

The study also reveals that unions and WGs do not always coordinate their activities or appear familiar with each other's strategies and activities, with the union likely to pull rank on WGs when a conflict of interests is suspected. One practical implication is that WGs need to take greater action to demonstrate their impact and worth to their unions. Likewise, unions may need to monitor WG activity in a more positive, extensive manner in order to recognize their wider value and to help disseminate mutual learning. In other words, both parties have to look outward in order to raise the stature of WGs. As WG achievements mount, this may happen over time. However, proactive measures would help to link WG activities into union strategies of revitalization in a more strategic fashion.

Of course, the findings also raise bigger questions as to how union vitality should be assessed. Union strategies of organizing, recruitment, and certain forms of restructuring (e.g., mergers) are often examined in terms of changes in membership size and density. The connection with qualitative characteristics of union strength (e.g., political influence, internal efficiency) is more oblique and thus difficult to quantify and trace in causality terms. Further, the assumption here is that the impacts of specific revival efforts can be isolated and measured. As shown earlier, however, many strategies work dynamically and in concert. The impact of WG presence as an identity-based mechanism, and of WG initiatives and approaches (both internally and in interaction with their union host), involves complex processes and phenomena that do not always sit easily with conventional union priorities. For instance, both WG and union aims include increased membership, yet the priority they place on engaging and involving members might differ in representation and mobilization terms. Many informants conceived that WGs generally tend to go further than many conventional union structures and procedures to accommodate the characteristics and circumstances of (women) members so as to stimulate their active involvement. Related to this, the ultimate measures of union strength thus need to reflect unions' capacity to effect change in all members' lives in the workplace and beyond, and not be limited to gauges of unions' own organizational parameters.

Indeed, WGs have particular contributions to make, not just in raising membership numbers but in campaigns relating to workplace concerns, furthering the representation of neglected constituents in union structures, and empowering them by this involvement within the union and via wider alliances. This analysis also stresses that those closest to WGs generally feel that they have the potential to make a larger contribution to union revival strategies. This is partly because of the growing experiences and achievements on which they are able to draw in response to criticisms of their existence by union traditionalists and various political slates, and to their widening spheres of interest and influence.

WGs thus hold multiple meanings for their unions in terms of different forms of revival strategy. It is clear that they have significance as union instruments for furthering extant strategies, thus appearing to travel the old tracks of conventional British union revival strategies. However, they also nuance and encourage changes to those strategies, and help develop additional ways forward via new or alternative "maps" that emphasize union inclusivity. WGs and other equality mechanisms, the evidence suggests, provide lessons for their unions to use in extending currently underdeveloped strategies (e.g., coalition building, structural reform and ways of working, cohesion among different constituency groups; see also Edelson's and Briskin's chapters, this volume). They also thereby underscore the lack of comprehensiveness of existing measures of union vitality that focus on quantifiable or overall union and labour movement indicators. This traditional emphasis has meant that much internal and sub-organizational and processual activity within unions, such as that carried out or represented by WGs, has been under-reported. A low level of WG and union monitoring in terms of impact assessment in turn makes their significance as union revitalization mechanisms more difficult to demonstrate. However, this analysis suggests that in many ways unions are in better shape than current conventional snapshot gauges of their vitality imply. One key challenge for them is to recognize and support WG developments that complement or critique their traditional modus operandi.

Notes

1 The focus here is on WGs that are recognized or whose development has been facilitated by their union (e.g., WGs with advisory or policy-making status in their unions, WGs with access to union resources). They thus differ from the independent development and operation of women's self-organizing groups. However, earlier research has shown that the former may spawn the latter while women's self-organizing groups may evolve into more formal, union-sanctioned WGs (Parker 2003).
2 "At least" denotes a conservative estimate because some sub-national WG numbers were not available.
3 The eight affiliates are the Broadcasting, Entertainment, Cinematograph and Theatre Union (BECTU); the national Union of Rail, Maritime and Transport Workers; the Graphical, Paper and Media Union (GPMU, now part of Amicus); the Union for Shop, Distributive and Allied Workers (USDAW); UNISON (the main public service union); Community; PCS; and the Transport and Salaried Staff Association (TSSA).
4 In the few cases where the WGs arose primarily in response to environmental and "other" factors, examples of such from the respondents actually emphasized union organizing and interest representation via special mechanisms.
5 On 1 May 2007, Amicus and the Transport and General Workers' Union (TGWU) merged to form Unite, the United Kingdom's largest trade union with more than 2 million members.

References

Aldred, C. 1981. *Women at Work*. London: Pan Books.
Arrowsmith, J. 2004. *Union Merger Momentum Continues*. European Industrial Relations Observatory On-line. http://www.eurofound.europa.eu/eiro/2004/10/feature/uk0410105f.html.
Baccaro, L., K. Hamann, and L. Turner. 2003. The politics of labour movement revitalization: The need for a revitalised perspective. *European Journal of Industrial Relations* 9, 1: 119-33.
Behrens, M., R. Hurd, and J. Waddington. 2004. How does restructuring contribute to union revitalization? In *Varieties of Unionism: Strategies for Union Revitalization in a Globalizing Economy*, ed. C.M. Frege and J. Kelly, 117-36. Oxford: Oxford University Press.
Cockburn, C. 1995. *Women and the European Social Dialogue: Strategies for Gender Democracy*. Equal Opportunities Unit. Luxembourg: European Commission.
Colgan, F., and S. Ledwith. 2000. Diversity, identities and strategies of women trade union activists. *Gender, Work and Organisation* 7, 4: 242-57.
–. 2002. *Gender, Diversity and Trade Unions: International Perspectives*. London: Routledge.
Cumbers, A. 2004. Transnational solidarity in the British and Norwegian trade union movements. *Antipode* 36, 5: 829-50.
Dickens, L., and M. Hall. 2004. Fairness – up to a point: Assessing the impact of new labour's employment legislation. *Human Resource Management Journal* 16, 4: 338-56.
Fichter, M., and I. Greer. 2004. Analysing social partnership: A tool of union revitalization? In *Varieties of Unionism: Strategies for Union Revitalization in a Globalizing Economy*, ed. C.M. Frege and J. Kelly, 71-89. Oxford: Oxford University Press.
Flynn, M., C. Brewster, R. Smith, and M. Rigby. 2004. Trade union democracy: The dynamics of different forms. In *Trade Unions and Democracy: Strategies and Perspectives*, ed. M. Harcourt and G. Wood, 319-51. Manchester: Manchester University Press.
Hall, M., S. Hutchinson, J. Parker, J. Purcell, and M. Terry. 2007. *Implementing Information and Consultation: Early Experience*. Research report commissioned by the Department for Business, Enterprise and Regulatory Reform's (DBERR) Employment Relations Research Paper Series. London: DBERR.
Hamann, K., and J. Kelly. 2003. The domestic sources of difference in labour market policies. *British Journal of Industrial Relations* 41, 4: 639-63.
Healy, G., and G. Kirton. 2000. Women, power and trade union government in the UK. *British Journal of Industrial Relations* 38, 3: 343-60.

Heery, E., and L. Adler. 2004. Organizing the unorganised. In *Varieties of Unionism: Strategies for Union Revitalization in a Globalizing Economy,* ed. C.M. Frege and J. Kelly, 45-69. Oxford: Oxford University Press.

Heery, E., J. Kelly, and J. Waddington. 2003. Union revitalization in Britain. *European Journal of Industrial Relations* 9, 1: 79-97.

Kelly, J. 2004. Social partnership arrangements in Britain: Labor cooperation and compliance. *Industrial Relations Journal* 43, 1: 267-92.

Machin, S. 2000. Union decline in Britain. *British Journal of Industrial Relations* 38, 4: 631-45.

Martinez Lucio, M., and M. Stuart. 2002. Assessing partnership: The prospects for, and challenges of, modernisation. *Employee Relations* 24, 3: 252-61.

Parker, J. 2003. *Women's Groups and Equality in British Unions.* Ceredigion, UK: Edwin Mellen Press.

–. 2006. Towards equality and renewal: Women's groups, diversity and democracy in British unions. *Economic and Industrial Democracy* 27, 3: 429-67.

–. 2008. The Trades Union Congress and civil alliance building: Towards social movement unionism? *Employee Relations* 30, 5: 562-83.

SERTUC WRC. 2004. *Waving Not Drowning – Hopefully: A Survey of Women and their Trade Unions.* London: SERTUC.

Terry, M. 2003. Partnership and trade unions in the UK. *Economic and Industrial Democracy* 24, 4: 485-507.

TSSA WiF (Transport and Salaried Staff Association, Women in Focus). 2007. *Women in Focus.* http://www.tssa.org.uk/article=1.php3?id_article=1620.

Waddington, J., M. Kahmann, and J. Hoffman. 2003. *United We Stand? A Comparison of the Trade Union Merger Process in Britain and Germany.* London: Anglo-German Foundation.

Wills, J. 2001. Community unionism and trade union renewal in the UK: Moving beyond the fragments at last? *Transactions of the Institute of British Geographers* 26, 4: 465-83.

Contributors

Patricia L. Baker (deceased) was Associate Professor of Anthropology at Mount St. Vincent University. She was awarded the Patricia Baker Award for Union Activism in 2008 by the National Union of CAUT for her tireless work in promotingequity for women in post-secondary education. She will be remembered for her research on women and unionization, and her contributions to her faculty association. She also served on the executive board of the National Union of the Canadian Association of University Teachers until her death in December 2007.

Linda Briskin is a professor in the social science division and the School of Women's Studies at York University (Toronto). She is currently researching worker militancies, union leadership, and strategies for ensuring equity representation inside unions. She has been a union activist for many decades.

Karen Brown is currently an associate consultant with a focus on organizational development within the community, government, and private sectors. Previously, Karen led the Finance Sector Union in South Australia/Northern Territory as state secretary for eleven years.

Marie Clarke Walker has been Executive Vice-President of the Canadian Labour Congress since 2002. She brings to her work a wealth of experience and skills in the promotion of equality and equity for working people and their communities in every aspect of their lives.

Miriam Edelson is a social activist, mother, and writer living in Toronto. Edelson has worked in the trade union movement since 1980, specializing in communications, community organizing, and human rights issues.

Janice Foley is Professor in the Faculty of Business Administration at the University of Regina. Her research interests include women and unions, globalization and unions, and healthy workplaces.

Mary Margaret Fonow is Professor and Director of the Women and Gender Studies Program at Arizona State University. Her research interests include feminism in unions and feminism and labour activism.

Anne Forrest is Director, Women's Studies, at the University of Windsor. Her areas of research include collective bargaining and women and unions.

Suzanne Franzway is Associate Professor in Gender Studies and Sociology at the University of South Australia. Her research interests include engineers and workplace culture, international labour movements and activism, and the impact of domestic violence on women's work.

Jan Kainer is Associate Professor at York University. She teaches in the Labour Studies Program in the Department of Social Science and in the School of Women's Studies. She has published in the area of pay equity and on equity initiatives in the Canadian labour movement.

Marie-Josée Legault is a professor of labour relations and labour studies at Téluq-Université du Québec à Montréal. Her fields of research include equity in employment and pay equity, and human rights and their effect on labour relations.

Anne McBride is Senior Lecturer in employment relations at the University of Manchester. Her research interests are the representation of women in trade unions, and workforce development issues in health care services.

Jane Parker is Senior Lecturer at Auckland University of Technology. She has published on gender equality in organizational settings, trade union organization and renewal strategies, social movement unionism, employee consultation, and occupational safety and health. She recently relocated from the University of Warwick, UK.

Barbara Pocock is Director of the Centre for Work + Life at the University of South Australia. Her research interests include gender politics in the workplace, the regulation of the industrial relations systems and their effects on inequality, and the changing nature of work and its intersections with changing household and social life.

Jeremy Waddington is Professor of Industrial Relations at the University of Manchester and Project Coordinator for the European Trade Union Institute, Brussels. He has written extensively on matters of trade union structure, organization, and activity.

Carol Wall is a long-time labour and social justice activist who spent seventeen years with the *Toronto Star* and held various positions within the Southern Ontario Newspaper Guild; the Communications, Energy and Paper (CEP), Local 87M; and community boards. She was the first CEP Human Rights Director for the Public Service Alliance of Canada.

Index

Johnson, Beverley: involvement in labour movement, 61-62; on lack of progress for equity, 75; link between Canadian labour movement and global equity struggles, 74; on linked oppressions, 140; only the appearance of power for equity committees, 66; on racism in the labour movement, 67-69, 71, 75; on recruitment of young workers, 70; on strategy to gain seats on federation board, 65-66

Kainer, Jan, 7, 113, 220
Kelly, J., 213
Kumar, P., 19, 97, 114
Kurtz, S., 141

labour force: Aboriginal participants, 8, 79; demographic changes, 1, 8, 79, 84; diversity of membership, 1, 79; feminization of, 1, 8, 219; segregation of women and women's work, 3, 108, 110, 111, 119; in unions, 79-80; unions' perpetuation of gender-segregated labour market, 3
Landry, Carol, 184
leadership: communication of equity issues, 131-32, 134-35; community support necessary for people of colour, 63-65; current leaders' disconnect from members, 70, 76, 80-81; diversifying labour leadership as renewal strategy, 8, 21, 25, 26, 29, 31-32, 81-82, 121; importance in women's committees in determining outcomes, 122-28, 130-31; necessary to reflect workforce, 82; need to increase women's activism, 182-83; obstacles for equity candidates, 130-31, 133-34; opportunity to improve effectiveness with union renewal, 4, 6, 8, 63, 97; role of formal leadership in advancing equity, 9; training and education in equity needed, 6, 8, 91, 130-31, 135, 140; women in leadership positions, 2, 6, 26, 119-20, 133, 161, 168; women's union leadership course (United Steelworkers), 178, 180-84. *See also* executive committees, representation of women
Ledwith, S., 27, 177-78, 206
Legault, Marie-Josée, 7, 120, 135
Liggett, M.H., 52
Liquor, Hospitality and Miscellaneous Workers Union, 169
LO. *See* Danish Confederation of Trade Unions (LO)

Mahon, R., 23
male domination in unions: challenges for women in male-dominated unions, 177; gender-segregated bargaining structures, 110-11; inequality deeply rooted in labour organizations, 21, 30, 32; male breadwinner ideal and gendered vision of social justice, 99, 101-2, 105, 106-9, 112, 115; masculinist traditions and practices (Australia), 158-60, 170; men's concerns and practices the norm, 178; pay equity demand and male resistance, 21, 33n5, 33n7, 109-10, 113-14; power struggles with women's committees, 127; reluctance to share power, 69, 88-89, 92, 121; segregation of women and women's work, 3, 108, 110, 111, 119; seniority systems' male bias, 8, 102, 110; sexual harassment issue, 20, 22, 138, 140, 161, 183-84, 187, 189, 227; two value systems, one for men and one for women, 108-9; WIMDOI conference, 178, 184-87. *See also* privilege within unions
Manufacturing, Science and Finance (MSF) union (UK), 201, 202(t), 203(t), 206, 207
Maritime Union of Australia, 164, 187
Marshall, T.H., 46
McBride, Anne, 10-11
McCarthy, J., 179
McDermott, P., 3
McKenzie, Roger, 85
Medoff, J., 103
membership: in Australian unions, 157, 158-59, 161-63, 171; in British unions, 192, 219, 222; current state, 15, 79-80, 114, 181; diversity, 1, 8, 74, 76, 119, 120, 140; need for equitable representation of diverse groups, 17, 40; union renewal an opportunity to capitalize on diverse membership, 6; unionization rates in service sector, 79-80, 162-63; women, 194-95, 219
membership participation: better communication as means of counteracting racism and sexism, 90-91; current leaders' disconnect from members, 70, 80-81; impact of women's leadership course, 182; increasing participation key to union revitalization, 1, 3, 6, 9, 10, 17, 18, 25, 31-32, 82, 91; issues unions should pursue to mobilize members, 9, 30-31; in model of equity progress, 132; need for leadership to reflect workforce, 82; training and education in equity

Pink Triangle Committee (CUPE Ontario), 144-46

Pocock, Barbara, 10

political activism: feminist view of unions as instruments of social justice, 2, 16, 30-31; history of feminist unionist–women's movement alliances, 19-22; pay equity fight, 21, 33n5, 33n7, 109-10, 113-14

Pollack, Marion, 142-43, 149

privilege within unions: justification of systemic barriers facing racialized workers, 87; lack of resources for equity committees, 65-67, 81, 88, 130; male breadwinner ideal, 99, 101-2, 105, 106-9, 112, 115; pay equity struggle, 21, 33n5, 33n7, 109-10, 113-14; reluctance to share power, 69, 88-89, 92, 121; segregation of women and women's work, 108, 110, 111, 119; systemic forms of gender and race dis/advantage, 65, 99, 108; white privilege, 9, 61, 65, 87, 88-89, 92. *See also* male domination in unions; vested-interest unionism

Provincial Status of Women Committee (BCTF), 146, 148

Public and Commercial Services (PCS) union (UK), 223, 224(t), 226, 228-29

Public Service Alliance of Canada, 128

Quebec Act Respecting Labour Standards, 42

Quebec Charter of Rights and Freedoms: articles on discrimination, 42-44; implications of equity requirements for unions, 7-8, 47-49, 50-52, 53-54, 135

Quebec Human Rights Commission, 42

Quebec Human Rights Tribunal, 44-46

racialized minorities: action plan to advance equity agenda, 8-9; choice of visible minority representatives by CLC, 67, 68-69; equity organizing by racial minorities, 26-27; increase in labour force, 8, 79, 84; job segregation by race/ethnicity, 103-4; limited progress in advancing equity for, 8; need for community to support labour involvement, 63-65; in population, 79, 82n1; significant inequity existing, 3; voiceless and invisible to a large extent in unions, 67-78, 84; workers in service sector, 79-80. *See also* racism in unions

racism in unions: amalgamation's impact on number of racialized local leaders, 71; anti-racist initiatives, 61, 65-67,

74-75, 76; difficulties experienced by women of colour in senior union positions, 62-63; discrimination couched in term "experience," 63; equity committees unsupported by senior leaders, 65-67; existence in the labour movement, 67-70; fear and suspicion of people of colour, 68, 72; history of, 84-87; in labour movement as in society, 1, 8, 86-87, 89; lack of acknowledgment of racism, 71; lack of support for racialized members' involvement in communities, 63-65; leaders removed from workers' positions on issues, 70; need for community to support labour involvement, 63-65; people of colour under-represented in union staff, 69; persons with power and privilege (white men) unwilling to share, 65, 69, 87, 88-89, 92, 121; reason for formation of black and Asian unions, 85-87; recommendations to combat racism and sexism, 90-92; recommendations to counteract racism and sexism, 90-92; systemic exclusion/discrimination, 73; young workers of colour absent from recruitment ads, 70, 91. *See also* Clarke Walker, Marie; Johnson, Beverley

Rainbow Committee (CUPE Ontario), 144-46

Randolph, A. Philip, 80

Rayside, D., 16, 120

Reitz, J., 112

renewal: challenges for unions to overcome, 80; changes needed to union culture, structure, and practices, 2, 4, 6; earlier contributions by women unionists, 1, 7, 15-17, 18, 31-32; equity essential for union survival, 1-2, 135; industrial unionism as obstacle, 115-16; new model of unionization needed, 1-2; organized labour's capacity for renewal, 5-7; themes in union renewal literature, 17-19; threats to renewal, 6-8. *See also* gendering labour movements; social movement unionism; vested-interest unionism

renewal strategies: addressing concerns of female membership and labour force, 21, 30, 31, 106, 138, 161, 171, 172, 195, 219, 227; current strategies same as earlier ones of female union activists, 1, 15-17; importance of women to union survival, 18, 97, 186; inclusive representation, 17-18, 40; influence of women's groups in coalition building, 221, 229-31, 232; influence of women's

Printed and bound in Canada

Set in Stone by Artegraphica Design Co. Ltd.

Copy editor: Judy Phillips

Proofreader: Stephanie VanderMeulen

Indexer: Patricia Buchanan